PROUD KATE

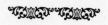

PROUD KATE

CHILD OF DESTINY

ISLE OF ESCAPE

FIFTY YEARS A WOMAN

LADIES OF THE PRESS

HIGHLAND TWILIGHT

MARRIAGE IN GOTHAM

PROMENADE DECK

PROUD KATE

Portrait of an Ambitious Woman

By ISHBEL ROSS

HARPER & BROTHERS * PUBLISHERS * NEW YORK

PROUD KATE

Library of Congress catalog card number: 51-11952

Contents

Acknowledgments

I am indebted to the manuscript division of the Library of Congress for access to Salmon Portland Chase's diaries, correspondence, journals, family memoranda and other documentation; to the Rhode Island Historical Society for letters, diaries, clippings and miscellaneous material bearing on the Sprague family; and to the Pennsylvania Historical Society for Kate Chase, Jay Cooke and Henry C. Carey correspondence.

Much source material also was obtained from the Cincinnati Public Library; the Ohio State Archaeological and Historical Society Library in Columbus; the Historical and Philosophical Society of Ohio in Cincinnati; the Chase College library in Cincinnati; the Providence Public Library; the New York Public Library (particularly the American History room); the New York Society Library; and the Chase National Bank.

I am also grateful to Orestes H. Caldwell for personal recollections of Governor Sprague; and to Mr. and Mrs. Henry H. Villard, Konrad Mueller and William A. Jackson, Library of Harvard University, for the use of excerpts from the correspondence of Henry Villard and Fanny Garrison Villard.

I. R.

PART ONE

Chapter I

A STAR IS BORN

JOVIAN TO his young wife, as one day he would seem to the country at large, Salmon Portland Chase suffered mightily and prayed hard on the hot August night in 1840 on which his daughter Kate was born. Nothing in the plain setting of the limestone house on a Cincinnati street where this event took place presaged the destiny of the child who, in time, would become the social leader of the Civil War era— the proud and brainy girl hated by Mary Todd, listened to by Abraham Lincoln, loved by Roscoe Conkling, admired by Presidents, generals and diplomats.

The clue to Kate's future lay in her inheritance. Almost from birth she was committed to a lifetime of consuming ambition centered on her father, who had grown to manhood with the conviction that in all things he must come first. His grandparents had trekked from Massachusetts to New Hampshire on foot, by horseback and canoe and their gifted sons had turned to the church, to astronomy, to politics, to law, to the arts or, like Salmon's father, Ithamar, to farming. Without exception, they had shown pride, ability and concern for their fellow men. In Salmon all these forces fused in relentless personal ambition.

In the year of Kate's birth he had already seen his goal. Nothing less than the Presidency would quench this rising fever. Champion of the slave and a soaring star in Western politics, he was passing from the visionary to the pragmatic in viewing himself as a national figure. His passion for power was to influence Kate from her earliest years; to affect

3

her course through life; to transmit a dream that she sought to make a reality.

At the moment his attention centered on Washington, which simmered in clouds of dust and an August heat haze, but reflected the liveliness of an election year. The Whigs were gaining ground, as Martin Van Buren sought to hold his office against the Indian fighter, William Henry Harrison. The contest for the Presidency was sparked by elements new to the spreading acres and growing cities of America. Torchlight processions and monster carnivals had caught the public fancy.

Pious, strait-laced, his towering figure always a little aloof from the crowd, Chase noted this native manifestation with faint disdain. It was not his nature to shout or cheer; rarely did he mellow into laughter. But next to the birth of his child, the election was of deep and compelling interest to him that summer. He was for Harrison. His campaigning had been interrupted briefly so that he could be with his second wife, seventeen-year-old Eliza Ann Smith, when her baby was born. His first wife, Catherine Garniss, had died of childbed fever while he was absent from home on political business.

As he watched over Eliza he had cause for concern. Not only had he lost Catherine, but the daughter who bore her name had died of typhoid fever only three months before Kate's birth. This time Chase was taking every precaution against the hazards of childbirth. Eliza's mother, Mrs. Edmund C. Smith, hovered around the canopied bed. A nurse, a physician and the wife of Flamen Ball, his business partner, stayed with her during her hours of labor. Chase prayed with fervor for the health and survival of Eliza and her baby. Always ready to scourge his soul, he paced back and forth in an adjoining room, flinging himself on a couch at intervals and turning to the Scriptures, while Eliza "bore her pain with great fortitude and was strengthened by her Heavenly Father to endure." From time to time he went in to see her, whispering words of consolation which, for once, were little heeded.

At two o'clock, while a thundershower splashed against the windowpanes, Mrs. Ball announced that he had a daughter. After looking at the baby and her tired mother, he returned to his study, knelt down and prayed God "to support and comfort my dear wife, to preserve the life of the child, and save both from sin."

The air was thunderous and oppressive and Chase in his exalted mood did not feel like sleep. He turned to Dr. John Eberle's new book *A Treatise on the Diseases and Physical Education of Children* and read until dawn. Then, satisfied that all was well, he went forth without sleep into a city where fifty thousand persons lived, loved and worked with all the vitality of a polyglot population reaching out for the benefits of the opening West. The streets were muddy from the night's rains. The gardens bloomed with August ripeness. The air was scented with roses, and on the hills girdling the city, Nicholas Longworth's grapes ripened in the summer sun. In spite of Mrs. Anthony Trollope, Chase thanked God that he had chosen Cincinnati for his home.

It was still a rowdy city in many respects, with filth in the streets, pigs wandering at will, gaudy saloons in shanty town and many incendiary fires and burglaries. But various civilizing factors were mellowing its rougher aspects. Studying the gentle arc of hills on which the city sprawled, the pewter sweep of the river, the bright-hued tangle of the Fifth Street market, where scores of wagons piled with dewy-fresh country produce stood wheel to wheel, the young lawyer strode along in a mood of rare elation.

Years earlier he had first traveled west to Ohio to join his uncle, Bishop Philander Chase, as student and helper. He was a stiff and earnest youth at the time, lofty-minded, penniless, fresh from his mother's farm in New Hampshire. Since then he had studied law in Washington, tasted the social life of the capital, attended levees at the Executive Mansion and become a man of affairs.

Now he was acutely conscious of the wheels that thundered, the machinery that roared, the vitality that sparked the scene. Cincinnati had church spires and spacious gardens. It also had factories, mills, eleven thousand workmen and eighty-eight steamboats on the river. A wide landing sloped from Front Street to the water's edge, where squat boats received and discharged their cargoes. The city had just taken over the waterworks. It was not many years since the early settlers had drunk from hillside springs and done their washing in the river.

Chase caught the significance of all these changes with sharp understanding. He was sensitive to the lot of his fellow men, in spite of his cold demeanor. As he walked to his office, townspeople greeted him in passing. He was already a familiar figure in the streets of Cincinnati. His looks would have drawn attention anywhere. He was more than six feet tall and cast in the heroic mold, with powerfully accented features —a face in which flesh and spirit stamped their separate impress and seemed at odds with each other. The long jaw, the heavily chiseled mouth, the burning eyes—deep set and proud, the Byronic lock of dark hair curling over a massive brow, the magnificent stature, would soon become familiar in councils of state, in the Senate, in the more fashionable parlors of Washington and on Civil War greenbacks.

Chase found his partner in a state of consternation when he reached their joint office. While Mrs. Ball was assisting at the birth of Kate, robbers had tilted a ladder against their home, swept aside the creeper and in a leisurely way had made off with their most valuable possessions. It took only one look at his partner, however, to persuade Flamen that the important news that morning was not the Ball burglary but the birth of a daughter to Chase.

Eliza did not question her husband's decision that the baby should bear the name of his beloved first wife and of the daughter who had recently died. She already knew the strength of the Garniss influence. But she worshiped and revered Salmon, as did many of the women whose paths crossed his throughout his life. Approvingly she watched him inscribe the name Catherine Jane Chase in the family Bible and make an entry in his diary which, along with his voluminous correspondence, was to create a singularly detailed picture of one man's progress through life: "The child is pronounced pretty. I think it quite otherwise. It is, however, well formed and I am thankful. May God give the child a good understanding that she may keep His commandments."

Kate was indeed well formed and, in time, was to show good understanding, but she was not destined to keep the Ten Commandments. Above all, she was to break the tenth, in coveting the Presidency for her father for more than twenty years. She was also to change the spelling of her name to Katharine, so as to nullify the Garniss influence.

Small promise of the hazel eyes, red-gold hair and remarkable white skin that were to distinguish Kate in later years showed in the small and restless bundle held by Eliza. Kate had the tow-colored fuzz and round blue eyes of infancy. But the nose that James A. Garfield, one of her admirers, was to describe later as "plain pug," already was a detectable feature. The child was restless from birth. There was no peace in her. Her father watched her struggling furies with curiosity but with no premonition of the driving force lodged in the small frame, the imperious pride that one day would channel her life, or the way in which his own future would be shaped by this vigorous child. He was more concerned about Eliza, and with reason. She wilted in the hot days following Kate's birth. The climate was miasmic. Fogs rolled up from the river. Humidity lay like a blanket over the city. Before the infant was a month old Chase hurried mother and baby off to Yellow Springs. But Eliza was still like a drooping reed when she returned to face the stern Cincinnati winter.

Their limestone house was wreathed with evergreens, their white pine window frames were stuck with frost, great logs burned in the fireplace and Kate looked like a healthy and cheerful baby on Christmas Day. Eliza walked to church with Salmon, then went on to have Christmas dinner at a friend's home. It was the last occasion on which she was to feel well. She developed a cold and before long had consumption. For the next five years she moved from one warm place to another, was cherished by her devoted husband and lavished much of her own failing strength on tireless Kate, who went everywhere with her.

It was a gay parade for Kate who, from her earliest years, liked the stir of life. She preened herself on carriage drives at the Springs. She was apt at learning new games and turns of speech when they visited cousins in New England. She found excitement in the well-dressed crowds, the mirrors, chandeliers and long tables of decorated game and sculptured desserts that she saw at the Astor House when they passed through New York. One winter they visited New Orleans. Hand in hand with her mother, she strolled through the narrow streets, caught glimpses of flaming scarlet flowers through gateways, heard drifts of songs from grilled balconies. These memories sank deep into the consciousness of the impressionable child. Staying at hotels, driving in public coaches, sailing in river boats, she became an object of attention. Already she was arresting, with a nimbus of reddish hair framing a white, intense face and sleepy eyes viewing the world through a heavy fringe of lashes.

Chase showered a wealth of affection on his small daughter when she was at home. He deplored the wandering life she led with her mother while he busied himself with his legal and political work in Cincinnati and Columbus. When they finally came back to stay, he was shocked to find how demanding she had become. Her mother was too frail to discipline so headstrong a child. Kate had grown willful, tempestuous and avid for love and admiration. Prayer and reason were the two antidotes best understood by the pious Chase. He sought to apply both to his small daughter. He bemoaned the amount of correction required. Entry after entry in his diary during this period mirrors Kate's tussles with the devil. He frequently read to her from Job, seeking to impress on her the virtues of patience, a grace she was never to make her own. Levity during morning prayers was a heinous offence at Kate's tender age and on this his comment was revealing: "Read after dressing a Psalm—the fiftieth, and first four chapters of Matthew. Some earnestness in prayer —was obliged to correct my dear little Kate—prayed with her."

Her father's earnest prayers and her mother's invalidism were Kate's earliest memories. Her Aunt Alice, Chase's sister, who arrived to help as Eliza's condition became worse, found her an "excellent girl, and bright and happy as a seraph." Mrs. Hamilton Smith, a Louisville friend of her parents, commented: "Funny Kate! She desires love."

By this time they had moved to Clifton Farm on the Lower Road outside Cincinnati, a magnificent region of hills and dales to the north of the Burnet woods. The blossoming orchard, the grassy stretches around the large old farmhouse, her kittens and chickens, the free and open life of the country, all delighted Kate. But death already shadowed the germ-ridden house where her mother lay by the hour, unable to attend to domestic tasks. Two more children were born and promptly died within the first five years of Kate's life.

A "nature cure," which consisted of a driving tour through Ohio with her brother, Edmund Custis Smith, who also had consumption, made Eliza worse. Again Chase sent Kate and her mother to the Springs. He wrote to his daughter from the farm, telling her that her chickens were growing tall and were fighting with each other and getting "their white dresses very dirty." He pictured Kate's kitten getting up a waltz for his benefit, chasing her tail and poking her nose into his cup of tea. These playful letters brought laughter and delight to Kate, who responded with hundreds of kisses for dear Papa. But by August, 1845, they were back at the farm and Eliza was desperately ill. Two months later she died at the age of twenty-three.

"Poor little Kate, she does not know how great a loss she has sustained," her father wrote.

From then on, Kate's picture of her mother faded, and she viewed her always as the slender figure in puffed gray satin with deep-ruched bonnet, whose likeness hung on the wall in second place to that of Catherine Garniss, until she reversed their order when she had established full authority over her father. Even within a year of her mother's death, Kate was showing an imperious spirit where he was concerned. Her cousin, F. C. Whipple, wrote to Chase: "Kate says she shall not write or send any word to you until you write her the letter you promised." She was far advanced for her years, and could read and write in a simple way at the age of five.

The winter after her mother's death was a grim one in Cincinnati. Day after day the temperature dropped to ten. There was sickness in the town and many deaths. Chase left Clifton at seven every morning, traveled to Cincinnati by omnibus and walked home in the evening, unless the snowdrifts were heavy. In that case he sleighed. Prayers were said after tea. Then Kate chatted and played with her father and the kitten and had a little pedagogic instruction before going to bed. Chase was always the schoolmaster in their moments of leisure, drilling and driving her as Aaron Burr did Theodosia. Kate was disciplined into intense application where her studies were concerned.

As time went on, she was exposed to many gentle influences through his friends. Chase belonged to the inner social circle in Cincinnati. He visited Nicholas Longworth, whose vineyards stretched along the hillsides. He was the protégé of Judge Jacob Burnet, a leader of the Ohio bar, and Kate sometimes called with her father at the fine old mansion where Lafayette, John Quincy Adams, Daniel Webster and Henry Clay were entertained. He was also the friend of William S. Groesbeck, a fellow lawyer who would one day plead Andrew Johnson's case before him in the impeachment proceedings. Groesbeck was married to Elizabeth Burnet, the Judge's daughter, and she was kind to little Kate, who sat politely in a tall stiff chair, her rosetted slippers neatly crossed, when she visited their home Elmhurst outside Cincinnati. She was much petted because of her motherless state.

Chase was deep in all the social and literary enterprises of the growing city. He helped to found the Lyceum, was a member of the Semi-Colon

Club, which met at Samuel E. Foote's until it dissolved in 1837, and he frequently went to Lane Seminary to visit Dr. Lyman Beecher and Mrs. Harriet Beecher Stowe. He was Sunday School superintendent in St. Paul's Episcopal Church, assisted by the three Blackwell sisters—Marian, Emily and Elizabeth, who was destined to become the first woman doctor.

The Cincinnati Kate knew was one of shaded hilly streets, of dim parlors in spacious houses, of austere churches and softly rustling silks. She was quite unconscious of the brawling keelboatmen, the corrupt politics, the beer and whisky that flowed from the distilleries and breweries, and the reveling frontiersmen. But from her earliest consciousness she knew what slavery meant. Chase talked freely to his small daughter about his work. He brought home his legal papers and studied them at Clifton. Kate never hesitated to walk into her father's study and quietly take a seat beside him as he inclined his noble head over his desk, studying books, briefs and reports.

As she grew older, he explained some of his cases to her. She found this more interesting than family prayers or chasing the kitten's tail. Chase was deeply immersed in political affairs and had already changed his party affiliations several times, a habit which was to persist throughout his life and contribute to his political misfortunes. He was a Henry Clay National Republican in 1832, a Harrison Whig in 1836, an out and out Whig in 1840, a Liberty man in 1844, a Free Soiler in 1848, a Democrat in 1851, a Liberty man again in 1852, a Republican in 1856. He was to make one more change of front in 1868, becoming a Democrat again when he saw he had no chance of nomination for the Presidency against Ulysses S. Grant on the Republican ticket.

As the years went on, Kate was to see no inconsistency in any of this, since her father maintained that on basic principles, except on the slavery issue, he was a Democrat all his life. On this he was firm and unshakable. Although he pulled away from the extremists, disliking the ranting touch, he fought their legal battles for the slaves and came to be known as the "Negro lawyer." Kate's favorite bedtime story in her early years concerned Matilda, the Negro woman whose case her father fought when she was seized as a fugitive while passing for white.

"There goes a fine young fellow who has just ruined himself," an onlooker remarked as Chase left the courtroom, after pleading Matilda's cause in 1837.

The name of John Van Zandt, the farmer who helped nine Negro fugitives to escape in his produce wagon, became as familiar to Kate as that of Matilda. She was seven when her father's dramatic plea for human liberty was presented to the Supreme Court in this famous case. Chase lost but focused national attention on the slavery issue.

And Kate had one of her earliest lessons in human values during this period, for she sat at her father's elbow as he wrote his lengthy brief. Sometimes he addressed her as if she were a judge, instead of a small attentive girl. Without understanding them, she learned to recite the words: "The law of the Creator, which invests every human being with an inalienable title to freedom, cannot be repealed by any inferior law, which asserts that man is property."

Kate understood that, in spite of her father's efforts, the case was lost. She grieved when Van Zandt died, ruined by a fine so heavy that all he owned did not meet it. She was to recognize him later as John Van Tromp in *Uncle Tom's Cabin*. It was long before she could reconcile the sequel with the brilliant part her father had played in the case. But even at seven she knew that he had scored a victory of sorts, notwithstanding the verdict. She heard him praised on all sides. He read her many of his letters. Important men sat at their table and discussed these matters.

Soon Kate was learning her father's history from the beginning. To her it had all the quality of a fairy tale, with its pioneering touches. He told her of his boyhood days in a two-storied yellow farmhouse in Cornish, New Hampshire, with a porch at the back, trees sheltering it, and a wooden fence shutting it off from the broad turnpike that threaded the Connecticut River Valley. Mount Ascutney emerged from the mists as Salmon fed the chickens in the early morning. And a "royal panoply of gilded clouds" often rolled across it as he milked the cows in the evening. He attended the village school and learned his ABC's from birch-bark pages. When the snowdrifts were taller than he, older brothers carried him to school. There were ten Chase children. Kate asked him often about Bessy Marble, the first little girl he remembered, aside from his sisters. She liked to hear how he gathered strawberries and wild flowers with her in the meadows and woods around his home.

Salmon was nine when the family moved from Cornish to Keene, where his mother's Scottish forebears had settled. His father died soon afterwards. He attended two district schools in Keene, then a private school in Windsor, Vermont. Later, he returned to Keene and studied Latin, Greek and mathematics. His mother, Jeanette Ralston, with her long Celtic face and Biblical admonitions, sewed his shirts, curbed his soaring flights of fancy with unfailing realism and exhorted him not to let his studies, friends and frivolities keep him from the love of God. His sister Abigail, observing his worldly leanings, wrote to him: "I confess I almost tremble for you, as I observe your desire to distinguish yourself, and apparent devotedness to those pursuits whose interests terminate in this life."

Chase was not a zealous student at this time, but he already longed for distinction. His life changed abruptly when his uncle, Bishop Philander Chase, invited him West to pursue his education. Nothing he told Kate interested her more than the details of his trip to Ohio through unsettled country, traveling by foot and on horseback, using the "ride and tie" system, then crossing Lake Erie on a novel craft known as the Walk-in-the-Water. In Cleveland he stopped to earn a little money ferrying passengers across the Cuyahoga.

Kate got a vivid picture from her father of the Bishop bringing Episcopalianism to the West. He had joined the great migration of advanced thinkers to Ohio, giving up a comfortable diocese in Connecticut to cope with swollen rivers, tough riding in the mountains and untamed land. At first he galloped around his diocese, preaching in barns, schoolhouses, courtrooms, out-of-doors or wherever he could gather together a group.

Her father found the Bishop an unyielding taskmaster when he joined him at his headquarters in Worthington. The youth was forced to chop and carry wood, to plant, sow and harvest, to milk the cows and drive them to pasture. He delivered meal and flour, and took wool to the carding factory. He prepared the Bishop's pork by plunging pigs into boiling water. On more than one occasion he used his razor on them when the bristles would not come off. The Bishop exacted his pound of flesh, and the Latin and Greek he learned failed to reconcile Salmon to the hard driving that went with them. When Uncle Philander became President of Cincinnati College and the youth followed him there, his education became more intensive. At last the Bishop resigned to go to England to raise money for a seminary of his own. He took Salmon East and left him with his family again, to the boy's great relief.

They were still miserably poor. Salmon's mother scraped and saved to put him through Dartmouth. He attended the academy at Royalton, Vermont, to prepare for admission, and taught during vacations to make money, but he told Kate that his pupils shouted him down and punched him into the bargain. He was suspended at Dartmouth for backing a rebellious classmate, but later returned and stayed to graduate, a Phi Beta Kappa. While in college he came under the spell of a revivalist who whipped up his interest in spiritual matters more effectively than the combined prayers of his mother and Abigail. He was to be profoundly religious for the rest of his life and, even in an age when scriptural injunction was customary in handling the young, Kate was to find her life affected by her father's devoutness.

From Dartmouth Chase went to Washington and asked another uncle, Senator Dudley Chase, to help him obtain a post in the government. The Senator had had nephews and cousins come calling before. He turned Salmon down and offered him fifty cents to buy a spade. Proud and indignant, Salmon advertised in the *Daily National Intelligencer* just before Christmas, 1826, that he was founding a Select Classical School. Candidates failed to respond, so he compromised and took over the boys' department of a well-known seminary in Washington, attended by the sons of Henry Clay and Attorney General William Wirt, and the nephew of Mrs. John Quincy Adams, as well as other Cabinet sprigs.

The handsome young man of towering stature soon was welcomed in the homes of Daniel Webster, Clay and Wirt. He studied law with the Attorney General, whom he recalled to Kate as "one of the handsomest men and one of the completest gentlemen of his time," even though he was a slaveholder. But Salmon, at this time, was more committed to social life than he was to his studies. He read law negligently and intermittently with Mr. Wirt, and barely passed muster when he became a lawyer in 1829.

Kate liked to hear about Mrs. Wirt, who was uniquely versed in the romantic history of flowers; about the four Wirt girls, whose musical evenings three times a week her father shared; and particularly about

Elizabeth, whom he frequently escorted to balls and levees at the Executive Mansion. On one occasion he went with her to visit Charles Carroll in Maryland, because she wished the last surviving signer of the Declaration of Independence to write in her album.

"Mr. Carroll kissed Elizabeth," Chase told Kate. "He seemed like a wonderfully active old gentleman, who ran up and downstairs like a boy, only that all his motions were as soft and gentle as those of a cat. He was over ninety but he rode every day."

Chase did not tell small Kate that he had been in love with Elizabeth Wirt and had begged her to marry him, but the penniless young teacher was not a promising match, and the link was broken when the administration changed and the Wirts moved to Baltimore. All the gentle arts and graces surrounding the Wirt family were Chase's first introduction to the pattern of living which was to be his when he returned to Washington with Kate.

He considered following the Wirts to Baltimore, but finally decided in favor of the West, saying: "I would rather be first twenty.years hence at Cincinnati than at Baltimore. As I ever have been first at school and college, except at Dartmouth, where I was much too idle, I shall ever strive to be first, wherever I may be, let what success will, attend the effort." But this confidence was transient. As he headed west, he wrote in his diary rather despairingly and with a closer approach to realism: "I have learned little and forgotten much, and really, to conclude of the future from the past, I almost despair of making any figure in the world. . . . I made much too little of the advantages which a residence in Washington at that time afforded."

His lofty aims were already beginning to show, along with his own dissatisfaction with his slow progress. He was then twenty-two and the year was 1830. He felt he had lost Elizabeth Wirt because he lacked ambition. He was never to overlook an opportunity again. He put all frivolity behind him and became the intense worker familiar to Kate. It was many years before she understood how significant the Wirts had been in her father's life, polishing the raw material into a worldly mold.

Cincinnati was young, growing, vitalized by men of drive from different parts of the country when he settled there. The atmosphere stimulated the youth from New England, who had drifted into the leisurely shallows of social life in Washington during the administration of John

Quincy Adams. In his new surroundings he studied law as if it were a brand new subject to him. He cultivated public men. He poured forth letters and kept a detailed diary. He fostered public movements, annotated the statutes of Ohio, contributed to magazines, lectured and became a pillar of the church. He adopted the cause of the Negro and took his stand with the liberals and reformers who were ringing the warning bell of a new era. Soon after Kate's birth he became a leading figure in the Liberty party and wrote its platform in 1843. For the first eight years of her life, he was organizing conventions, bolstering up the Liberty press and gaining stature in the national political scene.

Bit by bit, as they drove around in buggy or sleigh or Kate sat by his side on winter nights after her mother's death, her father's early life took shape and form before her like the pieces of a jigsaw puzzle. There was much she could not understand, but she caught the primary colors and broad outlines. She felt happy and important in her role of audience. Sometimes Chase called her his little hostess. He liked to talk expansively about himself and, although much of his conversation went over her head, the spirit of adulation already had her in its grip. She began to see her father as more than mortal man.

This unity of mood was rudely broken when he came home one autumn night in 1846, put his arm around her and told her gently that he was bringing a new mother for her to Clifton. He was startled to watch the fury that this announcement let loose in his small daughter. She wept, stormed and ran back and forth to look with streaming eyes at her mother's picture hanging on the wall—the slim, gentle figure in puffed gray satin. It took several hours and a good many prayers on Chase's part to soothe small Kate.

She stood in stormy rebellion some weeks later in the home of John McLean, Associate Justice of the Supreme Court, watching her father being married to the judge's niece, Sarah Bella Dunlop Ludlow. Kate was gowned in sunny yellow, her reddish hair was decked with flowers and she clutched a nosegay savagely as she stood beside Chase's third wife. She stared coldly through Bella's misty veil. The bride had no suspicion of the child's hostility. Or that Kate was having her first severe lesson in resignation. Her father's will had prevailed.

Chapter II

KATE'S LUSTER SHOWS

K ATE'S MOTHER had been dead little more than fourteen months when the third Mrs. Chase arrived at Clifton. She was surprised to find a small fury awaiting her. Kate hid the eggs, dodged out of sight in the orchard or climbed to a little hut she had in a tree and would not come down. But Bella was not intimidated by the fiery-tempered Kate. When kindness failed and coolness brought no response, she tried severity, making no attempt to conceal the child's rudeness from her father.

Kate's new stepmother had style and spirit, like Catherine Garniss. Her own mother was the most meek and undistinguished of Chase's wives, a circumstance that Kate was to resent bitterly in later life. But Bella Ludlow was the offspring of a pioneering family well-known in Ohio. She had money in her own right and was handsome to boot. Her grandfather, Israel Ludlow, was one of the founders of Cincinnati. The Ludlow mansion was a show place in the city. The Ludlow tradition was vigorous in the pioneering sense.

Her grandmother, Charlotte, had ridden through dense forests on her honeymoon and had helped Israel establish Ludlow's Station with its formidable blockhouse, armed against the Indians. There she had planted flowers and vegetables, learned to use a rifle, roasted pigs and held court, receiving all manner of guests, from Indian chiefs to presidential candidates. As the years went on, she earned both social and political prestige.

The bride who arrived at Clifton on a snowy winter day had some of her ancestor's dash and energy. Under other circumstances, it is likely that she and Kate would have got on. She planned to help Salmon in his political career and to become a potent hostess. She was worldly wise, spirited and intelligent, and everyone felt that she was a suitable mate for the rising young lawyer. He had met her first in his legal capacity. On the death of her father, James C. Ludlow, he was called in to settle what had once been an extensive estate. It had shrunk considerably, but he salvaged what he could for Bella and her younger sisters and brothers. Thereafter he managed their affairs. He had met Kate's mother in much the same way when her father died and his estate came to be settled.

Used to her father's undivided attention, Kate threw tantrums as capable Bella applied a firm touch to the Clifton household. Friends arrived in jingling sleighs, wrapped in heavy furs and wearing tall boots. The Ludlows were a gregarious tribe, loving parties, picnics, hops and soirées. Contrary to the tradition he had inherited, Chase, for a second time, had chosen a worldly wife. Only Kate's mother had been demure, and resigned in spirit.

Hurt and bewildered, Kate stood aloof from her stepmother's friends. Her father, conscious of her misery, still found time to hear "dear little Kate read verses," to pray and talk with her, to expound the philosophy of Job. He had many worries that winter and was face to face with financial difficulties, a state that was to become chronic for all but the period when Kate was riding the crest of the wave financially. He had much unrealizable property and was beset by mortgages and notes. Chase was both generous and improvident. He took slave cases for next to nothing. He turned down Nicholas Longworth's business when it was offered to him because he already represented banks that had suits involving the Longworth interests.

His legal work kept him in Columbus much of the winter, but every letter to Bella contained injunctions for Kate. The child listened sulkily as her stepmother read to her on a bitterly cold winter morning: "Tell little Kate she must be very particular about keeping herself perfectly clean, never forgetting her teeth morning or evening. Give my best love to her—bid her be a good girl."

During his absences the relationship between Kate and Bella grew much worse, and in spring, just as the orchards burst into blossom and the farm looked its most verdant, he entered a significant note in his diary: "This evening little Kate disobeyed her stepmother and made untrue representation; admonished her and promised to punish her, if I could not otherwise induce her to amend."

This was a grave step, since Kate had never been punished. Chase saw few of the scenes that raged between his wife and his daughter, but he was uneasily aware that the child was proving troublesome. By July he was openly disapproving and wrote to Bella, after receiving an unsatisfactory letter from Kate: "Studies which leave her no time to write correctly will, I am afraid, be of little benefit to her. Kiss dear little Kate twenty times for me."

With a new child on the way, Chase decided that Kate must be sent away to school. He was anxious about her education. He could no longer superintend each stage himself, for his wife made demands on his time when he made brief visits home from Columbus. He was also deeply concerned over Kate's growing antagonism to Bella. A baby daughter, whom they named Jeanette Ralston, was born in the late summer and almost immediately afterward Kate set off for New York with a simple wardrobe and her father as escort. This was the beginning of her life of independence.

It involved political excitement at the start. The Liberty party was holding a convention in Buffalo, so Chase took the northern route and left Kate with relatives who lived at Lockport, while he played an important part in the proceedings. He had written the keynote speech and he tried it out as they traveled through the Miami Canal. Kate gravely drank in the rolling phrases as their boat moved through the water. It was in this setting that she caught the first glimmering of the Executive Mansion in connection with her father. He told her he had been mentioned for the Vice-Presidency on the Liberty ticket. Kate readily grasped the thought and held on to it thereafter. At seven she was unconsciously preparing for her future career.

But New York was thrilling enough for the moment. She had lost all recollection of her early visits with her mother. A new world opened up before her as they toured the city in a barouche. They drove along Broadway past leafy poplars, through snarled traffic and heard the assorted cries of the street vendors. Her father pointed out the leading hotels, the shop displays, the homes of the famous and the better-known churches. They visited Bowling Green and surveyed the graveled paths, the autumn asters and the deep-hued dahlias of Battery Park.

Kate's brilliant hair was neatly tucked back under the stiff slats of a cambric bonnet. Her strange eyes had their usual catlike gleam. She was tall for her age, with tapering hands and small feet. Her only grief was that she soon would part from her father. She felt neither strange nor awed about entering the boarding school run by Miss Henrietta Haines at Madison Avenue and Forty-ninth Street. She curtsied with perfect assurance to the stately woman who sailed into the reception room to greet Mr. Chase.

Kate observed that Miss Haines was nearly as tall as her father. She was too young to note the compounded force and delicacy of her face, or to appraise the wise and remote glance directed at her. The head mistress's mouth suggested years of discipline for herself and others. She ran the most fashionable school for girls in New York at the time. It was also one where the discipline was tight and the academic standards high.

Miss Haines listened attentively while Mr. Salmon Portland Chase discussed Kate's Bible readings, her mother's death, her strong independence, her occasional tempers, his aversion to the theater and worldly pleasures, his wish that her upbringing should be simple, godly and serene.

He lingered as he went out, watching his daughter's tense white face, wondering if he were being cruel to her. But Kate took to her new surroundings with ease and assurance, once she had accepted the fact of her father's departure. She had lived a free and active physical life at Clifton, playing with her pets, running through the orchard, hunting for eggs, climbing trees, catching the blossoms in springtime, rustling through dead leaves in autumn, burying herself in the snowy mounds that banked up against the storm doors in winter.

This was a new world of routine, of watching clocks, where one girl was like another and the name Chase meant nothing. Kate shared a room with Mademoiselle de Janon, a French teacher who was to give her special care, attending to her clothes and deportment, as well as conversing with her in French. With her lively intelligence and quick mind, Kate showed superiority in all subjects. She became one of the best students in the school, and in time also emerged as a belle. The reports that went back to Cincinnati were pleasing to her father, for Kate studied diligently.

She remained at Miss Haines's school for nine years and made many friends among the daughters of established New York families. When the school was moved to Gramercy Park, more and more of these girls came in. Here Kate developed an early sophistication and a passionate interest in clothes. Soon her dressmaking bills were embarrassing to her father, and it was not until five years after she had left Miss Haines's that her accounts were settled in full.

The school routine was Spartan enough. The girls rose at half past five and studied until seven o'clock. They breakfasted on bread and butter, honey and café au lait, attended prayers, then walked outdoors until classes began. After the day's work, they paraded again at three o'clock, two by two, through the sleepy, tree-lined streets of the neighborhood. On their return, they sewed or studied, then dressed for dinner at five. After the one hearty meal of the day, they had French conversation and more study until tea and evening prayers. By eight o'clock they were on their way to bed.

They bathed twice a week, never opened their windows and often had colds. They used ginger poultices for toothaches or neuralgia, and got dental fillings if the emergency were dire. They were frequently awakened in the night by the bells that dingdonged persistently in the wake of the great fire of 1835. A sleigh ride through the snowy streets was a recurrent winter joy. And Kate, a country girl, treasured every sign of blossom and verdure when spring came around. On country drives she showed the girls how to string lilac blossoms into necklaces and make curls of dandelion stems.

Kate fell in love with Dr. Ogden Doremus, the handsome young man who gave lectures at the school. She practiced her études for her music master with zeal. But her chief interest was in history, taught by Dr. John Lord. And year after year she worked to perfect her handwriting, her father marking the improvement as time went on. Kate's eventual script was stiff and distinguished. Her letters were models of formal address. Rarely did she show her personality in anything she wrote—unlike her father, who bared his emotions with the utmost candor in his diary and correspondence. Miss Haines read and sealed all outgoing letters, so that no sentiment more disturbing than a hint of homesickness was likely to find its way into the violet-ink correspondence of the girls.

By degrees Kate was introduced to the works of contemporary writers —Whittier, Holmes, Lowell, Longfellow, Irving, Dickens, Hawthorne, Poe and Emerson. She knew that it would please her father if she were well read. Moreover, he numbered Whittier, Longfellow and Emerson among his personal friends, and he had helped to entertain Dickens on his visit to Ohio. Elocution was one of Kate's studies and she had a low musical voice well adapted to the reading of verse.

On Saturday afternoons the girls sometimes went by omnibus to the Hippodrome or to the distant pastures that eventually became Central Park. Dancing, skating and riding were offered by Miss Haines, and Kate carefully perfected herself in each. As she grew older, she rode with splendid carriage and was observed by some of the town's gay blades. She danced with poise beyond her years. Everything Kate did was done well.

Like all the other girls, she admired Miss Haines, who was both a mystery and an enthralling character to those who attended her school. Echoes of an old romance hung about her. She was one of seven children born to Elias Haines, a merchant whose home fronted on the Battery. One of her brothers became Governor of New Jersey and played a prominent part in pushing education in that state.

Tuesday was parlor evening and the girls had a good chance to observe Miss Haines in these more relaxed moments. They found her distant and attractive, like some Attic goddess. They had tableaux or music, and Kate always welcomed a chance to perform. Often they sewed, knitted or sketched until nine o'clock, embroidering silk cushions with white chenille and bunches of pearl grapes, making bands for their drawers, knitting slippers or pasting together valentines to send to mysterious boys who lived in distant parts, or whom they had met in the homes of their friends.

On Saturdays they were allowed callers and sometimes were invited out. As Kate's father grew in fame, he acquired influential friends in the East, and occasionally she would receive a summons to one of the more historic homes of New York. The girls learned how to comport themselves in the grand manner. Kate prepared for countless receiving lines in Washington by parading past Miss Haines and curtsying deeply to the slim, distinguished and acerbic-looking lady in black velvet and lace. The girls seemed like half-opened flowers themselves, with shirred silks, flounces and full skirts that were only a whisper of their mothers' hoops. Kate's hair, garlanded with flowers, was always noticeable in the line on parade nights. Her friends envied her her dazzling skin. She was not the most popular girl, although she had many friends. Kate's pride perplexed the simpler natures. But she always made an impression on the adult world, and she loved such whispers of it as reached the cloistered interior of the school or as she witnessed it on her Saturday forays. She relished the visiting speakers, from Cyrus Field to the Prince de Joinville, who came shortly before she left the school and whom she was to entertain later on in Washington.

But the theater and opera were Kate's greatest pleasures, and she finally conquered her father's resistance to these worldly diversions. She sat enthralled in tulle and apple blossoms through performances by Rachel, Talma and particularly Jenny Lind at Castle Garden in 1850. On one of his trips to New York, her father, by that time a Senator, was persuaded to take her to the Italian opera, just becoming fashionable. Kate took note of the costumes and jewels, the low corsages, the little caps festooned with pearls and coral and the masses of flowers piled high on the stage after the performance. She was conscious of carmine lip salves, pearl powder and perfumes ranging from the simple tansy to heavy patchouli. Studying the men, in full dress attire with white kid gloves, Kate was of the opinion that none matched her father, solemn and slightly disapproving though he was on this occasion. It was only a foretaste for Kate of the life to come, but she savored it with the hunger of her intense nature, from Thackeray's readings to Charlotte Cushman's acting.

She welcomed her Garniss grandparents with pleasure when they called to see how she was getting on, and at once inveigled them into buying her a forty-dollar cloak, a cambric dress and a muslin model with small bishop sleeves, white kid gloves with quiltings of satin ribbon and a velvet-covered spring to hold her radiant hair in place. Kate had learned to restrain her feelings when the name Garniss was mentioned. John P. Garniss—more amiable and forgiving than his hard-grained wife—wrote to Chase that Miss Haines was greatly pleased with Kate, and that her mother, Mrs. Elias Haines, who was staying at the school, was quite bewitched by her. "I think the elder Mrs. Haines one of the most elegant old ladies I ever saw," Garniss added. Thus Kate was schooled in the most formal traditions of the day. Her nature responded, her manners grew ever more polished and her conversation more pointed and adult. But when crossed, the termagant she was still flashed out.

During her years in school, Kate sampled every new fashion that came in and that Miss Haines would permit. On her social outings, she was viewing more expansive horizons than she had known in Cincinnati. Some of the girls invited her into their homes. She quickly absorbed the manners, customs and ideals of her new surroundings. Kate observed the beginnings of an ornate age of gilded settees, rosewood and mahogany pianofortes, velvet ottomans and parlors adorned with Etruscan vases, huge mirrors and sparkling chandeliers. Fortunes were being made and the results were beginning to show. The Gold Rush of '49 was still a fresh memory. Kate took to luxury with a single-mindedness that was to affect her entire life.

The fifties was a showy decade, with recurrent firework displays from ships anchored in the harbor. Miss Haines's girls became familiar with serpents, flower pots and wheels of colored fire sizzling across the night sky. Natural wonders, pantomimes and religious revivals, mesmerism and phrenology, all were part of this emotional era. The political scene was close and ever present on Kate's horizon. Her father's letters and the chitchat indulged in around her kept her well informed. Some of her friends were the daughters of men in public life.

At intervals she heard indirectly from Charles S. Sumner, her father's closest friend. Writing to Chase in 1851 he said: "Remember me to your intelligent daughter, who must be now a great comfort to you." The orator from New England rarely mentioned Kate without bracketing the word "intelligent" with her name. It pleased her to think that so great a man should view her in this light. Sumner had been in the public eye since his Fourth of July address in Boston in 1845 brought him to the front as a champion of the slave.

Chase's own political career developed rapidly while Kate was in boarding school. Sumner and he were drawing closer together on political issues, although Sumner was a Whig and an out and out Abolitionist. Both men were in accord on the basic issue of slavery, although Chase did not approve of extreme measures. "I am for union," he wrote to Sumner in the summer of 1847. "I care nothing for names."

The convention in Buffalo had spurred Chase on to work more energetically for a union of Liberty men with the Barnburners and other dissident factions in support of a strong candidate, with the result that Martin Van Buren was nominated for the Presidency in 1848 on the Free Soil ticket. "Free Soil, Free Speech, Free Labor and Free Men" was the campaign slogan used by this militant party against the Democratic and Whig candidates. James G. Birney's Liberty Party was taken into the fold. Chase backed Van Buren with the same zest he had shown for Harrison when these two men fought the log cabin, cider and frontier-life campaign in the year of Kate's birth. At that time Chase had characterized Van Buren as "cold, selfish, base and faithless." Now, in the blatant compromise of political life, he seemed a worthy candidate.

Van Buren was defeated again, as he was in the contest with Harrison. But Chase rode into the Senate in 1849 with a fused vote of Free Soilers and Democrats of various stripes. Some of the newspapers exploited the theory that he was party to a political bargain. Kate woke up to the bitter public criticism that a man in public life must face. She was only nine, and she did not fully understand it, although Chase wrote to her frankly. In time she was to become hardened to the abuse leveled at her father. But in her early innocence it stung.

Chase tried to make things clear to her when she went home to Clifton for the summer vacation. They all discussed their future life in Washington. Bella had just been waiting for the time when she could take her place by Salmon's side in Washington. Her uncle was a favorite in the capital and so was her Aunt Sarah, youngest daughter of Israel Ludlow. But Kate soon observed that her father was worried. The answer lay not in his political fortunes but in the deathly pallor of his wife. The doomed farmhouse was again working its own disaster. Bella, too, had developed consumption after the birth of Jeanette, and even Kate could detect the familiar cast of illness in her stepmother's face.

The birth of a new baby, Josephine Ludlow, made matters worse and the child herself was to die within the year. But Jeanette, now known as Nettie, was thriving. Kate began to observe her, not as a rival, but with friendly interest. The taming process at Miss Haines's was already taking effect. They were to be devoted sisters for the rest of their lives.

In September the Chases moved to Washington, returning Kate to her school. The best parlors were at once opened to the striking pair from Ohio and the McLeans launched Bella and Salmon on a festive season. Kate was to join them for Christmas and she looked forward to visiting the capital. But by December Bella was desperately ill. Once again Chase threw up his official duties to attend to an invalid wife. Three days before Christmas, he put her in a sanitarium in New Jersey, staying constantly by her side, while she sank, rallied and sank again. In the meantime, one of his sisters died and by the end of January he wrote dolefully to Sumner about his wife's condition and added: "What a vale of misery this world is! To me it has been emphatically so. Death has pursued me incessantly ever since I was twenty-five. My path has been—how terribly true it is—through the region of his shadow. Sometimes I feel as if I could give up—as if I must give up. And then after all I rise and press on. Have you ever experienced these feelings?"

But Chase wrote cheerfully to Kate, anxious not to disturb her in her school work, and feeling that she had had more than her share of melancholy. However, she noticed that his letters from Washington were not so buoyant as usual. Nor did he remember to include the usual admonitions. Actually, Chase was quite distracted, and things were not going well with him in the Senate. He had been snubbed for committee work and was not invited to caucuses by distrustful Democrats who thought him a turncoat.

Fierce debates raged over slavery in California and New Mexico. He cast in his lot with the antislavery group spearheaded by Senator William H. Seward, who had worked with him on the Van Zandt case, and his friend, John P. Hale, of New Hampshire. Soon they were to be joined by Benjamin F. Wade from Ohio and Sumner from Massachusetts. But Chase was ever doubtful of Seward and said of him: "I don't know what Seward will do. I have never been able to establish much sympathy between us. He is too much of a politician for me." Yet their fortunes were to be linked throughout the Civil War.

Chase was regarded by the Whigs as a dangerous radical and by the Democrats as a fanatic. He wrote to Kate about the deadly shafts aimed at him, but reminded her that he had withstood abuse through most of his public life and could take it at the seat of government. He stood like a rock on the Senate floor, already marked as a poor orator but a balky titan where conviction was concerned. Chase had a slight impediment in his speech, which lessened the impact of his well-assembled thoughts. He lacked fluency in an age of oratorical splendor. He was never to sway a crowd or move an audience by the sound of his voice—a disadvantage that Kate in time was to recognize as she helped him campaign for the Presidency. "Light without heat," one of his colleagues commented. "Mind without passion."

Her father's first notable speech in the Senate, Kate learned with pride, was on "Union and Freedom Without Compromise." Already she was following his public career with close attention and knew that he was in debate along with John C. Calhoun, Daniel Webster, Stephen A. Douglas and Jefferson Davis. Henry Clay, thin, ill, sardonic, about to step down from his pedestal and bow from the scene after his ultimate work on the Compromise of 1850, looked on with friendly interest. He remembered Chase as the pedagogue who had taught his son. Webster had known him for years; Chase had once been mildly enamored of his niece Emmeline.

Kate was on the outer periphery of her father's life during his early senatorial days, but he took her to Cincinnati with him for her summer vacations. And his letters often gave her glimpses of contemporary history. He wrote of Henry Clay's last speech in the Senate on the December day in 1851 on which his good friend Sumner took office. "I find no man so congenial to me as Sumner," he commented, "though I do not pretend to be up to his theories in all respects."

He urged Sumner to share a house with him that winter, but in the end Chase went into lodgings and took his meals at a boarding house. It was not the senatorial life that Bella had planned for him, but she was now helpless in a sanitarium.

During the spring vacation Kate visited her father and viewed both Senate and House from gallery seats. She had no difficulty in identifying the more outstanding personalities in the House. There was Joshua R. Giddings, her father's friend from Ohio, looking like a mighty oak with his barrel chest, broad shoulders and forthright manner. Horace Greeley happened to be present, round and cherubic, peering through crooked spectacles and looking childlike and innocent when Kate chanced to spot him. He was to be her friend for life.

Sam Houston whittled away at fresh timber, stopping now and then to take a pinch of snuff, or to send one of his wooden hearts with "Lady! I send thee my heart" to a favorite in the gallery. Kate knew all about him and wished that Sam, with his leopard skin vest, scarlet necktie and Mexican serape, would think of her. Charles Francis Adams looked cold and aloof, but Kate one day was to find him a most engaging friend and host in London.

In the Senate Kate looked long at Jefferson Davis, haughty, spare and erect, where the others lounged in their chairs. But the Senator who interested her most was Stephen A. Douglas, about whom her father had talked so much. His huge head and squat form, his dark burning eyes and square jaw, the long hair that he shook like a mane, made a lasting impression on Kate. She had heard that he was sometimes wild, drunk and disorderly, and that he had been known to fling himself into the lap of a colleague in the intensity of debate. Kate heard Douglas speak—short, sharp sentences punched out with withering scorn. She was already familiar with Webster's leonine head and the thundering sound of his voice. He was now in disgrace with Chase for compromising on the slavery issue.

This, then, was government—these whiskered snarling men in dark coats and light waistcoats, who lounged and yawned, took snuff and burst into angry talk. She had heard nothing that day that suggested noble purpose.

Kate must have turned with relief to her father and Sumner, whom he had welcomed to the Senate as a "brother colleague—one with whom I shall sympathize and be able fully to act." Certainly none compared with them in appearance. She walked down the Capitol steps between these two handsome Senators—both more than six feet tall, immaculately tailored in dark blue broadcloth coats with brass buttons, white stocks, light waistcoats and black trousers. Kate was familiar with Sumner's features from two portraits that hung in their home. One was in her father's study above that of Charles Carroll. The second was in his dining room with other political idols, put up in defiance of the pro-slavery men and as symbols of "faith and purpose."

Kate, looking up into the strong, melancholy, clean-shaven face of her early hero, no doubt was fascinated by the boldly chiseled features and thoughtful eyes that she was not yet old enough to detect as those of a zealot. Sumner treated her with courtesy, as if she were already grown up, and discussed the morning's debate as if she had understood it all.

Kate wore a pale green cambric bonnet lined with yellow. She felt important and happy, and gazed about her with the sharp awareness of her years. Her father drove her to Chevy Chase and Georgetown through tangled slopes where dogwood bloomed and the air was sweet with spring. He showed her the Executive Mansion and the Smithsonian Institution, Ebbitt House and Brown's Hotel, haunts of such Southern planters as the Chesnuts of South Carolina, who owned a thousand slaves, lived in state on their plantations and imported clothes from Paris. Brown's Hotel, which had been known as Indian Queen's Tavern, seemed unimpressive to Kate on a thoroughfare checkered with alternating gaps and shabby buildings.

Chase told Kate that Washington was improving. He recalled how it was in the late 1820's when he took the Wirt girls to balls and to levees at the Executive Mansion, so crowded that there scarcely was room to stand. Servants were knocked about. Food was spilled on the floor. One rarely went home with one's own hat. He thought John Quincy Adams "peculiarly unfortunate in his demeanor—cold and reserved, stiff as a crow-bar, with no perceptible polish, going through his part like a man who was sensible it must be done and who heartily rejoiced when finally it was over." He found Mrs. Adams a "fine-looking woman of liberal disposition." but had no great opinion of her sons, a judgment he later reversed.

"The town was quite ugly and unclean," he told Kate, "but immense crowds swarmed to the levees and the avenue would be jammed with carriages, in spite of the ruts and the mud. Music came from the East Room. At ten the supper room would be thrown open, displaying long tables covered with fine food and adorned with japonicas. *Home Sweet Home* was the signal that the levee was over."

Some time later Kate was able to visualize the scene when her father described in a letter the shocked silence in the Senate as Daniel Webster announced the serious illness of President Zachary Taylor and moved for an immediate adjournment. A tolling bell soon conveyed the news that he was dead. Eight white horses drew the cortege, and Millard Fillmore took office.

A change of Presidents was a significant event to Kate, who was now eagerly studying American history. She knew that she had a statesman for a father. She was no less sure that one day he might be President. But only one part of her father's life was in Washington. Clifton was still his home and his refuge, although his own personal tragedy was moving forward inexorably. Bella's disease had advanced. She was moved from one sanitarium to another. Her child Josephine died, but Nettie by some miracle survived. Chase lived "like Damocles, with a visible sword suspended over his head," he wrote to Sumner. Bella died in June, 1852, without having been able to take her place by his side in Washington. In seventeen years Chase had lost three wives and five children. When Kate joined him that summer, he looked older and sadder and his mood was one of persistent melancholy. He watched her with apprehension, fearing that she, too, might be stricken. But he was relieved to see that she was tender and kind with little Nettie.

Kate comforted her father as best she could in the grim months that followed. Just before his term in the Senate ended, he and Sumner fought the Kansas-Nebraska bill right in the teeth of the brilliant Senator Douglas, who had framed it. They drew up a manifesto, which was printed in some of the New York papers and was thoughtfully read by Kate.

Douglas tore it to shreds but Chase came back with a crackling answer. Their cause was lost, however, and as they walked down the Capitol steps after a seventeen-hour debate, they heard a cannon salute for the victorious slaveholders. "They celebrated a present victory," Chase commented, "but the echoes that they awoke will never rest until slavery shall die."

But the bell soon tolled for Sumner. On a May day in 1856, shortly before her graduation, Kate was horrified to read of Preston S. Brooks's physical attack on him in the Senate at the end of two days of relentless philippics by Sumner on the Kansas issue. It was the summer of 1860 before his sonorous tones were heard in the Senate again. His head was badly battered by his assailant's gutta-percha walking stick; his spine was affected and his recovery was slow.

Chase had been elected Governor of Ohio in the previous year, after a hard canvass, and he and Kate now talked quite openly in terms of the Presidency. With great pride she heard him speak at a Republican mass meeting in Cincinnati in August, 1855. He had suffered much abuse on the slavery issue during the campaign but on this occasion he insisted that his position was that of Washington, Jefferson, Madison, Adams and Franklin. When the votes were counted, he told a Michigan politician: "The elements required for a Presidential election have been harmonized in my election in Ohio." He enlisted the aid of the elder Francis Preston Blair, the sagacious Democratic adviser who had just turned Republican. But the bubble burst. The Chase organization never materialized and Kate had her first lesson in practical politics. Blair backed John C. Frémont as leader of the young Republican party. The Pathfinder was by this time famous for his explorations and expeditions in the Far West.

But James Buchanan won and Chase observed that the Republican party had "committed an act of positive injustice . . . in failing to take as their nominees men who truly personified the real issue before the country."

Failing the Executive Mansion, the Governor's mansion in Ohio had to do. "There's 1860 ahead," Kate reminded her father when he arrived in New York to see her graduate that June. In a frilled muslin gown, with her hair brushed out in gleaming splendor, she accepted her diploma and prize books with the easy grace that was now her natural attitude.

The years from 1847 to 1856 had marked Kate's development from a spoiled, tempestuous child to suave maturity, and the flowering of her looks from the insignificance of seven to a poised sixteen. Because of her height, she already seemed grown up, while still delighting in sticks of colored sealing wax or a sprig of jessamine from home to press in her album.

Miss Haines must have observed Kate with satisfaction, remembering the undisciplined child who had come to her nine years earlier and was now going forth with impeccable deportment and true charm of speech and manner. If the Executive Mansion already seemed a certainty to Kate, it must at least have had shadowy possibilities for her future in Miss Haines's shewd mind.

Kate went forth to her new life with her head poised high on her long and slender neck, like a bird in flight, eager and ready to soar.

Chapter III

GOVERNOR'S DAUGHTER

K ATE MADE the transition from schoolgirl to Governor's daughter
with ease when she settled in the leisurely city of Columbus as
hostess for her father. It was the start of a strong drive for power by both
father and daughter. Kate at last was to know Chase, not just as the
affectionate father, but as a man of boundless political ambition.

She was now to see how this taste was fed through his curious correspondence. It was like catching unexpected reflections in an all-revealing mirror. In her school days she had seen little of her father except
during summer vacations at Clifton. Even then she had often driven
with him to his office and had listened to his talk of politics and law.
From her earliest childhood, he had discussed such matters with her.
Sometimes she had understood; more often not. But she had always
liked to figure as his confidante.

Now she entered deeply and with uncanny understanding into his
political life. She caught the drift of his ambitions and made them her
own. In time the question was sometimes asked whether Chase or his
daughter pushed the harder toward the Executive Mansion. It was with
mental reservations that she heard him pray during their early days in
Columbus: "May God enable me to be content with the consciousness
of faithfully discharging all my duties, and deliver me from a too eager
thirst for the applause and favor of men!"

Humility warred with ambition in Chase. But pride alone governed
Kate. She was involved almost at once in intrigue. She had four years in

which to build up political strength. Already she realized that a strong organization was needed to prevent a fiasco like the Frémont nomination. Kate shrewdly concluded that such homely weapons as good fare, well-timed flattery and feminine charm might be added to political acumen in effecting this end.

Although her Aunt Alice ostensibly was housekeeper at first, Kate soon assumed command of the Governor's mansion and keyed up their household ways to the customs, hours and habits of the East. She ran up bills that appalled her timid aunt, engaged a Negro butler and leavened their hearty fare with a more sophisticated cuisine. Visiting politicians learned that they would be graciously dined and feted at the Governor's house. Kate's breakfasts became famous and visitors invariably were dazzled by their hostess. Few could believe that she was only sixteen.

She was so spectacular in looks and manner that she was talked about at once. All who saw her were struck by her style. She had returned to her native state with fashionable clothes and the inviolable poise acquired under the Spartan rule of Miss Haines. She stood tall and lissome in an era when curves were quite habitual. Kate was different. No bows, frills or fuss marked the harmonious picture. Her willowy lines were discernible even in the crinoline age, and all her clothes were fashioned to give them their due. Her hair was parted with stark simplicity and was drawn in a knot at the nape of her neck. When other belles appeared with garlands and flowers in their hair, Kate wore a single blossom or, quite often, nothing at all. The burnished effect was accent enough for her proudly tilted head. Her eyes were subtle, bold or soft, as the spirit moved her. Some observed that they glinted green like cats' eyes when Kate was aroused or angry. Her tilted nose was now an asset, although Kate never thought so and later tried to have this slight deviation corrected in Paris.

Her most striking characteristics at first glance were her proud bearing and the whiteness of her skin, an opaque pallor that gave intensity to her face. It was repeated in dazzling shoulders that were shown to good advantage in the crinoline age. Kate's step was light; her voice was low and memorable. Altogether her manner was one of well-considered charm, but it was her intelligence that men remembered longest. Her looks were incidental.

The Governor's house was a rambling building with chimneys, turrets and Gothic windows. The front porch led to a garden alive much of the year with flowers and shrubs. Columbus, Kate conceded, had pictorial charm, with its wide shade trees, cobblestone gutters and unpaved streets, hitching posts and roomy mansions. Its citizens were almost Southern in their leisurely manners and soft-spoken ways. Ladies shopped without leaving their carriages. The clerks brought bolts of silk and muslin into the open for their inspection.

Across the street from the Chase mansion was Dr. Francis Carter's home. Kate often watched his third wife, a flowerlike creature always dressed in white, with brown curls clustering around her face and a Spitz dog tucked under one arm. The Carter garden was brilliant all summer with roses. Goldfish swam in little pools and tropical plants thrived in a conservatory. The Carter house was to have special significance for Kate as time went on.

Nearby was the large square house with an ell, owned by Samuel Galloway, lawyer, educator, and congressman. He shared her father's views on slavery, education and temperance, but their ways were to part and he was to dismiss Chase as an impossible choice for the Presidency. Kate and Nettie often visited the Galloway house, in its shady framework of cedar, maple and poplar trees. Strings of onions and peppers hung like balloons in the cellar. Gooseberries, apricots and grapes grew to the rear of the house. Mrs. Galloway was kind and motherly to Kate, who already was showing her headstrong nature and had stirred up gossip behind the lace curtains of Columbus.

At Miss Haines's Kate had seen little of boys except at formal balls. Now they walked up and down the street in front of her home. They teased her, gibed her for her pride, commented on her haughty manners and elegant clothes. Kate scorned their clumsiness, their backwoods air and awkward ways. They repaid her in kind and stirred up her anger so that at least once she shed her dignity and was seen at the back gate, throwing stones at her tormentors and calling them names. "Kate the Shrew" they jeered in delight.

But it wasn't Kate the Shrew that William Dean Howells, then working on the *Ohio State Journal*, found at her father's dinner table when he ate his Thanksgiving turkey with the Chases. They were waited on by a "shining black butler" and Howells was charmed to play charades after dinner with "beautiful, vivacious young Kate Chase," who was already having her fling at amateur theatricals. Howells, an aspiring poet, had moved to Columbus and taken a smaller salary to get away from Cincinnati, which he found to be a "university of the streets and police stations, with a faculty of patrolmen, ward politicians and saloon-keepers." He was madly in love with Elinor Gertrude Mead, of Columbus, whom he was to marry in 1862.

James A. Garfield, eager, gray-eyed, alive with intellectual curiosity and desperately anxious to please, read Tennyson to Kate after one of her traditional breakfasts. The young president of Williams College was already an admirer of her father and she cultivated him zealously.

Ohio was a progressive and buoyant state, and before the Civil War Columbus had a constant parade of men of wit and talent. Legislators, lawyers, teachers, politicians, writers, paused to enjoy its leisurely charms or grind an axe. Reformers found it a sympathetic clime and a call on Chase was imperative. He presided with force and dignity. He was now forty-eight, and the Byronic flair of his earlier years was subdued to a more somber note, induced by grief and experience. His massive figure drew attention wherever he appeared, particularly when Kate stood by his side.

During their first year in Columbus, she and Nettie attended Lewis Heyl's Institute, studying art and French. Nettie had a talent for sketching. In later life she was to make use of this gift, illustrating stories for her children on a professional scale. Eventually she became a generous patron of the arts. Kate, with real powers of concentration and a good memory, learned languages with ease. She already spoke French fluently, thanks to her years with Mademoiselle de Janon, but both in Columbus, and in Washington during the Civil War, she continued her linguistic studies, so as to converse easily with members of the diplomatic corps. Later she became as accomplished in German as in French.

Nettie had spent much time with her invalid mother and her Ludlow relatives, and she was utterly different in temperament from Kate. She was amiable and easygoing, exacting nothing of anyone. In time, as Kate's ambitious demands for her father became insistent, he found more relaxation with his younger daughter. Nettie's affectionate, rambling letters, with the misspellings and flaws in punctuation that the pedagogue particularly deplored, gave him more comfort than Kate's correct but stilted ones.

Chase's first real worry on Kate's behalf developed when he heard that she was being gossiped about for associating with a married man. This was the start of a long series of flirtations, some minor, others more involved, that were to checker the Chase horizon from then on. Although susceptible himself to intelligent women and always craving the affection of the opposite sex, Chase was puritanical in his outlook, a moralist of the first order. He spurned the gossip in Columbus, sure that proud Kate could do no wrong.

She was to go her own way, then and later, loving admiration as she did. But most commentators of her era agree—and some were newspapermen who saw Kate under many different circumstances—that she was not deeply involved emotionally with the succession of men who appeared as her suitors, with the one exception of Roscoe Conkling, whom she may well have adored. She rarely spent her time on men of inferior mental caliber unless she thought they could help her father politically. She thrived on good conversation and easily became the pivotal figure in a gathering of any significance, but most often her seductive moods were used to woo support for her father's cause. Kate was never an idle flirt. She turned instinctively to men of affairs, and quickly steered a light conversation into political channels or let her bright intellect play over the current social picture. Kate could accept the personal flattery and gallantry of her era without being deluded for a moment. She stirred men's minds. They sought her counsel. But she did not readily fall in love.

And she was not in love with the middle-aged married man who took her driving in Columbus at every opportunity. It was common knowledge that his wife sat sobbing behind the curtains of the Carters' windows while she watched him drive up to the Governor's door and go off with Kate in his carriage. Kate was reckless, and indifferent to gossip. The drives came to an end when she tired of the man, not before. At about the same time, she showed her spirit, not only to the young boys of Columbus, but to some of the town's most respected matrons. As Governor's daughter she was invited to hold office in one of their charitable associations. When a local doctor, who was also a town gallant, came under fire, Kate jumped to her feet, her eyes glinting green, and with cutting emphasis condemned them as idle gossips. Then she walked proudly from the room, leaving a lasting chill behind her.

Since she was smarting from gossip herself at the time, her attack may well have been rooted in self-defense. From then on, the mothers regarded her with suspicion, but their daughters envied her spirit and independence. It was typical of Kate that she was all dignity and elegance when it pleased her, but could turn with temper on those who crossed her. The same shrew who threw sticks and stones at the boys over the back gate was in evidence in the parlor where the charitable society met.

Her closest friend was Lucretia Belle Hamlin, whose father, E. S. Hamlin, was a political aide of her father and a newspaperman. Belle, as she was always known, was tiny and had a heavy crop of red hair. When she and tall Kate walked together into a ballroom, as they frequently did, everyone turned to stare. During summer vacations at Clifton, when they were younger, they had haunted Kate's little hut in a tree, where they played great ladies of the theater. Kate was tomboyish then; her strength was not yet molded into grace. Belle Hamlin suffered, too, from Kate's hot temper, and in her aging years as a librarian in Ohio, she still remembered the flash of Kate's white teeth and the glinting anger of her eyes, as well as her striking looks.

Kate was slightly scornful of the social life of Columbus and felt that she dwelt in a cultural desert after the opera, theater and varied amusements of New York, and the parlors she had visited with her father in Washington. There was just one theater in the town and her father still was inclined to frown on this fleshly pleasure. The Dramatic Temple opened in 1855 but staggered financially and had dubious fare. The Beethoven Association was founded in the year of Kate's arrival and there were several halls where traveling opera companies appeared.

Kate was a born organizer and she sparked up an amateur theatrical company, serving as playwright, star and manager. Mrs. Galloway, whose son Todd was to become known later on in the theatrical world, backed her as patroness. The Galloways had not yet drawn away from the Chases with the animosity that was later to smolder between them.

But the event of most immediate interest to the Chases in 1857 was the opening of the new State House in Columbus. A crowd of ten thousand poured into town for the occasion. Governor Chase was the chief speaker, and Kate was in her element as hostess to the visiting dignitaries. Banquet tables filled the rotunda. There was dancing in the Senate Chamber, with Kate the toast of the evening.

By the age of eighteen, she had proved herself a stately hostess. There were government functions of various kinds—balls, soirées, receptions—during Chase's term, all conducted with Kate's skilled touch. By this time she was a definite force in her father's political life, and was so recognized by his visiting friends. They no longer treated her paternally, but bowed to Miss Kate as a peer. National figures moved in and out of her ken. All were interested in her, and some were amazed—not so much by her fresh grace as by her intelligence. She seemed to have a perfect grasp of the political picture and more skepticism than her father, whose appetite for flattery never was quite appeased.

Kate read much of her father's incoming mail with shrewd understanding. A great deal of his personal correspondence went from his home and she could not fail to note that many of his letters were evoked by the artful feelers Chase put out. His correspondence was a college course in political guile, to which Kate contributed liberally as time went on. Increasingly she gave him the benefit of her advice, often over the chessboard, at backgammon or even while they whacked in a leisurely way at croquet balls. Chase, a terrific worker, was as systematic about his relaxation as he was about his office labors. A daily ride. A game of croquet. An hour at chess, while he and Kate figured out political moves as they shifted their pawns. And time for prayers, for detached reading, for church, for quiet dinners with helpful friends.

From making Kate a sounding board for his views, Chase now turned to her seriously for advice. Her intuition, combined with a retentive memory and a cool head, opened up new avenues of thought for him. She soon saw that many of the politicians regarded her father as a shifting force. It outraged her that they could not see the noble design behind it all—that her father was consistent in principle in a period of political evolution, and that his ultimate goal was the welfare and freedom of man. Clearheaded in her analysis, she was forced to the conclusion that men of lesser honor were prone to shy from what they considered his holier-than-thou attitude.

Chase kept his lofty head above it all and wrote to Sumner: "As to all personal attacks I shall content myself with a simple appeal to the whole tenor of my past life and leave my vindication to Time and Public Reason." This was precisely the quality in Chase that alienated him from lesser men. Kate knew it and tried to humanize her father in the public eye, but she was up against a rock of dignity. As long as he lived, she was never able to reconcile this public coldness with the loving, and even sentimental, father that she and Nettie knew in the home. But in time she recognized its power for destruction in political life. Meanwhile, she studied the habits of other public figures.

There was Douglas, wild, dissolute, ardent, often drunk and disorderly, who for years had been able to charm a multitude. Kate knew that fierce censure had surrounded his private life until, in 1856, he married the beautiful Adèle Cutts. Already the transformation in him was said to be striking.

There was also awkward Abraham Lincoln from Illinois, whose debates with Douglas were magnetizing the country and were thoughtfully studied by her father. Kate went out to hear him when he spoke for two hours on the Capitol steps in Columbus on a September day in 1859. She thought he spoke with great humility, as he started out with deferential references to her father, to Thomas Corwin and to Benjamin F. Wade, all linked with Ohio.

He took issue with those who were "blowing out the moral lights around us; teaching that the Negro is no longer a man, but a brute; that the Declaration has nothing to do with him; that he ranks with the crocodile and the reptile; that man, with body and soul, is a matter of dollars and cents."

That same week, speaking in the bright moonlight in Cincinnati, a great crowd both hissed and applauded as he said: "I think slavery is wrong, morally and politically. I desire that it should be no further spread in these United States, and I should not object if it should gradually terminate in the whole Union. . . ."

Moncure Daniel Conway, the Abolitionist clergyman and writer, who was a friend of the Chases, found him "three times sublime to one grotesque" and was struck by his voice, his directness and his humor. Kate thought his delivery clear and high pitched, and his figures of speech well suited to the man he was. He towered six feet four, taller even than her father, and had the rough look of the frontier.

Neither Kate nor her father regarded Lincoln as a serious contender in the presidential picture. Seward, with his powerful New York backing, was the man they feared. Meanwhile Frank P. Blair, Jr. and Schuyler Colfax were building up a strong coalition around Edward Bates of Missouri. But Blair thought Lincoln's Columbus speech the best answer he had made to Douglas. And Samuel Galloway, after hearing it, urged Lincoln to be unobtrusive but receptive to nomination. He frankly said that Chase "would never do."

The elections in the following month were a repudiation of the administration. The Republicans won in Ohio and Chase was re-elected to the Senate. But his plurality this time was small and the fight had been close. Sumner wrote to him from Ostend, where he was recuperating from his injuries: "I am glad you are again a candidate. You must be elected, and persist in keeping Ohio on the side of Freedom. Don't forget to tell your daughter how constantly I remember her." And some time later, writing from Aix-les-Bains: "I am glad you went to Boston and stiffened our politicians there. They need it. And I am grateful to you for your continued firmness. Do not bate a jot. If I should not live to return (and more than once I have thought this probable) this is my legacy and benediction. I was glad to hear such good things of your daughters. God bless you."

Struck by the mortality of man after hearing from Sumner, Chase drew up a will in December, 1859. He estimated his fortune then at $128,250, mostly in real estate. He willed money to a sister, Mrs. Helen M. Walbridge, of Toledo, Ohio, and to his niece, Mrs. Jane Auld, The balance of $124,000 was to be divided between Kate and Nettie, which, with an inheritance of $15,000 each from their mothers' estates, gave them assets of $77,000 apiece. Although much of this was unrealizable at the time, Kate and Nettie were not without material resources as their father entered the lists for the Presidency.

It was not on the Senate that his eyes were fixed, although he had won his seat again. He was suffering increasingly from what Carl Schurz, the young German-American who passed through Columbus in the spring of 1860, called "presidential fever—a troublesome ailment, and sometimes fatal to the peace of mind and the moral equilibrium of persons attacked by it." He considered Chase its "noblest victim," yet he found such frank self-seeking disconcerting in a man of good sense. He knew precisely why Chase had invited him to the Governor's mansion. The Chicago convention was only a few weeks off and Schurz had a substantial German following in Wisconsin. Chase made no attempt to conceal his motives.

But Kate was a gifted hostess and made an indelible impression on the thirty-one-year-old Schurz. They remained good friends for years to come. So did Schurz and her father, although Schurz watched the great man's career with sympathy rather than awe. He saw him indulging in hopes and delusions that always proved deceptive, and wrote of him many years later: "He always knew that I thought his ambition hopeless and his efforts to accomplish its aim futile. But this never affected our personal friendship, for he knew also that I esteemed him very highly and cherished for him a sincere affection."

Schurz felt that Chase's ambition never corrupted his principles or vitiated his public morals, although repeated disappointments "pierced him and rankled in him like poisoned arrows." His first glimpse of this passion in Chase was always associated in his mind with a March morning in Columbus and Kate at the breakfast table. Before she appeared Chase took him into his library and avowed to him "with a frankness which astonished but at the same time greatly fascinated me, his ardent desire to be President of the United States." He bluntly told Schurz that he would like to have his opinion in the matter.

Schurz did not soften the blow. "If the Republican Convention at Chicago have courage enough to nominate an advanced anti-slavery man, they will nominate Seward; if not, they will not nominate you," he told him.

Chase looked stunned for a moment, as if he had heard the unexpected. Then he resumed the conversation in the best of temper, but Schurz knew he had disappointed his host, in spite of his cordiality for the rest of the visit.

Schurz had not yet been exposed to Kate, and he was dazzled indeed when she entered the breakfast room and let herself down into her chair "with the graceful lightness of a bird that, folding its wings, perches upon the branch of a tree." This is how he saw her:

She was then about eighteen years old, tall and slender and exceedingly well formed. Her features were not at all regularly beautiful according to the classic rule. Her little nose, somewhat audaciously tipped up, could perhaps not have passed muster with a severe critic, but it fitted pleasingly into her face with its large, languid, but at the same time vivacious hazel eyes, shaded by long dark lashes and arched over by proud eyebrows. The fine forehead was framed in waving, gold-brown hair. She had something imperial in the pose of the head, and all her movements possessed an exquisite natural charm. No wonder that she came to be admired as a great beauty and broke many hearts. After the usual commonplaces, the conversation at the breakfast table, in which Miss Kate took a lively and remarkably intelligent part, soon turned itself upon politics.

Kate broached the subject of the Presidency with more adroitness than her father. For the rest of his visit, she had Schurz in tow. He was feted and flattered and introduced to all the men who might have potent arguments in favor of her father. Her own expressive eyes were turned on him with their most seductive beams. He was not untouched by either of the Chases, and left persuaded that his host was a noble man and his daughter a ravishing creature with more than one girl's share of brains.

But in his solid way Schurz was quite unmoved on the presidential front and gave his support to Seward. This was Kate's first conscious attempt to effect an important coup for her father. She failed but made a lifelong friend. She had already learned the value of taking a blow and quickly recovering ground. This was an era when party fronts changed overnight, and today's Whig was tomorrow's Republican. Only toward Mrs. Lincoln, James G. Blaine, Samuel J. Tilden, Benjamin F. Wade, the Blair family and—in time—her husband, William Sprague, was Kate to be eternally unrelenting. Usually she was calculating for the future when she faced antagonism directed at her father.

But Schurz had raised some doubts in Chase and, when the Republicans of Wisconsin chose a pro-Seward delegation, he concentrated on Pennsylvania, New Jersey and Illinois. His free trade associations were not liked in the first two states and Lincoln's star was rising in Illinois. Kate took careful thought when an old admirer, Governor William H. Bissell, of Illinois, wrote to her father that spring: "You have not a few friends in this state, among whom I count myself, who would be very glad to have you nominated at Chicago as our presidential candidate, but . . . our folks have recently taken a notion to talk up Lincoln for that place. Of course, while that is so, it would be ungracious and

impolite to start anybody as his seeming rival. Lincoln is everything
that we can reasonably desire in a man and a politician."

By May Kate had persuaded her father that he lacked congressional
friends and must seek them in the direct manner by going to Washington. Knowing full well by this time that his hauteur did not help him,
she urged him to make himself affable on the floor of the House. But J.
M. Lucas, a Lincoln supporter, saw at once that he was acting out of character. Lucas sneered openly at the "cold and stoic aspect replaced by the
genial smiles, and the friendliest and most obliging manner." He considered Chase "chill, calculating and selfish, uniting a powerful intellect
with still more powerful ambition."

Chase was not particularly happy in this role. Actually, it put great
strain on his sense of the fitness of things. He tried his powers of
persuasion on grim-eyed Wade to see if that fighter from Ohio would
withdraw his own candidacy. He was rudely rebuffed. The Ohio Republicans were veering rapidly toward Wade. When Chase's best
friends tried to persuade him that his chances were poor, he reminded
them of his God-given mission: "I cannot change my position. A very
large body of people . . . desire that I shall be their candidate."

Even his old friend, Dr. Gamaliel Bailey, editor of the *National Era*
in Washington, who was to die within the year, urged him to withdraw
his candidacy and let Seward ride. Bailey's home had long been a gathering place for the radical forces and he was much beloved by Chase.
His Saturday night receptions drew such men as Greeley, Corwin, Wade,
Giddings, Conway, Hannibal Hamlin and Chase himself. He was the
publisher of *Uncle Tom's Cabin* and had been mobbed three times in
Cincinnati when editing the *Philanthropist*.

Both Kate and her father were baffled by the defection of intimate
friends and men of political sagacity. "Why?" Chase asked his daughter.
"When I would willingly forego every hope of personal distinction if I
could secure the adoption of the great principles of Right, Justice and
Humanity for which we are contending, by retiring myself to complete
obscurity, recognized of none but a few friends and God."

This was oblique reasoning, acceptable to few but Chase and his
ever-loving daughter. However lofty his motives, Kate knew that his
changes of political front were against him and that at the moment the
Know Nothings, whose favor he had courted, were incensed by his

efforts to round up the German-American vote. Not even to herself would Kate admit that her father left the public cold. But she could not shut her eyes to the fact that much of his support was lukewarm, and that some of his political helpers were sycophants and nonentities. Close study of his correspondence persuaded her of this. Kate was determined to bring men of power into the fold.

Seward, keen politician that he was behind a lackadaisical manner, had gone off to Europe, secure in the knowledge that Thurlow Weed would pull every possible string for him in New York; that he had strong newspaper backing, economic support and accredited political leaders in his camp. Kate was to become increasingly conscious of the hidden power of this subtle character whose heavy eyebrows, drooping upper lip and chronic look of irony, were a misleading front for a tenacious will. She knew that he had labored mightily for the prize, first with the Whigs, then the Republicans. Chase could not even be sure of Horace Greeley, although Kate was to cherish him for years, through thick and thin, for or against her father. She sincerely liked Mr. Greeley.

However unsuccessful the trip to Washington from the political point of view, Kate made the most of it socially. The dying moments of the Buchanan administration were also the dying moments of an era. Men still feasted and caroused, and women danced and made love a little madly as the war clouds thickened. But the social structure was rocking at its base. Kate felt the tension as she sat in the Senate gallery, observing the now familiar faces ranged in gloom, defiance and rage. She heard the angry debates, the shouted insults, and knew that Ben Wade had exhibited two pistols on the lid of his desk. Other Republicans kept their weapons concealed beneath their coats, and the more timid left the Capitol in groups. Echoes of John Brown's raid still exploded in the Senate. Sumner was back, looking fit. He had already voiced a mighty blast for his cause, but no Democrat had acknowledged his return. Both houses had daily verbal brawls and talk of duels. All attempts at harmony failed as North and South confronted each other with mounting emotion.

The ill will had spread to the more fashionable parlors of Washington. There were open breaks where a coating of ice had kept bad manners in check for several years. When the Marine Band played in the grounds of the Executive Mansion on Saturdays, ladies sat in their open carriages and talked of the art galleries of Europe, of the Paris shops, of Tennyson and Thackeray, to keep their minds from dwelling on impending doom. Or they drank chocolate from silver urns on the low tables that had just become fashionable and gossiped about the murder of Philip Barton Key by Daniel E. Sickles.

Some took tea with a spoonful of rum. Mrs. Douglas had launched the fashion of drawing the curtains and serving afternoon tea by candlelight and gaslight. It was considered a romantic innovation, even though the sun shone outdoors, and the crocuses and hyacinths were heralding an early spring. Mrs. Douglas's Saturday afternoon receptions, her dinners and dances, were always the last word in novelty and interest.

Fashions were fragile and illusory, Kate observed. Gauze and tulle were sprayed with white clematis, violets, honeysuckle, or Mrs. Douglas's favorite japonicas. Low, rounded necks and lace berthas set off white shoulders. Little caps of velvet and pearl, jet or coral, were worn on the hair, or garlands of flowers, trailingly repeated on billowing tulle skirts. Every steamer brought gloves, fans, handkerchiefs, silks and laces from Europe, often chosen by consular friends abroad. Silks from Lyons. Velvets specially woven in Genoa for a Southern hostess. The men wore sparkling studs, and diamond pins in their brilliant cravats. Their waistcoats were of velvet or satin, embroidered and brocaded. Mustaches were coming into vogue.

Kate was dressed in the height of fashion, as always. Her experience in Columbus had given her an easy familiarity with crowded assemblies. She was already known to the official set in Washington, having made a number of visits to the capital with her father. It was noted that Miss Kate had quite grown up in Columbus and that she was now a formidable belle. She was swept into the round of morning and evening receptions, the musicales, dinners, at-homes and balls. She found the play of political passion behind the social scene exciting, and was quite aware of chill winds that blew from the South for the daughter of Chase, the Negro protagonist.

Kate had her hair dressed by François, whose fame, aside from his skilled work, rested on the fact that he had filled the same function for Rachel. It pleased her to dine at a table where Gautier, the caterer, had spread his Roman chariots, cupids and swans. But it was not at the

Executive Mansion that Kate found these extravagances. The Buchanan functions were correct, but the imaginative touch was missing. There were few flowers in view, save for potted plants and stiff palms. The traditional glass plateau extended the length of the dinner table. From the center and each end rose epergnes filled with bonbons and cakes. Kate thought there was something bleak about it all, in spite of the fine French cooking and excellent wines. Did she dream how she would do it when her time came, as she sat at the Buchanan table and observed Harriet Lane?

Kate admired the President's niece, and Miss Lane approved of Kate and always received her when she was in Washington. So did Mrs. Douglas, although each disliked the other. Both these hostesses were engaged in a bitter feud. Mrs. Douglas had vowed to make Stephen's enemies her own. Grandniece of Dolly Madison and a grandee in her own right, she was quite capable of stealing anyone's social thunder. The competition was keen. The best opera seats invariably went to these two belles, who coldly turned their backs on each other.

Kate met both women on their own ground. She had the kinship of youth with Harriet, who was handsome and self-contained, made few social gaffs and gave able support to her uncle, the President. With her instinct for form, Kate approved Harriet's careful manners and thought she managed the Executive Mansion with dignity, if not with distinction. She watched her dancing with Lord Lyons, the British Ambassador, taking note of her white tulle dress wreathed in clematis. Kate, like many others, wondered how serious this romance was becoming. Harriet had the added luster of a European sojourn. She had been presented to the Empress Eugénie, and Kate had read of her attendance at one of Queen Victoria's drawing rooms wearing a "pink silk petticoat, overskirt of pink tulle, puffed and trimmed with apple blossoms, and finished off with a silk train."

Kate knew just how she must have looked, with her light hair, her clear complexion and rather full-blown figure—a wholesome and dignified, if not a wholly *elegant*, girl. She felt much in tune with Harriet, who had been carefully educated by her uncle, after being left an orphan. The President had watched Harriet's development as Salmon Portland Chase had labored over hers, from spelling mistakes to diplomatic tact.

Kate found it a piquant social situation that Mrs. Douglas should espouse her husband's quarrels so ardently and that tactful Harriet should lend herself to open rivalry with Addie Douglas. Here, too, was a belle with whom to reckon, more worldly than Harriet, formidable on every social level. She was credited with having tamed a savage, and the Senators looked on approvingly when she came down from the gallery to wrap his overcoat around wild Stephen as he dripped sweat in the wake of one of his oratorical outbursts. She prized the Little Giant.

Kate thought that Mrs. Douglas had a most seductive face, wide at the cheek bones, with a broad forehead, and humor and warmth in her eyes. Her chestnut hair was simply parted in the middle and was drawn to the nape of her neck, like Kate's, except that she frequently wore japonicas low in the back. She was placid and good tempered, and nearly everyone liked her. She dressed with great simplicity and chic. When Mrs. Roger A. Pryor, wife of the Southern Congressman, remarked to her: "You know, you are not really handsomer than the rest of us. Why do people say you are?" Mrs. Douglas replied: "Because I never trick myself out in diamonds, or use more than one color in a gown. An artist told me once that all those things spoiled a picture."

The two women were on friendly terms, although their husbands were at odds politically. Mrs. Pryor considered Kate, Mrs. Douglas and dark-haired Mrs. George E. Pugh, of Ohio, the unapproachable belles of the Buchanan regime, although she had expressed the opinion a year earlier that Kate was much too young to attend the ball given for Lord and Lady Napier, when these two popular Britons left the Embassy earlier than they had expected. The Ambassador was a friend of Lord Palmerston, but was not in favor with his successor.

Twelve hundred guests from different cities paid ten dollars apiece to dance at Willard's Hotel in the frescoed dining room decorated with the emblem of St. George and the Dragon. Paintings of Queen Victoria and George Washington faced each other. Gautier had spread his wares at one end of the room—oysters, boned turkey, ham, macaroons, champagne and the other makings of a feast.

Here North and South foregathered, with the fires banked down for the popular Napiers. Jefferson Davis, spare, autocratic, stayed a little aloof. Seward drifted sadly through a quadrille and Robert Toombs openly snubbed the North. Sam Houston danced with a Massachusetts belle. Nerissa Saunders, a Buchanan favorite, played the harp. James Gordon Bennett, who liked to be invited to all the important parties, chatted with Mrs. Douglas, whose white tulle flounces were looped with bunches of violets, the flower she also wore in her low coiffeur. Dion Boucicault whispered gallantries to Mrs. Pugh, striking in crimson velvet with rubies at her neck and pomegranate flowers in her hair.

Lady Napier, a Scot who deplored all ostentation except on state occasions and then outdid the most lavish, wore white brocaded satin with a Juliet cap of pearls. She greeted young Miss Chase with kindness. Kate was in white silk tissue, embroidered with moss rosebuds. Years later, Mrs. Pryor with the dark gulf of the Civil War between them, wrote of her:

She was extremely beautiful. Her complexion was marvellously delicate; her fine features seeming to be cut from fine bisque, her eyes bright, soft, sweet, were of exquisite blue [sic], and her hair a wonderful color like the ripe corn tassels in full sunlight. Her teeth were perfect. Poets sang then, and still sing, to the turn of her beautiful neck and the regal carriage of her head. She was as intellectual as she was beautiful. From her teens she was initiated into political questions, for which her genius, and her calm, thoughtful nature eminently fitted her.

The Napier ball was only a memory as the nation raced toward war and Abraham Lincoln campaigned with quiet persistence to be first among his fellow Americans. So did Salmon Portland Chase. The rush and stir of their visit to Washington that spring swept both Kate and her father into a cloud of optimism. Such was the welcome given Kate that the perfidious Wade and the hostile Congressmen failed to dampen her hopes. She went back to Columbus, leaving an image of grace behind her and bearing with her the finished picture of the role she would play when her father became President.

Chapter IV

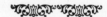

"A GLORIOUS GIRL"

KATE'S AMBITIONS were checked for the time being when the telegraph clicked the news into Columbus that Abraham Lincoln was the nominee of the Republican party at Chicago. Her father had made a poor showing. Even his own state had failed to give him its full strength. It had thrown the votes from Chase to Lincoln that gave the man from Springfield his majority.

Carl Schurz, who had backed Seward, thought of his friend Chase with sympathy as the city of Chicago "shook with triumphant cheers for Lincoln." He pictured him waiting expectantly near the telegraph in Columbus. Not only had his prediction come true but it had "become more terribly true than I myself had imagined."

"No doubt he had hoped, and hoped, and hoped against hope," wrote Schurz, "and now came this disastrous, crushing, humiliating defeat. I saw that magnificent man before me, writhing with the agony of his disappointment, and I sympathized with him most profoundly. I should have pitied him, had I dared to pity such a man."

Kate did not writhe. She was coldly angry, but kept a proud front before observers. Her father, she knew, would stick to his Olympian heights in face of disaster and ignore its implications. Only to his daughters did he show bewilderment or agony of spirit.

For the next few days, Kate read with bitterness of the scenes in Chicago and the ovation given the Rail Splitter. She could picture it all—the big, ugly auditorium festooned with bunting, rosettes and evergreens; the huge charcoal sketch of Lincoln and the garish portraits of American statesmen; bands playing and delegates milling about like ants; the Wigwam put up for Lincoln's supporters; Seward's cannon ready to boom for his own victory, and their Ohioan "friends" scuttling the ship in favor of Wade.

Joshua Giddings wrote in conciliatory vein to her father afterwards but Chase felt that his name had been trifled with and his prestige impaired. It was a bitter pill for him to swallow. His record as Governor was good. His entire career had been tied up with the state of Ohio. His moral probity was unquestioned. He was a man of importance and influence. His daughters and friends were truly baffled by the defection of his own state.

Kate realistically saw that both her father and Seward had been outgeneraled in the national scene. The only satisfaction she could wring from the situation was the parallel downfall of Seward. The reverberations in his case far exceeded the Chase debacle. His campaign had been strong and showy. It had boomed up to the last minute in Chicago, where the delegates were wined, dined and flattered by politicians from New York; where a parade was engineered but proved disastrous when the Lincoln supporters got ahead of the Seward men and packed the convention hall.

Kate carefully weighed the elements that had entered into the campaign. While her anger burned at white heat, she stored away impressions for the future. She did not underestimate political expediency, or the fact that Lincoln stood midway between the radical and conservative elements. It was clear to her now that his campaign tactics had been sound too. He had traveled four thousand miles that year and made twenty-three speeches. He had written to numerous men of "potential political usefulness." But so had her father. She thought of the network of correspondence in which she had taken a hand.

The Lincoln-Douglas debates beyond doubt had taken the public by storm. Kate herself acknowledged their fascination. She knew that copies of Lincoln's speeches had been freely circulated among influential Ohioans. Moreover, his Cooper Union speech had made him a figure in the East, and the rail-splitter legend born at Decatur in May had caught the public fancy. Kate was well aware that her father lived on

Parnassus, whereas Lincoln created a telling effect in the market place—to some of rugged grandeur, to others of apelike awkwardness.

The headstrong Edwin M. Stanton, who was to fight the Civil War with Lincoln, had declined to take a legal case with him, saying he would not be associated with such a "damned, gawky, long-armed ape as that." But Gideon Welles, who also would enter Lincoln's Cabinet, was more perceptive and wrote of Lincoln when he visited Hartford: "He was made where the material for strong men is plenty, and his huge, tall frame is loosely thrown together. He is in every way large, brain included, but his countenance shows intellect, generosity, great good nature, and keen discrimination. He is an effective speaker, because he is earnest, strong, honest, simple in style, and clear as crystal in his logic."

Kate had enough political wisdom by this time to recognize Lincoln as a man of strength. She simply could not see him pitted against her father. But she was silent, except to Chase, whom she privately consoled. His followers in Ohio were dumbfounded that he should have made so poor a showing at the national convention. Little groups gathered in Columbus and Cincinnati to commiserate.

But Kate, with detachment and strength of purpose, sought balm in gentler matters. Decorative as she was on a ballroom floor, like her father she loved the soil and outdoor life. She persuaded him to visit the farm for a brief respite. Practical in moments of crisis, she busied herself making quantities of crabapple jelly. There had been much rain and the grass and foliage were intensely green. Their roses, kept cut down, were blooming late and plentifully. Their strawberry beds were thriving. Only the fig trees, which they were trying hopefully to cultivate as an experiment, seemed to languish in the northern clime.

Kate watched her father's tension ease as they worked together in the garden. He became a more human and pliable person in these surroundings. Kate, too, underwent a transformation when she wrapped an apron around her muslin dress, and her white skin became faintly flushed as she bent over jelly pans. In the cool of the evening she played backgammon or croquet with her father or they read poetry and the classics. The artful correspondence that preceded the convention had subsided for the time being. Both had the knack of turning their backs on failure. Chase brushed off his defeat as if it had never taken place. Kate smarted but held her peace.

By September she was caught up again in the social round. She went to Cleveland with her father to attend the dedication of the Oliver Hazard Perry monument, commemorating the defeat of the British on Lake Erie. Since Perry was a Rhode Islander, one of the speakers was Governor William Sprague of that state. At a ball given in a local hotel on the night of the ceremonies, Richard E. Parsons, of Columbus, presented him to Kate. The slight, dark-haired youth, known as the Boy Governor, was fascinated by Chase's daughter and danced with her as often as she could spare him a number. He was not a brilliant talker, but he extolled her father, had strong political views and caught her interest by his earnestness. Actually, Sprague was extremely susceptible to women, but he had none of the arts or graces of the professional gallant with which she was becoming familiar. However, he piqued Kate's interest.

"What a charming man Governor Sprague is!" she remarked as the ball came to an end. Before she went to bed that night, she learned that he was known as the Cotton King of New England and that his family lived in almost feudal state on Rhode Island. This did not diminish Kate's interest in the young governor.

A month later Baron Renfrew was the guest of honor at a ball given in the Cincinnati Opera House. The belle that evening was Rebecca Groesbeck, who wore a white tulle dress puffed at the waist, and spurned her mother's jewels, hastily offered when they learned that the Baron intended to dance with her. No supper was served, the party broke up early, and the occasion was not one of the Prince's gayer memories of America.

Like all her young friends, Kate followed his progress across the country with interest. His reception was compounded of good will, acid observation and gush. His tapering trousers with lapped seams, the knickerbockers he was popularizing, his sack coats and elegant waistcoats, his clean-shaven rather sulky face, all drew comment. Kate, who studied the current periodicals, like the wideawake young politician that she was, noted that Harriet Lane took him to Madame Smith's school for girls in Washington, where he played a game of tenpins. However, he declined to stay on the White House balcony and watch the fireworks when they kept fizzling out later that evening.

Kate heard from some of her old school friends in New York of the ball given in his honor at the Academy of Music—of the three thousand guests crowded together, the pink and white muslin decorations, the great blaze of gaslight from twenty-five chandeliers and the belles in their finest attire. All wrote with horror of the huge vases that toppled and the section of floor that collapsed in dangerous proximity to the Prince, without ruffling him in the least.

The social picture dimmed when he sailed from Portland, Maine, on a day late in October. Kate, reading the latest installment of Dickens' *Great Expectations* in *Harper's Weekly* on the same date, might have drawn her father's attention to a significant editorial: "If the peace can be preserved between Great Britain and the United States it matters very little what other powers may do. France, Russia, Germany, Italy, Spain and the Asiatic Powers may war as they please without troubling us, or risking the cause of truth and civilization—so long as we keep out of the conflict."

President Buchanan wrote reassuringly to Queen Victoria that the young Prince had made an excellent impression on a "sensitive and discriminating people." But the President had graver problems. Tall, ruddy, his head cocked to one side, he was seen pacing the porch of the Executive Mansion muttering: "Not in my time, not in my time." His administration was ending with bad blood on all sides. The Dred Scott decision was still a burning issue. The Treasury was depleted. The fuse of war was ready for the match.

Sectionalism was in full flower at the Capitol, with thin, proud John C. Breckinridge in the chair and eager for the Presidency as the candidate of the Southern Democrats. Violent passions blazed intermittently. All pretense at amity had ended. Roaring abuse, mutual contempt or the quick flash of defiance, were standard manners between North and South. Men dared not leave their seats lest they lose their votes on vital issues. Pink-cheeked pages with cambric collars stood by, ready to rouse Senators for the calling of the roll.

Soon after the election of Lincoln, President Buchanan was attending a fashionable wedding when he heard shouts in the street. He soon discovered the cause. South Carolina had seceded from the Union. By nightfall the dining rooms of the hotels were misted with blue cockades, and Southern leaders were celebrating at the home of Jefferson Davis before going to call at the Executive Mansion. By February the seven states of the lower South had seceded and formed their own government—the Confederate States of America, to be headed by Jefferson Davis throughout the war.

By this time Kate was concentrating on a Cabinet post for her father. The assistance of James S. Pike, Washington correspondent of the New York *Tribune*, was enlisted to stir up Horace Greeley and Charles A. Dana on the subject. Pike was an old friend of the Chases and indeed, before her marriage, his second wife, Lizzie, had been much enamored of Chase.

On the last day of December, her father showed Kate a telegraphed message from Lincoln in Springfield, saying: "In these troublous times I would like a conference with you. Please visit me here at once."

Chase reached Springfield on January 3 and the President-elect, waiving all ceremony, called on him at his hotel. Chase studied the weary, deep-hewn face with interest, and later gave Kate a detailed account of his interview.

"I have done with you," said Lincoln, "what I would not perhaps have ventured to do with any other man in the country—sent for you to ask you whether you will accept the appointment of Secretary of the Treasury, without, however, being exactly prepared to offer it to you."

Lincoln told Chase bluntly that he was making Seward Secretary of State. Had Seward declined the post, he would have offered it to him, he said. Chase was deeply offended. Not the Presidency. Not the chief Cabinet post, except as second choice. Moreover, he knew that Simon Cameron had been slated for the Treasury, but that last-minute opposition had made Lincoln pause over this appointment. After listening to Alexander K. McClure, editor and legislator, talk for more than an hour against Cameron, Lincoln had just written to his appointee revoking his offer and suggesting that Cameron send in a letter of declination.

It was a galling situation for Chase, although he did not know all the circumstances at the time. He told Lincoln coldly that he was "not prepared to say that he would accept that place if offered" and he desired to ask the advice of his friends. In actual fact, he wanted to talk it over with Kate and to consult Sumner and his newspaper friends on Park Row.

Kate was wild when she heard all this. It was incredible that her father should receive such treatment on top of defeat. To some it seemed as if Lincoln were doing a generous thing in appointing his rival candidates to the Cabinet. But not to Kate.

Lincoln parleyed with him for two days and Chase, paying a return call in his austere home, found him, as did McClure, "ill-clad, ungraceful in movement, and his rudely chiselled face, always sad in repose, clearly portraying his fretting anxieties." He wore snuff-colored pantaloons, an open black vest held by a few brass buttons, a straight coat with tight-fitting sleeves that exaggerated his long bony arms—"all supplemented by an awkwardness that was uncommon among men of intelligence."

But, as in the case of McClure, Lincoln's earnestness, sincerity and candor made their impression until he "forgot all the grotesque qualities which so confounded me when I first greeted him" and learned to respect, if not like, the man. On his return to Ohio and after a talk with Kate, Chase wrote to Thaddeus Stevens: "Mr. Lincoln conversed frankly and fully. He is a man to be depended on. He may, as all men may, make mistakes; but the cause will be want of sufficient information, not unsoundness of judgment or of devotion to principle."

Lincoln had at least wrung lip service from Chase. Kate, stifling her resentment, decided that a half loaf was better than none. And her father might help to checkmate Seward. Dana had the same idea. "With Mr. Seward at the head of the State Department, we must have a firm hand, an immovable will, and an unyielding power of refusing in the Treasury, or we are lost," he wrote Chase. Dana knew that Thurlow Weed was trying to create a friendly Cabinet around Seward and to exclude Chase.

When Sumner added his potent persuasion, Kate knew that the battle was won and that her father would accept the secondary post, if need be. She foresaw more national fame for him in the Cabinet than in the Senate. And national fame was what he needed for the next campaign.

But the Chase arrival in Washington in February was not the triumphal affair that Kate had previsioned a year earlier. Her father came in without the cheers for a President-elect, although a few days later Lincoln himself was to arrive in even deeper silence. Washington had a dreary look in the gray February light. The cobbled pavements of Pennsylvania Avenue were rough and uneven. The roadbed oozed mud. The scattered buildings to the south looked raddled. The fashionable stretch of shop, hotel and restaurant was to the north, dressed up by a brick sidewalk, the town's promenade.

The Treasury Department, where Chase would take command, boasted a new extension. Next door was the State Department, housed in a nondescript way and closely resembling the old-fashioned buildings to the west of the Executive Mansion. Kate looked with special interest through the iron fence and gateways at the now familiar dwelling, conscious of the straggling sheds and red brick barn, the conservatory to the west and the wooded lawn. No doubt she felt that there was much that she could do with this establishment, both indoors and out. She had had ample chance to observe it during the Buchanan regime. From what she now heard of Mary Todd and Abraham Lincoln, little need be expected there.

The Capitol loomed unfinished, with derricks and a network of steel rope girdling the base of its cast-iron dome. There was little else to view in the way of public buildings, save the Smithsonian Institution. No one edifice seemed related to any other. There were gaps on every street. But Kate knew that soon the Rock Creek area would be blossoming, that there were fine estates on the outskirts of the city, that the Pryors often went calling at the pillared mansion of Colonel Robert E. Lee across Long Bridge and that Francis P. Blair, who had failed her father so badly, summered at beautiful Silver Spring. In the city proper the hotels were gay, rowdy and overcrowded, if not impressive to look at; the shops catered to the transient needs of a capital city; and Kate hoped earnestly that she had come to Washington to stay.

Rarely had so handsome a father and daughter appeared on the national scene. Kate was aware that a new life had begun for her. She could now give her father the home setting he had lacked in his senatorial days, when he stayed in dismal boarding houses. She already had friends of high estate and she planned to plunge at once into the social whirl. But her first task was to find a suitable mansion.

The farewells of the Southerners were still being said when Kate settled in Washington. Though she was the daughter of the radical Chase, she had friends among them. She was too diplomatic to be outspoken in her views, however deeply she might feel on the slavery issue. She watched the baggage wagons trundling through the streets, piled high with boxes and trunks filled with the finery of the Southern hostesses. No one could visualize better than Kate the parties and high moments they represented.

Carriages banged along the rutted highways and messengers moved fleetly from point to point as one family after another headed for the wharf. Their blooded horses were shipped South. Hotelkeepers watched the exodus with dismay. It was like the breakup of an old and powerful dynasty. Some hated to go. Mrs. Clement C. Clay could do nothing but weep. Before long she was to weep much more and for better cause. Others left with elation, because the deadlock was ended, and they saw a new day dawning for the South.

Kate pictured these women with all their fine clothes going back to great plantations to recline on their piazzas behind scented barriers of Lamarque roses, while small slave girls switched the flies from their vicinity with little besoms. She was party to the Northern conception of Southern life and had no real belief that the day of bloodshed was at hand, although she had listened to more inflammatory talk than the average girl of her age. Hotheads had always surrounded her father, but his own radicalism was purely of the intellect. He was a conservative in practice; at times even a snob. Kate resembled him in this respect.

She saw at once that most of the mansions owned by the Southerners had been closed up. No longer would extremists gather at the homes of Senator John Slidell or Senator James Henry Hammond, who had taunted Northern sympathizers in 1858 with the phrase: "Cotton is King." No longer would Mrs. William M. Gwin, wife of the proslavery Senator from California, spend $75,000 a year running her home at Nineteenth and I Streets, or have fashionable Washingtonians studying volumes of colored engravings to find original costumes for a fancy-dress ball.

Mrs. Pryor, a favorite of Kate's, was still in town, but the days were running short when she would entertain Secessionist friends, serving them canvasback duck, oysters, terrapin, flummeries and tea; or when Roger would hold political court late at night over bourbon, hot water and lemons. On New Year's Day Mrs. Pryor had brewed a mighty bowl of punch with "arrack proportioned rightly and enough toasted crab apples." Virginians and other Southerners had swarmed in and some Northerners too, for the Pryors had kept friends on both sides of the chasm. It was gloomy outdoors but within, music, gay attire and bright conversation concealed the unrest. The long-haired Pryor had decided to stay for Lincoln's inauguration, but he wrote that "o'er all there hung a shadow and a fear."

Kate took careful note of the picture and mapped out the course she would follow. Mrs. McLean gave her kindly advice. She was a sage woman with hearty Ludlow blood in her veins and she was glad to see clever Kate become her father's hostess. She had worried greatly over the machinations of some of the women who fluttered around Chase. The McLeans were a liberal and generous pair, and Chase would always bless John McLean for dissenting on the Dred Scott decision, but he, too, soon was to pass from the scene.

Things had changed greatly in Washington since Kate's visit the previous spring. The social vista had narrowed. A new leader was needed. She gave little thought to Mrs. Lincoln, the strange wife of the President-elect, about whom whispers already were spreading in Washington. Nothing was expected socially of the backwoods pair. Nor was there much promising hostess material in the Republican ranks. Seward's wife was an invalid, although Kate was already well aware that his three-story brick mansion on F Street was a fortress of intrigue. His fastidious suppers of turkey, game, shad and champagne had spelled votes in his senatorial days. They would not fail him now. His small gatherings of potent figures took in men of all stripes, for Seward worked obliquely without open animosities.

While Kate looked for a house, she and her father took rooms at Willard's, to be close to the presidential picture. After Lincoln's arrival official calls were made, back and forth, and her father was much in evidence. Kate heard echoes of the parade. President Buchanan. The Judiciary. Mayor James E. Berret, a Breckenridge man. The Common Council. General Winfield Scott, whose great frame scarcely unbent as he doffed his plumed hat to the new President. Senator Douglas, strong and magnetic, gazing up darkly at the giant Lincoln. And a long parade of editors, office seekers, politicians, delegates and sycophants.

It fell to Chase's lot to present John Tyler and the delegates attending the so-called peace conference initiated by the Virginia Legislature. Not even General Scott could have injected more majesty into the occasion. But the conference was petering out inconclusively and the delegates were in low spirits. It was not a happy gathering. After this reception the ladies passed in review, and Kate bowed proudly to the man who had worsted her father. This was probably Lincoln's first glimpse of the famous Miss Chase, unless he had spotted her in Columbus.

When Mrs. Lincoln finally arrived just before the inauguration, few of the official ladies showed up to receive her. But Kate was among the little group that courteously welcomed her, and Mrs. Douglas brought warmth and cordiality to bear on the woman who had rejected Stephen and settled for Abraham Lincoln. Kate had only fleeting consciousness of a round and tired face, of hurried exchanges and of a certain nervousness of manner. Later she and her father discussed the President-elect and the impression he was making. Chase had been quick to observe the spirit of levity that confused more serious men. But Lincoln had remembered names, made apt comments and expressed himself uniquely, if rather coarsely.

Both Kate and her father were aghast when they learned that he had challenged Sumner to stand back to back with him and match their inches—a playful pastime sometimes indulged in by Lincoln when he met an uncommonly tall man. The Abolitionist from New England had snubbed Lincoln outright, reminding him that the time had come to unite their fronts against the enemy and not their backs.

"He is a good piece of a man," Lincoln commented without rancor, adding that, although he had never had much to do with churchmen, Sumner was his idea of a bishop.

Still smarting from her father's defeat, Kate made cool appraisal of the political leaders who had gathered from far and near to cotton up to the new President. In particular she kept an eye on Seward, who was determined to freeze her father out of the Cabinet. For several days the clash of interests on this point was severe. Lincoln listened attentively, made few comments and stood his ground on Chase, although Seward persisted and finally came out with the flat statement: "There are differences between myself and Chase which make it impossible for us to act in harmony."

On March 2 a delegation of Seward's friends arrived to protest the inclusion of Chase the radical in the Cabinet. They said that Seward would never work with him. Lincoln told them bluntly that the prime need of the nation was the hearty co-operation of all good men and all sections. He suggested that he might make Seward Minister to

Great Britain instead of Secretary of State. "No Chase, no Seward," he later told his secretary, John G. Nicolay. "I can't afford to let Seward take the first trick."

By March 4 Seward had accepted the inevitable. He wrote: "The President is determined that he will have a compound Cabinet and that it shall be peaceful and even permanent."

Greeley applauded in print, saying that the "ablest Republican living" had received the Treasury appointment, thanks to the "determined courage and clear-headed sagacity of old Abe himself, powerfully backed by [Hannibal] Hamlin, who is a jewel." It was a rare experience for Kate to see her father get what she considered his due in the public prints. She was becoming hardened to newspaper abuse and political intrigue.

But from then on she was to keep close watch over Seward. He was always to remain an enigma to Kate, and one of the most unmalleable of her father's enemies. Neither her dislike nor her blandishments were to have any effect on the cool and detached Secretary of State. He continued to treat her with smiling courtesy and, in time, with reluctant admiration. Kate was suspicious of the smooth deference and guarded manner he showed to friend and foe. When scarred, he smiled and took another pinch of snuff. His speeches were as carefully planned and as flatly delivered as her father's. But they spread good cheer and reassurance. Both Kate and Chase had carefully studied his whip-up speech on January 12, which struck them as being too conciliatory to the disunionists.

In the days of maneuvering before inauguration, a number of the Republican leaders took note of Kate. She shone like a star in the small company of official ladies. And Seward, for one, was well aware that she was doing some smooth "politicking" on her father's behalf. She already had good friends in the newspaper world, and Kate was never to miss a chance with members of the press. Greeley's crowd were unalterably opposed to Seward. Kate pushed this advantage.

Almost from the moment of their arrival in Washington, Nicolay and John Hay, the President's handsome young secretaries, were alert to Miss Kate, the sprightly crinolined creature who sailed through the lobby of Willard's with her head in the air and made shrewder comments than any other woman on the scene. She was "Fair Lady" to

General Scott, as were most of the females upon whom his eyes lit in his old age.

The General was worried as the day of inauguration approached. Through his ironclad hide was seeping the knowledge that Washington was ill prepared for the unforeseen, although he preferred to think of it as an unassailable fortress. Attempts at conciliation between the time of Lincoln's election and his installation had failed dismally. There were whispers that he would not live to serve as President. The General set up a showy military display for March 4, calling on every soldier in the city. He planned to parade personally with a battery of artillery and take up his stand near the north entrance to the Capitol.

The excitement had become intense by Sunday, and Kate and her father had to push their way through the crowds outside Willard's as they set forth for church. That evening fifteen hundred persons dined in the hotel. All day long crowds in motley attire milled about in the city, and many slept that night in the open, while cavalry platoons patrolled the streets. Rarely had Washington seen so mixed a crowd as swarmed in for the inauguration of Abraham Lincoln. Kate took note of the large number from the West, and the few Southerners within sight or hearing. They had shut themselves up in disapproval.

Monday morning was chill and cloudy, with a sharp northwest wind blowing and whippets of dust rising from the streets. By noon it had calmed down and the sun shone brightly. As Kate, all in blue, drove with her father to the Capitol, she was well aware that not all the homes were en fête. She saw closed shutters, unfriendly faces and scathing glances, as well as flags and bunting. Observing the glittering epaulets of General Scott's officers, the prancing cavalry, and the blue scarves, white rosettes and gleaming batons of the mounted marshals, she knew that green-coated riflemen also were concealed on rooftops along Pennsylvania Avenue.

The public had been trudging for four hours toward the Capitol, but only the elect entered the Senate Chamber and saw Lincoln ushered in, beat the dust from his clothes and genially greet the waiting dignitaries. The procession moved to the flag-draped platform at the East Portico. Senator Edward D. Baker, of Oregon, an old friend of the President's, introduced him and he prepared to speak, while fifty armed men mounted guard beneath the platform.

It was Kate's first view of a presidential inauguration. She had every reason to take careful note of what transpired. Lincoln fumbled for a moment with his tall hat, not knowing where to put it, and Senator Douglas took it from him and held it during his speech, a gesture that Carl Schurz and Henry Watterson, who sat nearby, later described as symbolic. Lincoln then drew out his steel-bowed spectacles and delivered his first inaugural speech in clear, high-pitched tones that carried his lucid phrases to the farthest reaches of the crowd. Kate caught the phrases: "In your hands, my dissatisfied fellow-countrymen, and not in mine, is the momentous issue of civil war. The government will not assail you. You can have no conflict without being yourselves the aggressors. . . . We are not enemies, but friends. We must not be enemies. Though passion may have strained, it must not break our bonds of affection. . . ."

"I think there's a clank of metal in it," George Templeton Strong, lawyer and civic worker, commented afterward. To the Secessionists the speech was like a declaration of war. To Chase it was a mild pronouncement on the slavery issue. To Kate it was the speech that her father should have been delivering. And what must she have thought as the senile Chief Justice Roger B. Taney tottered forward and shakily administered the oath of office to the man who had so unexpectedly become President? Whatever she felt, Kate's manner was composed and gracious to the other ladies as the official set dispersed. Lincoln drove with Buchanan to the White House, past crowds that now clung to railings, mounted fences and even hung from the branches of trees.

With this climactic event over, Kate and her father faced congratulations on their own account, as it became known that he was to be Secretary of the Treasury. Office seekers swarmed around him at once. Flattering letters poured in. Kate, reading many of them, again had a sense of her father's national stature. She quickly took note of a letter from Anna Ella Carroll, a woman whose name was whispered with awe in Washington for the power she was supposed to wield with important men. She, too, wanted a favor from her old Ohio friend. Chase answered her on March 11: "I am not seeing anyone just yet on the matter to which you refer, but of course will see you. You have my grateful thanks for the great and patriotic services you have rendered and are still rendering to the country in this crisis."

From this time on, red-haired Anna, with her documents and pamphlets, her Carroll inheritance and her mysterious power, was to be in and out of the Chase home as it quickly became the gathering place for the radicals who formerly met at Dr. Bailey's. Kate was to hear much about the Tennessee Plan and Miss Carroll before the Civil War was over, although there is no evidence that there was close sympathy between the two women. Miss Carroll was a person with a fixed idea, who was alternately disliked and respected by men in public office. Chase, always courteous to women, happened to be one of those who listened attentively to her insidious talk, although he was not an advocate of the Tennessee Plan.

Kate soon found the home she needed—a mansion at the corner of E and Sixth Street Northwest. Her father leased it for twelve hundred dollars a year, and Kate rounded up a staff of six servants, enough for a start. Chase was greatly worried about finances. He had moved to Washington deeply in debt. He tried to sell his home in Columbus and urged Flamen Ball to get rid of his holdings in Cincinnati. But real estate was in a slump. Kate's grocery bills still followed him from Columbus and he was harassed by overdue notes.

To set up his new ménage, he borrowed ten thousand dollars from his own appointee, Hiram Barney, Collector of the Port of New York —a sordid fact that depressed the sensitive Secretary of the Treasury but did not cloud the blue sky for Kate as she set off for New York to buy furniture for her new home. She stopped off in Philadelphia to visit her father's banker friend, Jay Cooke. She had known his brother, Henry D. Cooke, in Columbus. After her visit Jay wrote enthusiastically to Henry: "Kate Chase spent Tuesday night with us. She is a glorious girl."

The glorious girl was to thread her way in and out of his life for years to come, as he and her father worked closely together on financial matters. He was to market the government bonds that financed the Civil War, to serve as fiscal agent to the Treasury and to finance the construction of Western railroads in the post war days. Kate was now to add bankers to her growing guest list. They were not such ready talkers over the dinner table as her political, judicial and newspaper friends, but they soon loomed large on her father's horizon and, therefore, also on hers.

Chapter V

MARY TODD BOWS TO KATE CHASE

K ATE CHASE and Mary Todd greeted each other with warm smiles and chill thoughts at the first levee held at the Executive Mansion in March, 1861. It had been widely rumored that Kate "was bound to make her father President" and the meeting of the Lincolns and the Chases in public was observed with more than passing interest.

There was little doubt that Kate's languid eyes, hazel flecked with green, caught the bold blue challenge and latent wariness in Mary's counter glance. It was noted that her fingers lingered longer in Lincoln's white-gloved hand than in his wife's. A smile softened her lips in their moment of greeting.

Although uncommonly tall herself, her figure rising in slender grace from a rustling crinoline of stiff white silk sprayed with jasmine, Kate was forced to look far up to Abe, to incline slowly toward Mary. She could find nothing but gentle courtesy in the President's sorrowful face, and gallantry in his stiff bow.

He, in turn, must have studied twenty-one-year-old Kate with interest. This was not his first glimpse of the daughter of Salmon Portland Chase. He could scarcely have overlooked her at Willard's. His newly appointed Secretary of the Treasury stood on the sidelines, proud of Kate and treating the President to the benevolence that was to grow into what Nicolay later described as an "attitude varied between the limits of active hostility and benevolent contempt."

Kate's approach was finer drawn. She was deferential to Lincoln and

63

dignified with his wife, but both already recognized her as a foe, young though she was, and captivatingly fresh among the more mature beauties of the capital. Lincoln may have been amused, but clearly Mary Todd did not like it. Nor could she see why everyone was dazzled by Miss Kate.

As this stellar guest moved out of range, Mrs. Lincoln spoke fast and shrilly to the next in line. To those nearby it seemed that in Kate's brief passage she had dimmed the evening for the President's wife. Mary's rose moiré antique seemed slightly vulgar now. The garland of red flowers resting on her dark hair gave her a top-heavy look. She was short, abundantly curved and overadorned. Her pearl and gold necklace, earrings and bracelets rattled as she tossed her head and shook hands. Mary's pet vanity—her shoulders—rose white and softly rounded from the low sweep of her dress, but her arms looked thick and strong beside the porcelain delicacy of Kate's.

In the midst of her duties Mary saw that her guests kept turning to watch the progress of this stately girl across the room. Her dress was perfect in line and fit. There were no flowers in her hair to detract from its burnished simplicity; no jewels to draw attention from her statuesque throat and shoulders; no frills to mar her splendid carriage.

Kate, schooled in social decorum at Miss Haines's, and during the closing days of the Buchanan administration, had scored heavily over Mrs. Lincoln, who moved already in a fog of distrust, and chattered loudly to cover her dismay. One social era had died; another was being ushered in with the Lincolns. Kate was fated to spearhead the radical element that gathered around her father, but she had no intention of letting past magnificence die. Good manners, fine feathers and sumptuous living were to distinguish the Chase ménage.

No one understood Kate's reasoning better than the sybarite who now led her toward the flash and dazzle of the diplomatic corps. Sumner knew that her poise was a screen for hidden fury. He had watched her grow from childhood. He respected her intelligence, approved her manners, and took pride in her intractability—a quality she shared with him. It was no secret to Sumner that the girl on his arm believed with all her heart and soul that her father should have stood that night where the gaunt giant of Springfield held court; that she, Kate, should have been the hostess on this occasion. He shared her conviction, but he accepted the fact that Lincoln was the victor. So far, the President had borne himself like a humble and forthright man, if somewhat lacking in dignity. However, he still had to prove himself to Sumner on the slavery issue. His inaugural speech had given sanction to the enemy.

Sumner, at last recovered from his injuries, and only recently back from Europe, was now Chase's most honored friend, bound to him increasingly by scholarly interests and radical sympathies. Chase's lust for the Presidency was an old and, at the moment, a bitter tale to the Senator from Massachusetts. But he saw that it now raged dangerously in Kate on behalf of her father. Sumner knew how strongly these two proud spirits reacted to the sting of defeat. But it was his hostess he pitied as he watched the foreign set warm up to Kate. He was to be Mrs. Lincoln's friend and advocate for years to come. Curiously, two of the men closest to Kate—Sumner and Sprague—were to like and be liked by Mary Todd, in spite of the deadly enmity that soon fanned into flame between the two women.

Kate's spirits rose as the evening wore on and gallantry stirred her pulses. Time was on her side. Her reign was just beginning. She had merely to look around to see that the Lincolns were being snubbed. There was uneasiness in the air. Deep passions had been stirred to the point of eruption. The pick of the social crop was absent. The powerful belles of the South, already scattered, had left a vacuum. Top Army and Navy officials, and old-guard conservatives of all types, had decided to ignore the black Republicans. Kate mentally made comparisons with a Buchanan reception.

But how might it have been had Salmon Portland Chase been elected? Kate must have drawn sharp comparisons between her courtly father, noble in mien as a Roman senator, and the rough-hewn President, shuffling uncomfortably in his new role, his white kid gloves wilting on his aching hands. What black treachery had cut the cards in Lincoln's favor when her father was so eminently suited to lead the nation? When she might have stood by his side as hostess?

Mrs. Lincoln soon was aware that Miss Chase was holding a levee of her own—the first of many that were to widen the breach between these social rivals. Soon she was to complain openly and bitterly that Kate came to her receptions and held court. It was not in Mary's nature to play second fiddle to another woman, however ridiculous the comparison, from the standpoint of age, looks, intellect or any other factor.

Kate was not yet aware of this quality in the President's wife, although soon she was to feel its menace. At the moment she looked dramatic—even to Mary, who caught the impact of her dead white skin, her proud bearing, the reddish hair that Mrs. Pryor likened to tassels of ripened corn. Seasoned observers saw at once that a lady of quality had come in time to take the place of the veterans from the South. With Mrs. Seward out of the running, Kate automatically became the premier Cabinet hostess. None so dynamic—with the triple endowment of youth, style and brains—had yet assumed this role. None had wrapped more pride and envy into her approach to the President's wife.

Before she went to bed that night Mrs. Lincoln learned from her cousin, Mrs. Elizabeth Todd Grimsley, that Miss Chase had drawn her aside and questioned her searchingly about their life in Springfield— how Mary ran her household, how the boys behaved, what the President liked for dinner, their style of furniture and table appointments, the type of entertaining they favored.

Was she showing common courtesy, or was there deadly intent behind this interrogation? When Mary heard of it she was in no doubt whatever. But Mrs. Grimsley, flattered by Kate's interest, had given her a wealth of detail. "I know she admires you, Mary," she consoled the infuriated Mrs. Lincoln. "I heard her talking to Mr. Lincoln later— she told him she thought you looked like a fashion plate. She said she never expected to see one come to life—right out of Godey's."

Mary was in tears. "Oh, Lizzie, for mercy's sake, don't be such an eternal fool. Can't you see Kate Chase was only making fun of me—of all of us?"

By degrees it dawned on Lizzie that Kate had deftly extracted from her the most intimate details about the Lincolns. That smooth-faced girl. It was hard to believe. She was stricken with remorse as she watched Mary tear the red flowers from her hair and rant with rage. The President's wife already was suspicious of Kate, and with good reason. Tonight she had felt the cold wind of the girl's superiority blow across her. She was never to know ease with her again, or cease to malign her.

But however bitter her attacks on Kate, they had no effect on Lincoln. He continued to honor and admire the proud girl, to value her opinion, to single her out for conversation. Knowing how Kate and her father felt, he forgave them freely and cherished the slightest evidence of their good will. He knew already that his crown was one of thorns, and none need envy him.

Kate, driving home from the levee with her father, was thoughtful. She gave Mrs. Lincoln credit for more social competence than she had expected; for pleasing Kentucky speech; for passable, if not fluent French; for unsophisticated but becoming attire; for being less the vulgarian than rumor had made her. But the levee, like the inaugural ball in the hall which promptly became known as the White Muslin Palace of Aladdin, had seemed to Kate an untidy and undistinguished affair. She and her father had put in a brief and belated appearance at the earlier function and had shared Henry Adams' opinion that it was a melancholy occasion. The plank structure had rocked, the gas chandeliers had swayed dangerously, the Marine Band had thundered out music for quadrilles danced heartily by the people. Society had been conspicuously absent, but the Lincolns had been kindly surveyed. Mary had worn blue silk with pearls and had led the grand march with her old suitor and her husband's debating antagonist, Senator Douglas.

Tonight had been little better. The scramble for hats, coats, sticks and mantles had been severe. Crinolines had been squashed. Garlands had been knocked awry and possessions lost. Rules of precedence had suffered in the general crowding. The new Secretary of the Treasury was thoughtful and tired. The cares of state were heavy enough at the moment to obliterate the social picture, which to him was a mere shadow on a steadily darkening canvas.

In his own mind the burden lay on him, not on Abraham Lincoln. Both he and Seward already considered themselves the brains that must run the country. It was to take many months of patient work on Lincoln's part to persuade these self-appointed titans that he was in command. But in the early days of uncertainty, the Lincolns made little headway and calumny gathered around them at every turn. Kate gave ear to the gossip and whipped it up in strategic quarters. It was easy to put Mrs. Lincoln in the wrong. She floundered in a hostile atmosphere, gave her confidence indiscreetly, nagged the President, had frenzied scenes with the servants. Stories spread like wildfire—about her manners, her tantrums, her extravagance, her tears, her vanity and her passion for buying clothes.

Kate had embarked on a calculated social program of her own. What she said about Mrs. Lincoln carried weight, since she was already held in high esteem. As an honored member of the Cabinet family, she had ample opportunity to observe, for she caught her rival at the greatest disadvantage—on the social bastions, where her own worldliness made a lesser figure of the strident, high-pitched mistress of the Executive Mansion. Both women were busy with machinations. They had come to Washington with parallel ambitions—one for her husband, the other for her father. They wasted no time in setting the stage. But Kate was hardheaded, cool and intelligent, where Mary's emotions ran riot. Mary was the President's wife, but in battles of wit, in social counterplay, Kate took the honors. The social boycott of the Lincolns deepened.

But the scramble for office was on and long lines of men with their hats in their hands filed into the Executive Mansion and up to the offices on the second floor, within full view of the Lincoln living quarters at the other end of the hall. No one gave thought any longer to Lincoln's safety, although the capital seethed with talk of treason.

Kate calmly pursued her social program, furnishing her new home, accepting invitations and preparing to entertain on her own account. The spell held throughout March. Then, as spring spread a blanket of green over Washington and the crocuses, hyacinths, tulips and snow-drops bloomed, war came like a thunderclap and dazed the population, in spite of all the premonitory signs. It found the capital unready and the President unsure. Like Buchanan, he had followed what seemed to be a vacillating course, but one that history showed to be a policy of forbearance and delay in the hope of ultimate amity.

Night after night Chase came home with echoes of the anxious Cabinet meetings around the long oak table in the President's shabby office. The Army was against relieving Fort Sumter. The Navy was for it. So was Montgomery Blair, the new Postmaster General. But Chase advised Lincoln: "Let us not rush headlong into that unfathomable gulf." General Scott, knowing how small his army was, could not face the thought that the nation was on the brink of war.

Kate set forth for the first state dinner late in March, knowing that her father was full of foreboding. She wore pale yellow and was instantly spotted as something rare by William Howard Russell, the bulky and cynical correspondent of the *Times* of London, who was little impressed by the dinner arrangements or the Republican guests. He found Mrs. Lincoln homely, but more agreeable than he had expected. Before the evening was over, he saw that she was markedly outshone by Miss Kate Chase, whose conversation was as choice as her coloring. The President made jokes and exchanged some banter with Kate as he tried to keep his anxiety in check. But after dinner he took the Cabinet members aside for further consultation, then lay awake for the rest of the night, weighing the mighty problem of Fort Sumter.

Next day, after a Cabinet meeting, he signed an order for the preparation of an expedition, to be used if necessary for Fort Sumter. Seward went him one better and ordered a similar expedition for Fort Pickens, but was courteously put in his place by Lincoln, who showed plainly that he was in command. Seward accepted the reproof with his usual flexibility and before long was able to say: "The President is the best of us." Chase from time to time was to make the same concession verbally, but it is doubtful that he or Kate ever fully believed it. As time went on, Kate was credited with being the one who stiffened her father's resistance to Lincoln. With Mary Todd continually reminding the President that Chase was his enemy, filled with envy and determined to succeed him in office, and with Kate stirring up unrest in Chase and belittling Lincoln, the feminine tug of war must inevitably have affected the relations of these two men. It did so visibly in the case of Chase who, from time to time, was all but won by Lincoln's great good will. Then a talk with Kate would renew his suspicions, whip up his envy and annihilate the germ of friendly response. It is likely that Mary's strong drive had much less effect on Lincoln, who had vast tolerance for his wife, as for his fellow men. He continued to put up with Chase for his fine services and because he seemed to have deep-rooted respect for the man. Nor did he ever fail in courtesy to Miss Kate—Lincoln's way of addressing the daughter of his most troublesome Cabinet officer.

The President appeared, jesting as usual, at Mrs. Lincoln's levee on the afternoon of April 6. Kate recalled his mood when her father told her later that he had just ordered *The Star of the West* to proceed with food for the garrison. Chase said that now it was a matter for prayer. Roger Pryor was dramatically proclaiming in Charleston that if a shot were fired, Virginia would join the Confederacy.

The shot was fired from land batteries and on April 12 the bombardment of Fort Sumter got under way. The garrison surrendered next day and the Civil War had begun. The news reached Washington by telegraph and it spread like flashes of lightning through the city. Bulletins were posted in all the hotels. Crowds gathered around the telegraph office.

Kate was at home when her father was summoned to an emergency Cabinet meeting. He returned hours later like a man who has faced disaster. As always, he turned to prayer. Kate joined with her own petitions. The Chases, more quickly than most, accepted the fact that the nation might be in for a long and costly struggle. The Secretary of the Treasury knew that to finance a war was a problem beyond his dreams. He had nothing on which to build. Since taking office, he had been working hard to organize the Treasury and devise ways of filling its empty coffers. The nation was as bankrupt in funds as in military strength.

The public thought that all would be over in three months' time. The panoply of General Scott, however hollow, still sustained them. But Chase shared in the fearful anxiety of those who knew better. And although he had drawn back at first from the "unfathomable gulf," he had given his confirmation on the Fort Sumter question and now accepted the inevitable.

Kate had a long and solemn talk with her father as war became a reality. Always methodical in his reasoning, Chase reviewed the years of antislavery agitation in which they both had shared to some extent. He recalled the oratory of Webster, Jackson, Benton, Clay and Calhoun—for, against and in the middle of the road. He cited the Van Zandt case, the Dred Scott decision, the Kansas-Nebraska Act, the mobbings in Ohio, John Brown's Raid, the attack on Sumner, the passionate discord in House and Senate.

Chase spoke of the great men the South had nurtured—fine orators and noble statesmen. He reminded her of the South's resources—its cotton, tobacco, sugar-cane fields, cattle and horses, its variegated scenery and vegetation. Now the rapid industrialization of the North stood in opposition to the patriarchy of the South, with little hope for concord.

The South functioned almost as a separate nation, with tariff and domestic policies widening the breach, aside from the dark and persistent shadow of three million slaves, of human bondage against human freedom.

It was talk that Kate had been hearing from childhood—familiar, matter of course. Only since coming to Washington had she seen how deep was the gulf that separated North and South, how violent the emotions that divided the country. She had seen it reflected in the women, as powerfully as in their husbands.

Now the conflict was actually upon them. It was a sobering thought for Kate, who saw at once that her father faced a colossal task. For a few days the capital seemed suspended in the deathly quiet that followed the first excitement. Lincoln issued his proclamation asking the loyal states to send him seventy-five thousand militiamen. Jefferson Davis summoned one hundred thousand volunteers from the Confederate states, and his Secretary of War predicted that Washington would be theirs by the first of May.

Tension deepened in the capital as the impression spread that the Confederate Army was marching north. General Scott insisted that General Pierre Beauregard could never take Washington. General Robert E. Lee had ridden away from Arlington Heights to join the Confederate forces and win eternal fame. Maryland hesitated. As Roger Pryor had predicted, Virginia was veering toward the Confederacy and the capital was badly exposed.

Small scattered efforts were taken to stem a tidal wave. Ammunition was distributed. Blue-caped pickets rode through the streets, and guns were set up to protect Long Bridge. Willard's, which still harbored Southerners, was guarded, and the Frontier Guards, a motley crew of vigilantes, drilled and slept in the Executive Mansion. The pictures and statues in the Capitol were boarded up. Chase, between Cabinet meetings, busied himself with plans to make the Treasury a citadel for the President and Cabinet. General Scott had approved a plan for holding Executive Square. Iron bars were already being hammered across the Treasury doorways. Sandbags were piled on the portico. Two thousand barrels of flour were to be stored in the basement. Many of the shops had been shuttered. Homes were deserted. Hotels were emptying out. Transients fled to their native states. Secessionists moved South. There was a great exodus by train, steamer, carriage, truck and even wheel-barrow.

News reached Kate fast, as her father moved between the Treasury, the Executive Mansion and the War Department, where Simon Cameron presided and General Scott hovered with lofty detachment but deep inner concern. His gout troubled him and the military situation was completely out of hand.

Sixteen states had responded at once to the President's proclamation, promising men, money and arms. Local recruiting was under way but all Washington waited for the arrival of trained soldiers to save it. They seemed long in coming, while rumors spread like wildfire and no one knew what actually was happening.

Kate kept busy during these troubled days of isolation by setting her new home in order and waiting for her father to come in for a few hours' rest before the next bout with Lincoln, the Cabinet and the baffled General Scott. All the normal functions of housekeeping were breaking down. Deliveries were disrupted. Certain foods were scarce. Kate was an excellent manager and in moments of crisis she always applied herself to practical problems. Many of the women and children were leaving the city, but she announced at once that she would stay with her father, whatever happened. There was little rest or sleep for anyone.

Finally a company of militiamen from Minnesota and several companies of poorly armed Pennsylvania volunteers arrived, after running a barrage of stones and jeers in Baltimore. They were quartered in the Capitol. Cheers greeted the Sixth Massachusetts Regiment, the first well armed volunteers to reach the capital. They, too, had battled in Baltimore and their coats and knapsacks were roughed up. They bunked in the Senate Chamber and had arrived in time to see Washington cut off from railway and telegraph communication by Baltimore Secessionists who were determined to stop the flow of Yankee soldiers through the city. The acute tension lessened with the arrival of the Seventh New York Regiment, gentlemen in gray, spruced up and gleaming with accouterments. Next day more soldiers arrived from Massachusetts and Rhode Island, and the Union Army was already in the making.

One of the first states to respond to Lincoln's call for men was Rhode Island. Governor William Sprague had telegraphed, offering twelve hundred men and his own services. It happened that he was a confirmed student of military tactics. As a boy of ten he drilled classmates during the Dorr Rebellion on Rhode Island. As a youth he joined the Marine Artillery of Providence and took much pride in drill and parade. In early manhood he went abroad, visited the French and Italian battlefields and interviewed Garibaldi. He was welcomed home like a military hero and rode through the streets with plumed hat and sweeping cape. On top of this he became Governor. He had already organized the Rhode Island Militia, which was well drilled and fully equipped, largely from his own funds.

When war was declared, he jumped at the chance to move into action and ordered the militia, with Colonel Ambrose E. Burnside commanding, to proceed to Washington. The Rhode Islanders looked keen and martial in their blue shirts and gray trousers, with hats turned up at one side. They went through their military paces smartly at ceremonies held at the Patent Office for the dedication of the large new flag donated by the Department of the Interior. Lincoln hoisted the halyard and received the salute. The soldiers marched into quarters singing a patriotic air.

Like the men of the New York Seventh, many of the Rhode Islanders were said to be millionaires. Governor Sprague unquestionably was, and Kate watched him with close attention as his regiment paraded past. She remembered him well from the night they had danced together in Cleveland. He, in turn, had thought often of the entrancing Miss Chase.

Their glances met as he rode past, more impressive on his white horse than on the dance floor, where his small stature and slouching gait did not show to good advantage. Even when mounted and wearing a yellow-plumed hat, he looked more poet than soldier. His dark hair swept to his collar in the prevailing fashion. He had a thin drooping mustache, a deeply indented chin and stone-gray eyes that suggested melancholy but actually were nearsighted.

The word had spread that the Boy Governor of Rhode Island was the richest young man in New England, if not in the world. It was thought to be astonishing that he should drink from a tin cup and bunk on the ground with his men. His youth and romantic aura whipped up more cheers than greeted the hearty Colonel Burnside, a splendid military figure, whiskered, strong and genial, who had traveled the hard road from tailor's apprentice to West Point graduate.

The soldiers brought reassurance to Washington. Communications were restored. Men drilled in blossoming parks and slept a little uneasily in the halls of government. During May bands blared in the streets, soldiers marched to drumbeat, flags flew and the capital not only revived, but whipped up a show of gaiety in the first white heat of war before the fire was felt and the people burned.

With the coming of the soldiers, there were ceremonials of all kinds—flag raisings, drills, dress parades, regimental serenades and dances. Kate had never been so busy. By June she was the acknowledged belle of Washington, the officers' favorite dancing partner, the most observed and admired of all the beauties who cheered the soldiers as they marched past. Officials from the President downward took note of her bearing and liked to have a word with Kate, who usually had something thoughtful to say. General Scott observed that young Governor Sprague, of Rhode Island, hovered often in her vicinity. His conduct was quite marked during one military display when he rode over to the Chase barouche to pay his respects.

It was not the kind of social life she had bargained for when she moved to Washington, but it held its own excitement, and brought dashing and gifted men from different states into Kate's vicinity. There was keen competition for her favors. Huge boxes of flowers were delivered at her home—wreaths for her hair, trailing vines, bouquets for her wrists, festoons for her skirts—each of one variety in the fashion of the day—moss roses, lilies, violets, japonicas, honeysuckle or clematis. But Sprague, her favorite suitor, soon learned that Kate did not deck herself with flowers from shoulder to hem.

While these frivolities still persisted, Cabinet officers struggled with unheard-of problems. Chase now worried more about his empty Treasury than the safety of Washington. Kate heard little about the Presidency, much about finances, in the early months of the war. She was quick to grasp the intricacies of her father's financial problems. The national debt on July 1, 1861, was $90,000,000. The balance in the Treasury was $2,000,000. Chase had already adopted the policy of issuing government bonds and making financial appeals directly to the public.

When President Lincoln asked that $400,000,000 be placed at the disposal of the government for war purposes, Chase proposed to raise $80,000,000 by taxes and $240,000,000 by loans in the first fiscal year. Congress authorized a national loan of $250,000,000; levied on the states and territories a direct tax of $20,000,000; and made provision for the balance by an increased tariff and an income tax.

But the Civil War, like all wars, ran high in costs, and for the last quarter of the year expenses averaged nearly $50,000,000 a month. In August Chase told Kate that he wished her to accompany him to New York, where he was going to talk the principal bankers of the nation into a great national loan. He called them in from various cities and spoke eloquently of the country's dire need. The days that followed were full of excitement for Kate. She shopped, went to the theater, met her old school friends and in the evenings dined with some of the leading bankers of the day. Her father was tense with anxiety through it all. He was finding it extremely difficult to put across his will. The bankers came up with objections, great and small, until at last he said to them firmly that unless they gave him their support he would go back to Washington and issue notes for circulation—"for, gentlemen, the war must go on until this rebellion is put down, if we have to put out paper until it takes $1,000 to buy a breakfast."

Then one evening he returned to their hotel and told Kate that he had won. He promptly formed a syndicate of banks which advanced the Government $50,000,000. When this loan was successfully placed, he raised another $50,000,000 from the same source, the Government paying seven and three-tenths per cent for the money. This was just the beginning of benefits to come.

It was a brilliant and difficult coup at the time, and Kate returned to Washington more proud than ever of her father. This was only one of several trips that she made to New York during the first year of the war, although it was by far the most significant. Both she and Mrs. Lincoln traveled back and forth to buy furniture for their homes and clothing for their already well-clad backs. Mary Todd went early in the year, running up bills at A. T. Stewart's, ordering lavishly, picking up whatever her fancy dictated.

Soon the Executive Mansion was refurbished but no one cared, since the war overshadowed all else. The woods were revarnished. The chairs and sofas were upholstered in crimson satin brocatelle. The walls were ornately repapered. The windows were hung with Swiss lace curtains and draped with fringed and tasseled brocatelle that matched the chairs. The East Room had a huge carpet with a flowered design. The French wallpaper for this stately room was to lead to a woeful scene between the President and his wife, since Mary had far outrun the congressional allotment for her expenditures on the Executive Mansion.

Kate heard these rumors and knew that Mrs. Lincoln had been buying at a dizzy pace. All the official set gossiped about the dinner service with coat of arms, the Bohemian cut glass and the massive ornaments that arrived at the Executive Mansion as soldiers paraded past it. This in no way deterred Kate from her plans. With little money to spend, but the same inconsequent touch as Mrs. Lincoln, she went on a shopping spree.

On all her trips to New York, she stopped off in Philadelphia to stay with the Cookes. Like Carl Schurz, she found them "good hearted people of frank and simple manners." They had morning and evening prayers and Kate knelt in the hall while Jay conducted devotions. After "Amen" he jumped up in his hearty way, clapped his hands and cried out jovially: "Now, let's be jolly."

Chase and Cooke were already fast friends, but Cooke was not oblivious to the further benefits to be derived from sticking close to the Secretary of the Treasury. He now planned favors, which Kate accepted with more equanimity than her father. Chase firmly returned a closed carriage which Cooke sent on with a receipted bill, after Chase had asked Kate to order a carriage but not to be extravagant about it.

"I must accept no presents beyond those which the ordinary intercourse of society prompts and allows from a friend," he wrote to Cooke, setting the pace for their future relations.

But Kate was only faintly embarrassed to have the Cookes send her book brackets for her bedroom, copied after some she had admired in their library. She remarked that she must not openly comment thereafter on their possessions. However, she was happy to have Governor Sprague's support when she selected her heavy piled carpets at Stewart's on her second visit to New York that year. The Secretary of the Treasury's daughter and the rich young Governor from Rhode Island were most cordially received by Alexander T. Stewart himself. Come what might, Kate was determined to have her home in good order for the opening of the social season of 1861-62.

Actually there was no lull all summer. Mrs. Lincoln held court through June and July, receiving an endless parade of soldiers not yet baptized in blood. The special session of Congress called by the President brought politicians back to the capital early in July. Douglas was missing. He had died of typhoid fever in June. Breckinridge, of Kentucky, was still in the saddle but wavering. Washington was almost unrecognizable to the returned legislators. Encampments ringed the city. Caissons rattled through the streets. There was bugling, drilling and drumming all over the place. Rifles cracked for target practice, sometimes in dangerous proximity to the civilian population. Soldiers were billeted in the most unlikely places. In one afternoon four thousand men with glittering bayonets marched into the city from three separate states. The Union Army was growing. So was the confusion.

Twenty thousand men marched in the broiling sun on Independence Day. Chase stood in the reviewing stand with the President and his fellow Cabinet members. Kate looked cool in pink organdy and caught one of the bouquets tossed by the Garibaldi Guard. She was now a practiced observer of the glowing colors of the new regiments, could appraise the bands and pick out one plumed drum major from another. She had officer friends in many of the units.

Kate had inside knowledge, through her father, of the vast operations going on behind the scenes to feed, house, clothe and finance Lincoln's militia. Freight jammed the railways and the navy yard. Wagon trains laden with provisions and ammunition were dragged through the unpaved streets. Simon Cameron was handing out war contracts that were soon to be under attack, until "shoddy" became a Union byword. Chase slaved at the Treasury, but kept an eye on all other departments too. He was increasingly persuaded that Lincoln was not the man to run the country in such a crisis. Even more than Seward, he kept a finger in every pie.

The shops did a brisk trade. The Marine Band played as usual, but often was drowned out by the regimental bands. Fife and drum were ubiquitous. The giddy Zouaves were mourning the death of their commander, young Colonel Elmer E. Ellsworth, who had been buried in state from the White House. The Garibaldi Guard flitted about the town like wandering gypsies. Mounted orderlies rode between the encampments and the War Department with requisitions and dispatches.

There was heavy drinking, and fastidious Kate shrank from the filth and degradation she saw as she drove through the city. Washington stank as the summer heat threw up its miasmic steam. But in the cool of the night, driving home from a hop, this picture was blotted out and she saw only the winking lights of the tents, like teepees poised on the hills. The Rhode Islanders were quartered now in Sprague Camp. They had huts, roofed with felt, close to a cemetery. Kate often rode out in the daytime to visit the Governor there. At night he came in to town to dance and flirt with Kate at the innumerable parties held for the visiting officers. No one feared invasion any longer, with Washington bristling with soldiers and arms, even though General Beauregard's army was within a day's march of the city. The farmers brought in their produce from Virginia. The bridges were open, although guarded. People crossed into the adjoining state at will.

The Chase home was open to visitors all day long. Kate continued her Columbus custom of having breakfast guests to talk to her busy father. When he hurried off to the Treasury, she took over, before going out to make morning calls. Office seekers from New York and Ohio besieged him at his home, as well as at his office. Already complaints about Lincoln were being welcomed in the Chase ménage. They crept into the Secretary's mail. They tinctured the dinner table conversation and loomed large at breakfast parleys.

Mrs. Lincoln came in for her share of innuendo over hot chocolate or cold drinks in the afternoon. Kate delicately but persistently whipped up the spreading feeling that the President's wife was maladroit. She passed on the latest morsels about her financial embarrassments and her unfortunate association with dubious employees. She knew that John Hay privately called Mrs. Lincoln the Hell Cat or Her Satanic Majesty. Sprague, listening to Kate, felt sorry at times for Mary Todd. He had a kind heart, and to her dying day Mrs. Lincoln thought of him as a "truly good-hearted man" and of Kate as a heartless wretch.

Their conflict showed itself in various ways. Once it involved young Julia Taft, who spent much time at the Executive Mansion along with her brothers, Bud and Holly, who were the favorite playmates of Willie and Tad Lincoln. The Tafts were the children of H. N. Taft, Chief Examiner in the Patent Office during the Buchanan administration. He had given his office to Governor Sprague and his staff when the two Rhode Island regiments were quartered at first in the Patent Office.

Julia, aged sixteen, was much enamored of the Boy Governor. Mrs. Lincoln noticed this and told her one day to have the gardener in the conservatory make up a special bouquet and present it to Governor Sprague with her compliments. Julia watched the man tie the short-stemmed camellias on broom straws and build up a bouquet to the proportions of a cabbage, with an edging of forget-me-knots and ferns. It was finally thrust into a stiff paper holder. Then, wearing a dotted Swiss dress with blue sash but no hoop and feeling very happy, she set off for the Patent Office, rehearsing the little speech she intended to make. On the way she met Miss Chase, swinging along between two officers.

"Where are you taking these flowers, child?" Miss Chase inquired.

"Mrs. Lincoln gave them to me to take to Governor Sprague," said Julia.

"I will hand them to the Governor with Mrs. Lincoln's compliments," said Kate imperiously, taking the bouquet from the girl.

Many years later Julia wrote of this incident: "She was very handsome, beautifully dressed, and accustomed to have what she wanted, and she took the bouquet from me before I could get up enough spunk to resist. I went back to Mrs. Lincoln in wrath and tears."

The President's wife comforted Julia and said she could have another bouquet and take it to the Governor when Miss Chase was not around. But, as Julia sadly related, Miss Chase was always around and eventually married him.

Julia was one of the three girls at Madame Smith's school who played tenpins with Baron Renfrew on his visit in 1860. When she made a ten-strike, he bowed to her with his hand on his heart. She received a rose in a pot as a memento of the occasion. Her half brother, Charles Sabin Taft, was the surgeon who tried to stanch President Lincoln's wound after he was shot. Her mother was a belle whose bonnets aroused Mrs. Lincoln's envy.

Julia had many memories of the President—sprawled in a big chair in the sitting room with an old worn Bible on his lap; looking from the window toward Long Bridge and sighing deeply; stepping over her brothers and his own boys as they played on the floor; and finally lifting Bud up to see Willie before he was put in his coffin.

She was an alert observer of the period but she did not again encounter Kate, although she often heard rumors that she was likely to marry the Governor. So persistent were these reports that they finally appeared in the papers, and Ohio friends wrote to Chase asking for confirmation. But Kate was not yet engaged to Sprague. She had many cavaliers. Some had more intellect, were handsomer and more entertaining than the Governor. None, however, matched him in dollar value. Kate kept him on her string. He was ever in attendance.

Bit by bit the ladies of the North learned what the ladies of the South were doing. As in Washington, things still were gay in Montgomery, Charleston and Richmond. In July Mrs. Pryor was at The Oaks, seventy miles from Richmond, looking out at broad acres of tobacco and an old-fashioned garden with box-edged crescents, stars and circles. She embroidered her husband's shoulder straps with heavy bullion fringe and filled knapsacks with oilcloth, underclothing, white gloves, collars, neckties, and handkerchiefs. Roger was colonel of the Third Virginia Infantry.

There was much philandering on the piazza of the Spotswood Hotel in Richmond and the Southern girls, wearing Palmetto cockades, sewed by day and danced by night with the soldiers of the Confederate Army. The men of the South were rushing to arms, and the women were forming sewing circles in churches, homes and public buildings. The churches became depots for flannel, muslin, strong linen and uniform cloth. The first officers' uniforms were of the finest cadet cloth and gold lace. The women embroidered cases for razors, and morocco holders for needles, thread, and court plaster. War was still in the making. Little blood had been shed.

The air was laced with the perfume of violets, jasmine and early roses, as Mrs. Mary Boykin Chesnut looked out toward a deer park where horses, sheep and Devon cows grazed on blue grass. The huge family coach was ready to take her to White Sulphur Springs to recover from the winter of secession in Washington. Small footmen stopped playing marbles under the trees to mount the coach as she drove off for her annual refreshment.

"This water is making us young again," she wrote a few days later. "Women from Washington come riding into our camp, beautiful women. They bring letters done up in their back hair, or in their garments. . . . An antique female with every hair curled and frizzed is said to be a Yankee spy."

Soon false hair was removed and searched at the boundaries. Crinolines were reversed for hidden pistols and bustles were stabbed with long pins. No one doubted any longer that women spies were busy. Kate had already encountered Mrs. Rose O'Neal Greenhow in fashionable parlors during the Buchanan régime. The aunt of Mrs. Douglas had worked hard over the Republicans, flattered Chase and made some headway with Seward and Henry Wilson of Massachusetts.

Kate watched this bold and handsome woman with interest, for the whispers were that she was a traitor, and her name was strongly linked with some of the New Englanders who were close to the Chases. She was soon in prison, but the talk about Mrs. Lincoln went on. It was widely reported that she was a spy and Confederate sympathizer. Before long there were shouts in the street to this effect as she drove past in her carriage. Mary Todd had the misfortune to lose three half brothers and a brother-in-law in the Confederate Army before the war was over, but she never dared to say that she was sorry.

Chapter VI

❧❧❧❧

THE MUSIC DIES

THE PICTURE changed abruptly and the dance music faded in the North after July 21 when General Irvin McDowell's forces were defeated at Bull Run by the Confederates, led by General Joseph E. Johnston and General Beauregard. Washington wakened up to the reality of war.

None could deny that it was an ignominious rout for the Union Army. Mrs. Greenhow later was credited with giving warning of the attack. Untrained soldiers scattered in all directions; the retreat became a panicky flight. Soldiers abandoned their haversacks, their guns, their coats and caps, and limped, staggered or rode back to Washington, leaving slaughter behind them.

The optimists who had gone out to watch the battle from the hill at Centerville overlooking Bull Run, with lunches, bourbon and wine, as if for a proud parade, slunk home angry and dismayed. Chase was not among them but Henry Wilson, Ben Wade and Zach Chandler—who had led the cry "On to Richmond"—returned to Washington with grim faces. Jeering Mr. Russell of the *Times* of London soon let the world know how the Union had fared.

Colonel Burnside rode up to Willard's without his hat and Captain Sprague came in with his saddle, a chastened warrior. He gave Kate his own account of the rout. When the panic began, he rode in front of the men and struck down their muskets to a level with the enemy. He then tried to lead a charge, but his horse was shot from under him. No other officers were in sight and the men scattered in all directions.

"But the artillery remained, and I with it," the Governor related. "I received the full blast of Johnston's reinforcements, not twenty paces off. For ten minutes I supplied a gun with ammunition to give confidence to the line. Bullets whizzed past me and made holes in my loose blouse."

Sprague insisted that he was ordered to take a white flag and surrender, but that he "spurned this miserable and cowardly proposition." He finally left the field with his saddle, and bullet holes in his clothes. Kate heard from the disheartened Governor about officers in tears and a shocking collapse of morale.

He was never to go into battle again, although he raised more regiments, poured money into the war coffers and supported the Union cause with good heart. He was deeply hurt when he was censured, like all the other officers, after the Battle of Bull Run. Kate comforted him, and her father announced within two weeks: "Sprague is to be the hero of the war, not perhaps the great hero, but the one about whom there will be more romantic stories and more admiring interest than any other."

In this Chase was a false prophet. Sprague had had his day as the romantic hero while the bands played and the capital was enacting the prelude to war. But when death and defeat became commonplace, he did give practical aid. The President listened to him at times on military tactics and gave him several missions to fulfill. He was much in the Chase orbit, which brought him close to Lincoln.

Washington for several days was in a state of utter confusion. The groans of the wounded were heard in the streets, as a long procession of ambulances moved in. Public buildings were turned into hospitals and all were asked to help. Kate drove forth in her carriage, bearing fruit for the wounded, but she shrank from the start at the sight of blood and suffering. She did not faint, like Mrs. Chesnut on her first hospital rounds in the South. She simply avoided the points of concentration as time went on. But she always wore the air of the good Samaritan as she visited the officers in their camps, when order finally was restored. At times she was drawn by her father into an errand of mercy. When the sewing circles were organized and relief societies busied themselves in every city, town and village in the country, Kate made a point of taking foodstuffs, lemons, tobacco and other comforts to the hospitals. When one of her officer friends was brought in wounded, she went to his bedside, shutting her eyes as well as she could to the surrounding gore and anguish.

She soon took note of the hammering Mrs. Mary Clemmer Ames, of the New York *Independent*, was giving Mrs. Lincoln: "While her sister-women scraped lint, sewed bandages and put on nurses' caps, and gave all to country and to death, the wife of the President spent her time in rolling to and from Washington and New York, intent on extravagant purchases for herself and the White House. . . .

"But just as if there were no monstrous national debt, no rivers of blood flowing, she seemed chiefly intent upon pleasure, personal flattery, and adulation; upon extravagant dress and ceaseless self-gratification."

Actually, as the war went on, William O. Stoddard, the presidential secretary assigned to handle Mrs. Lincoln's mail—much of which was so vituperative that it was thrown away without her ever seeing it—pictured her as working zealously for the soldiers. He built up a strong case for the President's wife to offset the shocking criticism. Thereafter she was heralded as taking fruits, foods, wines and all manner of gifts from the Executive Mansion to the wounded. Criticism continued, however, and Mrs. Lincoln seemed a heartless creature to the public.

Kate's aloofness from the scene of suffering, on the other hand, was treated apologetically in the press. The powerful Mrs. Emily Edson Briggs, who, as Olivia, wrote for the Philadelphia *Press*, excused her in fatuous terms: "She is a flower of immortality; not perfect, it is true, as other letter-writers say, but she happens to be placed in a sphere where perfection is expected, and she is mortal like the rest of us. She shrinks from the hard and lowly task of visiting the wretched hut, the sick and the afflicted. So do Victoria and Eugénie, whose fame is wafted to us across the great water."

Just as Mrs. Lincoln could do no right, Kate could do no wrong. She might scorn the needle, avoid the hospitals and continue her French lessons with M. A. Mot, but she was a strong force behind the political scene and an unofficial adviser to some of the Generals. She was frequently seen holding forth on army matters in the camps that ringed the city. With a bonnet tied under her chin, a small parasol tilted to protect her delicate skin and wearing a long cloak and sensible boots to protect her from the mud, Kate spent many hours at camp headquarters, sur-

rounded by bearded warriors. Most often they were men in top command, although she was to develop a great detestation for General
George B. McClellan. He, in turn, regarded her with distrust.

Kate soon acquired a workable grasp of military tactics, adept in this
as in the political field. Her suitor Sprague was an excellent tutor in the
practical aspects of warfare. It was one of the few subjects on which he
was fluent, and Kate was relieved to find a topic on which the young
Governor and she could converse. The well of intellectual discovery
had long ago dried up between them. Kate was aware that all too often
Sprague preferred to sit in sodden silence.

The social picture darkened after Bull Run. Even Mary Todd gave up
and went off to Long Branch after the White House dinner held in
August for Prince Jérôme Napoleon Bonaparte. No women were present
but Mrs. Todd and Mrs. Grimsley, since the Princess Clothilde was in
mourning and stayed in retirement in New York. However, Chase sat at
Mrs. Lincoln's left and was able to report to Kate on what went on between the Prince and the President's wife. Any social awkwardness displayed by the Lincolns in public was promptly noted by Kate and made
use of, sooner or later. Lord Lyons was there and expressed his regret to
Chase that his daughter was not among the guests.

As usual, she wanted to know what Mrs. Lincoln wore. Something
white, Chase recalled, and Lizzie wore pink. But the papers were more
explicit. Thus Kate learned that Mrs. Lincoln looked "elegant" at this
important state dinner in white grenadine over white silk with a long
train and that Mrs. Grimsley wore salmon tulle with fresh flowers.

Kate felt sure that the unctuous paragraphs appearing in the New
York Herald about the function were written by Henry Wikoff, the
polished but unscrupulous character who haunted the most fashionable
parlors in Washington as an observer for James Gordon Bennett. He
always flattered Mrs. Lincoln and on this occasion wrote:

"Her state dinner to the Prince Napoleon, on Saturday last, was a
model of completeness, taste and geniality; and, altogether, this Kentucky girl, this Western matron, this republican queen, puts to the blush
and entirely eclipses the first ladies of Europe—the excellent Victoria,
the pensive Eugénie and the brilliant Isabella."

This must have been gratifying reading for praise-hungry Mary Todd
but it was merely amusing to Kate, who discounted almost anything that

appeared in Bennett's paper and swore by Horace Greeley. She was much too sure of herself by this time to be discomposed by any such allusion to the President's wife. Kate was only one of many who believed that she was destined to be the American counterpart of Eugénie.

Her father was pressing her hard about Sprague. He was already making the Governor a family figure. When Kate was out of town, he shepherded him around the more fashionable parlors when the day's work was done. He wrote to her on one occasion that the Princesse de Joinville "had taken possession of Governor Sprague" on one of their social sorties. In this same letter, he warned Kate, who had gone to New York for more shopping, to be careful in her purchases. It was hard work to make both ends meet, he pointed out, and if circumstances should compel him to resign, his expenses would have greatly exceeded his income.

"If it were not the name of the thing it would not be worth while to hold prominent position, involving little else than incessant labor with the privilege of finding oneself," wrote the disillusioned and overworked Chase, who by this time was at loggerheads with Lincoln on nearly all public issues.

But his wily plans continued. In September he wrote to the Governor about a little flyer he was taking in gold through Joshua Hanna, whom he described as a "sagacious and careful man." "I would offer the half of my little venture to you," he said, "but I should hate to be laughed at if disappointed and, besides, am already fancying your amusement at my small operation."

He also suggested that Sprague join him in buying Seven Oaks, a house with twenty acres, outside Cincinnati—"since my means, you know, are not really abundant." There is no record of Sprague going in on this deal but Chase took possession of Seven Oaks and Kate scratched her name indelibly on one of the window panes with a diamond ring. It was a whim of hers to leave her mark behind her. She later inveigled Horace Greeley into carving his name with hers on the piazza of Canonchet, her home on Rhode Island. Now and again the dignified Kate gave way to frivolous impulses.

On her return to Washington, with her wardrobe complete for the coming season, her curtains bought in Philadelphia (costing $504) and everything else in order in her home, her father showed her a pile of letters he had saved for her to read. They were mostly from Ohio and were lurid with abuse of Lincoln. Out West a revolution was threatened. Lincoln had been burned in effigy in Cincinnati. His picture had been torn from the walls and trampled under foot.

Joshua Hanna, enraged over the curbing of General Frémont, wrote from Pittsburgh in November, 1861: "The common expression is, Chase is the only man who does his work honestly with a view to the future, and the only one competent to meet the crisis—if he was at the head confidence would return more and more, would flow in beyond the wants of government—therefore my friend, be advised, let every tub stand on its own bottom. . . ."

There were dozens more in the same tenor and the presidential fever burned anew in the Chase home, in spite of surrounding chaos. It tinged Kate's manner with fresh disdain as she faced Mrs. Lincoln for another season. She had made great headway in the intervening months, while Mary groveled deep in scandal. Kate was ready to challenge her. She now had a well-appointed home and was an experienced hostess. Her wardrobe was unmatched in point of taste. She had a host of admirers, in addition to the faithful Sprague. She had prestige and glamour, good health, youth and vitality. Kate did not need the electrical apparatus that Mrs. Clement C. Clay and other Southern hostesses had been known to use to stir up their tired bodies at the height of the season. Moreover, she had no fear of responsibility.

"If one learns to like responsibility, it will rest easily upon one," she told Nettie years later, in turning over her father's housekeeping to her half sister.

Kate gloried in it, as she did in power and influence. She never consciously entered into competition with Mrs. Lincoln—she was too assured. But Mrs. Elizabeth Keckley, the Negro dressmaker who sewed for the President's wife, left plenty of her own brand of testimony as to Mary's concern over Kate. She wished ever to outshine Miss Chase in her formal party costumes. In refurbishing the Executive Mansion, she worried lest the knowing girl question her taste. It was a concentrated social feud in the midst of cataclysm.

Handsome Mrs. Keckley, once a slave and now the confidante of Washington hostesses, saw pathos in Mrs. Lincoln's strivings for pre-eminence. But she also took note of the ferocity with which the President's wife struck at the Chases in conversations with her husband. He would wander in during fittings, fling himself on a sofa, read a newspaper, make comments on the dress or grieve over the war news, which during that period rarely was good. His wife never failed to jab at Chase and Seward, but Chase, having Kate for a daughter, was doubly damned.

On one occasion, while pulling on his gloves before going downstairs for a levee, the President remarked, according to Mrs. Keckley: "Well, Mother, who must I talk with tonight—shall it be Mrs. D.?"

"That deceitful woman! No, you shall not listen to her flattery."

"Well, then, what do you say to Miss C.? She is too young and handsome to practice deceit."

"Young and handsome you call her! You should not judge beauty for me. No, she is in league with Mrs. D., and you shall not talk with her."

"Well, Mother, I must talk with some one. Is there any one that you do not object to?"

"I don't know as it is necessary that you should talk to anybody in particular. You know well enough, Mr. Lincoln, that I do not approve of your flirtations with silly women, just as if you were a beardless boy, fresh from school."

"But, Mother, I insist that I must talk with somebody. I can't stand around like a simpleton and say nothing. If you will not tell me who I may talk with, please tell me who I may not talk with."

"There is Mrs. D. and Miss C. in particular. I detest them both. Mrs. B. also will come around you, but you need not listen to her flattery. These are the ones in particular."

Was Mrs. D. the beautiful Mrs. Douglas? Miss C., beyond doubt, was Kate. It was natural that both should be gracious to the President, and it is likely that he enjoyed their amiable conversation. Mrs. Douglas was warm-hearted, good to look at and she seemed to relish his jokes. The Lincoln humor was still being critically discussed in Washington. Kate might not always see the funny side of things, but she was spirited and keen. One could sound her out on politics or army matters and she always was ready with an opinion. Usually it was based on logic and common sense.

Moreover, the President had observed that none of the ladies but Mrs. Gideon Welles, wife of his Secretary of the Navy, was as courteous to his wife as Mrs. Douglas. This only angered Mary, who was in wild rebellion against being steered by lofty ladies who thought her a rustic nitwit. She preferred to make her own mistakes, whoppers though they might be, and she bitterly resented their undervaluation of her own not inconsiderable social training, her gentle upbringing and fair education.

Kate was sure that Mrs. Lincoln whipped up feeling against her father in the family counsels. In this she was not mistaken, as Mrs. Keckley made amply clear. Hay was alive to it too. It sometimes amused him. The Hell Cat constantly niggled away at Chase. She prided herself on her judgment about people, and the President good-naturedly humored her. But even when her attacks on Chase were fully borne out by surrounding evidence, the President gently reminded Mary: "Do good to those who hate you and turn their ill-will to friendship."

Mrs. Keckley considered Kate a "lovely woman, worthy of all the admiration she received," as she reported on the conversations she heard between the Lincolns bearing on Chase. One of Mary's hottest attacks came as the President lay on a sofa, reading a newspaper and feeling discouraged over the war news:

"Father, I do wish that you would enquire a little into the motives of Chase."

"Mother, you are too suspicious. I give you credit for sagacity, but you are disposed to magnify trifles. Chase is a patriot, and one of my best friends."

"Yes, one of your best friends because it is his interest to be so. He is anything for Chase. If he thought he could make anything by it, he would betray you tomorrow."

"I fear that you are prejudiced against the man, Mother. I know that you do him injustice."

"Mr. Lincoln, you are either blind or will not see. I am not the only one that has warned you against him."

"True, I receive letters daily from all parts of the country, telling me not to trust Chase; but then these letters are written by the political enemies of the Secretary, and it would be unjust and foolish to pay any attention to them."

"Very well, you will find out some day, if you live long enough, that I have read the man correctly. I only hope that your eyes may not be opened to the truth when it is too late."

Kate was by no means blind to Mrs. Lincoln's assets, but she never lacked for a fresh tale to hang on her. One day she drove up to the Executive Mansion in time to see Mary shaking hands with a Negro woman and personally ushering her through the front door. All Kate's early training in the Chase household failed her at this point. Her animosity to the President's wife outweighed her humanity.

Rebecca Orville was a teacher who had asked Mrs. Lincoln for an interview and had promptly been invited to tea. She was campaigning for a school for Negro children. The money had been raised, but all her efforts to move further had been blocked. The children were being taught in the Presbyterian Church to which she belonged.

When Miss Orville arrived at the front door, Edward, the doorman, who was dismissed eventually by Mrs. Lincoln, sent her round to the kitchen entrance, although she showed him her invitation. The President's wife was furious when she learned from a pantrymaid what had happened. She swept down in mauve silk, had Miss Orville ushered at once into the Red Room and told a reluctant servant to serve tea. Then she listened to her story, with gravity and understanding. She assured the harassed teacher that she would bring the matter to the President's attention.

"My people will never forget you for this," said Miss Orville.

Mary escorted her to the door, determined that she should not be subjected to further rudeness. She was shaking hands with the Negro woman when she saw a carriage draw up at the entrance. In a flash she identified the mulberry uniform of the coachman and the elegant equipage. It belonged to the Chases. The Secretary of the Treasury had just arrived for a Cabinet meeting. He passed Mary with a courteous bow.

Beneath a silk parasol sat Miss Kate, all in white, her hazel eyes glinting green with malice. She had taken it all in. She bowed too, but Mrs. Lincoln vanished swiftly as Miss Orville stepped out into the sunshine.

Had the President's wife caught the catlike gleam? She was to hear about it again when Miss Chase made veiled observations at the next Cabinet dinner about making too much of the Negro. Yet Kate's idol had come to fame through championing the Negro cause. The Van Zandt case had made her father's name known throughout the nation. At times Kate was inconsistent on the slavery issue, although much beloved by her Negro servants. Ironically enough, they were to be her only pallbearers at the end of her troubled life.

Chase heard Kate's observations and caught their meaning. He must have disapproved strongly as he watched her across a centerpiece of white sugar doves and iced roses, tipped by a gilded eagle with spread wings, for he turned kindly to Mrs. Lincoln, who sat flushed and angry at his side. Kate had been needlessly cruel and, for her, uncommonly indiscreet, since she usually had a guarded tongue in public. He must take her to task. But of what avail to question Kate about anything she saw fit to say or do? He was fast realizing that she was a stronger force than he, man of destiny though he assumed himself to be from the magnifying reflection of his own mirror.

General McClellan was the lion at the first evening levee opening the 1861-62 social season at the Executive Mansion. On his arm was his wife Nell, whose hazel eyes and vivacious manner were noted with interest by Kate. Her father was already grumbling about McClellan. There was dissatisfaction all around with the military operations. Ball's Bluff was an angry memory. Chase and his radical friends were furious with Lincoln for curbing the dashing frontier raids of General Frémont as head of the army in the West. Frémont had come to Washington in December. He had many supporters, and the band played to slightly jangled undertones as the guests filed past President and Mrs. Lincoln.

It was a showy company, nevertheless. The gold braid in Washington had increased a thousandfold and McClellan liked pomp and circumstance. He was enjoying his new role and was drilling an army into shape, even though it still was a passive force. When he dashed through the streets on his black horse—stocky, with close-cropped hair, high color and bright blue eyes, he seemed a whirlwind of controlled power. He was usually followed by a string of aides, traveling like a small cavalcade and leaving dust and clatter behind them. Studying him on this occasion, Kate decided that McClellan, like Sprague, looked his best on a horse.

The Chases were close friends of the McDowells, and Kate invited Mrs. McDowell to receive with her on New Year's Day after the Lincoln reception. A distinguished company gathered at the Chase home, where Kate held court in her freshly furnished domain. For once the diplomats were outshone by the glitter of the army. The women noted how skillfully Kate had furnished her home and how imaginative all her arrangements were. Lord Lyons was her special care that afternoon. Relations with Great Britain were at a crucial stage. The Confederate commissioners to Great Britain and France—Senator James M. Mason, of Virginia, and Senator John Slidell, of Louisiana—had been taken from the British mail steamship *Trent* and were now imprisoned at Fort Warren in Boston Harbor. Lord Lyons had just demanded their release through Seward on behalf of his government. The Cabinet was debating the matter and Chase was deeply troubled.

The British Ambassador was singling out Kate for attention as he had once paid court to Harriet Lane. She found him an engaging companion, for she loved good conversation, sharp wit and his particular brand of cynicism. As time went on, she was to be credited with helping to swing British sympathy away from the South through Lord Lyons. She may at least have been one of several factors, but she found a formidable counterbalance in another of her friends, Russell of the *Times*, who sent devastating pictures of the North to his London paper. Lincoln was known to like Lord Lyons, almost from the start.

After her reception, Kate kept some of her guests for a turkey dinner. In soft candlelight, wearing pink moiré, her hair burnished and her eyes alight with animation, she conversed with Sumner about his experiences abroad. He told her of meeting George Eliot at a dinner party, and of running into George Sand on a ship plying between Genoa and Marseilles, reporting that she was small, thickset, and clumsy looking in a Spanish costume.

He had met the Disraelis in Munich and he gave Kate an entertaining account of their conversation. Kate always enjoyed meetings with Sumner, who could talk with equal facility on foreign relations, abolition, old lace, authors, intaglios, verse, ceramics or any one of the fine arts. His house was now being stocked with treasures from abroad and he consulted Kate about some of his housekeeping problems. She found him a stimulating companion, and his courtly manners and liking for her father all were points in his favor. He was the only one of the extreme Abolitionists well liked by Kate. Like Chase, she abhorred sensationalism.

Sumner invariably sought her out at public functions and she sparkled in the company of this Chesterfieldian figure, with the abundant locks of hair turned gray since his illness, the Greek nose, strongly modeled features and violent opinions. He was no less courteous to Mrs. Lincoln, who besieged him with notes, invitations and flowery compliments

When she eventually summed up the characters of the men who surrounded her husband—Andrew Johnson a demagogue, McClellan a humbug, Ulysses S. Grant a butcher, and Chase a cheat—Sumner emerged unscathed, the spotless knight, the paragon. Governor Sprague ran him a close second.

The winter of 1861-62 was cold and gloomy, dark and rainy, and the President moved about in a daze of depression, studying army plans and maps, breaking the tension of Cabinet meetings with an occasional jest. Chase and Seward both were giving him trouble. Britain seemed to be favoring the Confederacy, the army was in a stalemate, criticism mounted steadily and his wife had stirred up a hornet's nest of trouble.

Kate moved through the season with perfect command of herself in all situations. She gave *matinées dansantes* by candlelight, much frequented by the young officers. Wednesday evenings were devoted to dinners and receptions for her father's friends. All was good form and convention under Kate's rule, although the Chase home was fast becoming a gathering ground for western soreheads and radicals. Kate came and went while the parleys were on, a sight for her father's friends from out of town, whether she wore a brocaded crinoline or her riding habit. She had dozens of beaux—officers, aides to the President, handsome young men who vied with one another to escort her on her daily rides. Such was her vitality that she could dance all night and set forth at seven in the morning, her hair like a bonfire, her eyes glinting green and her white skin faintly flushed with elation.

One of her favorite riding companions was Garfield, now colonel of an Ohio volunteer infantry regiment. He liked to canter slowly beside her in the Rock Creek region and talk of books or of her father. He happened to be one of the young men who reverenced Chase, which she found an endearing quality in him, considering the abuse heaped on her noble father in other quarters. Kate and Garfield were old friends. She had known him both as teacher and legislator in Ohio, and she appreciated the sturdy quality, good looks and good brains of this young man who had sprung from a log cabin. He was an ever welcome guest at the Chase home.

Garfield escorted Kate to army camps and galloped through country lanes with her in the early evening. He considered her a "splendid rider," although, unlike most of her men friends, he never flattered her about her looks and, indeed, appraised them rather harshly: "Kate is quite a belle here. . . . They have a fine residence and live in splendid style. . . . She is a woman of good sense and pretty good culture—has a good form but not a pretty face, its beauty being marred by a nose slightly inclined to be pug. She has possibly more social influence and makes a better impression generally than any other Cabinet lady."

There was no doubt that she made a far better impression than the President's wife who, by this time, was in deep water. Criticism that had begun idly as gossip over the dinner table had strengthened into serious charges. There was nothing too severe to say about Mary. She was mad, she was vain, bad tempered, stingy, extravagant, vulgar and spiteful. She preyed on the President to push her favorites and paid off grudges by meddling in appointments. She surrounded herself with fools, flatterers and knaves. She was deeply in debt. Above all, she was supposed to have Confederate sympathies, since three of her half brothers were fighting for the South.

By this time Lincoln was receiving letters from all parts of the country telling him not to trust Chase, and Chase was receiving a lesser number of letters condemning Lincoln. Their feud was much discussed in Washington, just as the occasional clashes between Kate and Mrs. Lincoln made gossip for the sewing circles. By this time their hostility was out in the open.

Kate was overheard remarking as she moved with her usual stately air through a pushing line at a levee: "Such a crush! Doesn't it make you feel quite dreadful having all of us come just to stare at you, Mrs. Lincoln? Though I must say you look as though you were enjoying it. Doesn't she, Mr. President?" One of Kate's shabbier tricks was to appeal to Lincoln when she wished to embarrass his wife.

Mary cut in coldly: "Being stared at is something one gets used to, I expect."

"I daresay you're right, Mrs. Lincoln. Personally I find it very trying—but then, of course, you've had so many more years of experience than I."

Kate sailed off, leaving vain Mary in a fury. She was about to hold her own last morning reception before Lent, and she wrote to Jay Cooke in Philadelphia: "I am especially anxious while paying off all my debts to make it an attractive and agreeable occasion. Will you in some of your pilgrimages up town stop at Van Zant's where you find the best fruit and have a basketful of the best and prettiest grapes, pears, oranges, apples, etc. sent me by Adams Express Monday night to my address so that they may arrive here without fail early Tuesday morning. Please send the bill with them. Pardon me for giving you this trouble, but I could not think of anyone who would do it quite so well. Nettie is improving all the time, and we are all as usual busier than bees."

Soon Kate received an invitation to a large private party to be given by the Lincolns. Five hundred cards were sent out and again a storm of criticism broke around the hapless Mrs. Lincoln. As usual, she had gone about everything in the wrong way. Her idea was to telescope her entertaining, give up state dinners because of the war and merge the levees. The press was not invited, another tactical error in that particular era. Criticism burst forth on a widespread scale, and a wounded soldier wrote a dirge about Mrs. Lincoln's party.

The fact of the matter was that the Southern hostesses had taken the props from the social structure in Washington when they left with their husbands. Mrs. Lincoln had failed to build up confidence, and the official set was snubbing her parties to the point where Seward advised a dignified affair by invitation. On one occasion every woman stayed away save the generous-hearted Mrs. Douglas. Kate wickedly pleaded a last-minute headache and when her father made her excuses Mrs. Lincoln rather tartly remarked: "It's such a pity, and I can fancy her disappointment at not being able to come. Still, there is one consolation. I'm quite certain Miss Kate will hear all about the party. She's fortunate in having so many admirers among the gentlemen who are here."

The President was disturbed over the reaction to Mary's proposed private party. "I don't fancy this pass business," he commented. *Leslie's Weekly* did not help matters by whooping up the affair as a symptom of Northern social supremacy, observing that "no European court or capital can compare with the Presidential circle and the society at Washington this winter, in the freshness and beauty of its women . . . the dingy, sprawling city on the Potomac is bright with the blue of northern eyes, and the fresh, rosy glow of northern complexions."

Mrs. Lincoln's Five Hundred, according to this publication, represented "intellect, attainment, position, elegance." The New York *Herald* suggested that she was bent on sweeping out the "long-haired, white-coated tobacco-chewing and expectorant abolitionist politicians." Ben Wade rudely refused to attend. The story spread that he had answered his invitation in curt terms: "Are the President and Mrs. Lincoln aware that there is a civil war? If they are not, Mr. and Mrs. Wade are, and for that reason decline to participate in feasting and dancing."

Such was the outcry that the invitation list was stretched at the last moment to take in the press and other Washingtonians who, presumably, lacked the absolute requirements for the widely advertised function.

For the Lincolns it was a night of great anguish and even Kate, passing along the receiving line in shadowy café au lait lace, dropped her cold front to Mary for a moment and inquired quite gently about her son, ill upstairs. She had just watched Nettie through a bout of scarlet fever at the Cooke home in Philadelphia and had been ill with fever herself. She was in an unusually sympathetic frame of mind.

Several times during the evening, the anxious President and his wife went upstairs to see how Willie was faring. The capable Mrs. Keckley was nursing him. At the last minute, they had thought of canceling the party, but the President ruled: "It's too late to change now. We must go through it somehow. If we cancel the invitations, it will only make more talk."

When all was said and done, Mary staged a party of some dimensions and the top brackets in every field were represented. The assemblage was impressive. Many of the officers were soon to die. Others were to go down in history as failures. Chase and Sumner stalked like gods among the guests. General Frémont looked moody, while Jessie laughed and chattered. Kate talked in their own language to the Comte de Paris and the Duc de Chartres. These two young princes of the House of Orléans, exiles from France and now blue-uniformed officers in the Union Army, were popular in Washington. Kate particularly liked the Comte de Paris, fine featured and intelligent, but most of all she enjoyed good conversations with their uncle, the Prince de Joinville, who was interested in the American scene and tried hard to be part of it. The two younger men were attached to McClellan's staff.

Kate observed that Mrs. McClellan looked handsome that night in a white tunic dress, with bands of cherry velvet and a headdress of white illusion. Mrs. John J. Crittenden, of Kentucky, who had bridged the chasm between North and South, wore black velvet and diamonds, with a headdress of crimson flowers.

Mrs. Lincoln took little satisfaction in her costume on this occasion, although it was one of her more dramatic effects. The story circulated that she was wearing half mourning for Prince Albert, a gesture aimed at Lord Lyons, who was among the guests. Her white satin gown had a deep train swathed in black Chantilly lace. She wore a wreath of black and white crape myrtle, pearls around her neck, and more of the myrtle trailing down her dress. The *décolletage* was as low as Mrs. Lincoln liked it to be, and only that evening, as Mrs. Keckley dressed her, the President had wandered in, taken up his stand with his back to the fire and looked with some amazement at his wife.

"Whew! our cat has a long tail tonight," he observed.

Mary said nothing.

"Mother, it is my opinion if some of that tail was nearer the head, it would be in better style."

It could have been Mary's night of triumph. Actually it was one of uneasiness and woe, although she smiled and greeted friend and foe effusively. Lovely crinolines floated past. Men in uniform or formal evening attire bowed low over her hand as she received with the weary President in the East Room, while the Marine Band played softly in the vestibule. The Red, Green and Blue Rooms all were filled with people and gayly decorated with flowers. Dancing was ruled out.

Mary led the promenade on her husband's arm around the East Room before supper, and Kate for once avoided holding a levee. But men flocked around her again in the dining room, drew her toward the Japanese bowl filled with champagne punch and eased their way toward the feast that Maillard's of New York had set up. Kate had heard that a ton of game had been ordered, and she could well believe it, as she surveyed the turkeys, hams, duck, pheasant, venison and partridge dressed for the kill.

The confectionery effects, in an age when the pastry cook flourished, were arresting and struck the patriotic note. Kate noticed a sugar model of Fort Sumter on a side table provisioned with dressed game. The frigate "Union" was in full sail on a stand supported by cherubs and draped in the Stars and Stripes. Water nymphs made of nougat supported a fountain and sugar beehives foamed with charlotte russe.

After supper the promenading went on until three o'clock in the morning. The band played "The Girl I Left Behind Me" and, although there was no dancing, the press later compared the function to the Duchess of Richmond's ball in Brussels on the night before Waterloo.

"Well, Mother, it was a nice party," said the President, as it ended. "I was proud of you tonight."

The President paid most of the bills out of his own pocket. It was just another of Mary's ill-advised impetuosities. He was smarting at the time from the fierce criticism that had followed the publication in the New York *Herald* of advance portions of his speech to Congress in December. Mary and her friends, the Chevalier Wikoff and John Watt, the head gardener, all were said to be involved.

The nation seemed to be skidding toward bankruptcy. The cry of corruption in the War Department would not be stilled. The President was under attack on all fronts and his suffering face showed that he felt it. But all other issues were wiped from his mind, and Mary's too, when Willie died a few days later. His fever had proved to be typhoid.

"It is hard, hard to have him die," said President Lincoln, lifting the cover from his son's face as he lay on his bed, with Mrs. Keckley mounting guard. And to Nicolay he said in anguished bewilderment: "My boy is gone, he is actually gone!" and wept.

Mary went wild with grief and Kate heard of terrible scenes in the crape-hung mansion. She paid a formal call, but only Mrs. Welles could get within range of the President's wife. A great storm blew on the day of Willie's funeral. Mary could not attend. It was months before there was any fashionable display in the Executive Mansion again. His mother refused to enter the room where Willie died, or the Green Room, where he was embalmed. She stopped visiting the hospitals for a time and gave way completely to her grief. At her request the Marine Band no longer played in the White House grounds. Flowers were banned because they reminded her of Willie.

Kate had liked this blue-eyed boy, bright, candid and better mannered than little Tad, who drove the White House aides to distraction with his mischief. Tad had a defective palate, lisped and was much behind his years in general deportment. Chase thought that all the Lincoln children were badly spoiled. He knew the President's philosophy that the young should be free, happy and unrestrained. "Love is the chain whereby to bind a child to its parents," said Lincoln.

Kate often conversed with Robert, the oldest son, a personable and intelligent young man, with a greater sense of dignity than his mother. But she, too, shared in the talk that Mary was determined to keep him out of the army. Many of the young officers she knew thought likewise. Robert was popular, nevertheless.

After Willie's death Mrs. Lincoln became alternately violent and melancholy, and every few days Kate heard some new tale of her irrationality. In July the President moved to the Soldiers' Home, where Mary dabbled in spiritualism and made such scenes that her husband on one occasion pointed to the asylum in the distance and told her he would have to put her in it unless she calmed down. But she continued to meddle in politics and particularly to pound at Chase. She wrote from the Soldiers' Home to her friend, James Gordon Bennett, telling him that she favored Cabinet changes and would do what she could to bring them about. She mentioned Governor Sprague as being her ally in this respect, although it is highly unlikely that Kate's most ardent suitor had any thought of unhorsing her beloved father. There was much good will between them, and Sprague was at all times deferential to Salmon Portland Chase, even when most deeply upset by "Katy," as he now addressed her.

Confiding, sincere and trustful himself, Lincoln refused to let anyone pick at his Cabinet, even one member at another, as they constantly tried to do. But public opinion had forced him to oust Simon Cameron and replace him with Edwin M. Stanton as Secretary of War. On several occasions he found it necessary to restrain Seward and Chase, both powerful, antagonistic to each other and bitterly divided about McClellan. Seward backed "Little Mac." Chase thought he was losing the war for the North.

Both he and Kate watched every move made by the McClellans. Kate, who circulated freely and had friends in every camp, came home with tale after tale of the social doings of the General and his wife, of the fine fare at their dinners, of his bay horses and splendid carriages, of the extravagant party given in February by Mrs. McClellan soon after Mrs. Lincoln's ill-starred venture. Unlike most of the generals, he lived away from camp. He had a house on H Street close to Seward's. His cavalcade for taking the field was like a small army in itself. He often dined at Wormley's and his own dinners, served in the late afternoon to selected groups with political implications, became noted for their good food and wines. Stanton, who had cleared the War Department of much of its corruption and substituted honest woolen uniforms of two-toned blue for shoddy, wrote: "This army has got to fight or run away, and while men are striving nobly in the West, the champagne and oyster suppers on the Potomac must be stopped."

Stanton and Chase were two Cabinet members who were in sympathy in some respects. Both were radicals. Both disliked McClellan. Kate was well aware that the Secretary of War was the only real friend her father had in the group around Lincoln. The radicals who met late at night in the Chase home matched the McClellan display against the nation's suffering. Polished buttons and smart quick-step were no substitute for fighting men.

Finally, when the President in the midst of his grief over Willie's death, ordered a military advance in April, the slow crawl down the peninsula began. Shiloh that month was another deadly blow, and criticism swung from McClellan to Grant. The pressure on Lincoln increased but he would not budge on Grant. Sickened by McClellan's indecision he exclaimed: "I can't spare this man; he fights."

Kate knew that her father was much involved in the military maneuvers as well as in the nation's finances. He was leading the attack on McClellan. He kept up a running correspondence with the generals in the field. And he went on a revenue cutter with Lincoln and Stanton to Fort Monroe to reconnoiter immediately prior to the Merrimac incident. Many of his complaints, voiced to Kate, were also written to Horace Greeley. During this period he and the editor were corresponding back and forth about the poor use of the cavalry, the inadequate forage, the needless waste in every department and the defection of McClellan. Late in May Chase wrote to Greeley: "McClellan is a dear luxury—fifty days—fifty miles—fifty millions of dollars—easy arithmetic but not satisfactory. If one could have some faith in his competency in battle—should his army ever fight one—if not in his competency for movement, it would be a comfort."

The silent testimony of the Quaker guns and weak fortifications when the Confederates evacuated Manassas came as a shock to the country.

Worse still, during the last week of June, the Army of the Potomac, at last within range of Richmond, engaged in the bloodshed of the Seven Days' Battles. The final score was 15,849 Union, and 19,749 Confederate, casualties. Lee drove McClellan back. The final engagement was at Malvern Hill on the first of July. Again the capital was in mourning— and in some despair.

Chase insisted that his daughters leave the city at once, but Kate stayed long enough to distribute comforts and give a little aid as the wounded arrived in droves and suffering reached a new peak. Battered men, in desperate need of attention, were now quartered in homes, hotels, schools, seminaries, warehouses and churches, as well as in hospitals. Kate took in one of the wounded and he stayed at the Chase home through most of the summer, even after she had left. Church bells were silent on Independence Day, so as not to disturb the suffering men who lay beneath them. Washington had been stripped of its living army. It now received the dead and dying.

Things were even bloodier in the South, where wounded men lay on verandas, in the halls and drawing rooms of stately mansions, as well as in every public building. Mrs. Pryor moved from hotel to hospital, trying to shut out the dreadful sights she saw in the streets, such as open wagons piled with the dead. She had found Roger in a tent ill with malaria after Seven Pines, earlier in the year, and had taken him to the Spotswood Hotel, where all her underwear, napkins, her green and white chintzes, her tablecloths, sheets and dimity counterpanes were rapidly being transformed by the sewing circle into bandages.

"Too much blood, too much death, too much anguish," wrote Mrs. Pryor at the close of the blistering week late in June. "The dreadful guns shook the earth, and thrilled our souls with horror."

Negroes ran about the streets with messages. Newsboys shouted "Extras" for papers printed on the short slips of yellow Confederate paper. Coffins topped with cap, sword and gloves were borne through the streets. Military bands played their dirges without cessation. Richmond was filled with sorrowing people, and few could feel that this was victory. Gold was scarce. Confederate currency had declined in value. Many of the women had moved on to the Carolinas or to other native states. Markets were poor. The blockade was beginning to tell. No longer did the people of Richmond feast on oysters, terrapin and canvasback duck from Chesapeake Bay. Jefferson Davis dined on beef stew, potatoes, coffee and bread. The gardens of Richmond glowed with brilliant blossoms, birds sang in the foliaged streets, but drums were muffled and the women wept for their men lost in battle.

By this time Mrs. Greenhow was in the Southern capital. After her stormy imprisonment in Washington, she was "exiled" in the spring of 1862 and was warmly received by Jefferson Davis, who told her: "But for you there would have been no Battle of Bull Run." Kate had heard that she was much annoyed with Mrs. Douglas, her niece, because Addie had visited her only three times during her imprisonment and had been cold to her. She also knew that Mrs. Greenhow detested Mrs. Lincoln, and had made disparaging remarks about her dress, as well as her appearance, saying she had a "short, broad, flat figure, with a broad flat face, with sallow mottled complexion and exceedingly thin pinched lips." She had seen her in a shop in "very grand" attire. "Yet I don't think that Eugénie or Mrs. Davis would have selected it for the hour and occasion," commented Mrs. Greenhow.

Kate heard a great deal about the operations of the spies. The Chase home was a stronghold of Abolitionist sympathizers. Miss Carroll was in and out. News of the South and the sufferings there seeped up, as well as tales of profiteers and frivolers. Prisoners spread their stories. Kate heard of old friends who had left Richmond and gone back to their native states, of supplies they sent in to town from their plantations, of the sewing and knitting they were doing for the soldiers. There was much talk, too, of the materials being carried secretly from the North to the South. One woman's hoop was found to conceal a roll of army cloth, several pairs of cavalier boots, a bolt of crimson flannel, packages of gilt braid and sewing silk, cans of preserved meats and a bag of coffee. There were tales of shirkers and cowards, both in the North and the South. But all agreed that Mrs. Robert E. Lee was an indefatigable worker.

Kate for once debated her own course of action when her father put pressure on her to leave Washington with Nettie after the Seven Days' Battles. Life had become insufferable in the hot, crowded and saddened city. Repeatedly Chase came home with tales of Cabinet conflicts, to add to his own particular woe, which was a national debt of $524,000,000 on July 1, 1862. He was locked in grim combat with the President, insisting that money could be raised only if the public had confidence in its generals. He and Stanton were pressing Lincoln hard on McClellan.

At last Kate agreed to visit her friend, Mrs. Helen McDowell, at Buttermilk Falls, near Troy. With or without forethought she packed some of her more elaborate costumes for a simple stay at a simple farm.

Chapter VII

CIVIL WAR BELLE

BY THE middle of August, the aged and the ailing, the convalescent officers, the grumblers and other idlers who felt they could spare the time to take the waters at Saratoga, were aware that the creamy-skinned girl who strolled along Broadway under a lace parasol or sat on her hotel piazza surrounded by cavaliers, was none other than Miss Kate Chase from Washington.

Broadway was used to belles of various vintages. It was only a few years since Madame Jumel, the siren of the Revolutionary War, had been fighting her years at Saratoga with false hair, jewels as big as pebbles and costumes designed for youth. She was now close to ninety and ap-proaching death, but Kate listened with interest to the Jumel legends in the relaxing atmosphere of the spa, where the bands still played, there was dancing, and fine feathers were more common than mourning. She unpacked her trunks and entered into the spirit of all the entertainment. As usual, she became the center of the stage without the slightest effort.

Kate had not lingered long at Buttermilk Falls. In fact, the General's wife was much upset by her behavior and wrote to Chase to say that she had gone off almost at once to Saratoga—suitably chaperoned, of course, by friends who had stopped en route to the spa.

"Nettie, I think, has enjoyed her visit but it is very dull for Kate," wrote Mrs. McDowell. "Our hours do not suit her—and the cooking does not agree with her. When the opportunity offered (to go to Sara-toga) I was glad she took advantage of it, for she would have been ill, I think, if she had remained here."

Mrs. McDowell was worried about her husband, who had fallen from grace and was under heavy fire in Washington. She was little interested in whipping up excitement for Kate at so grim a moment in the country's history. But she was a sensible woman, who understood that Kate had become used to luxurious living, to sophisticated food and to admiring men. Indeed, Kate was never to be satisfied with less until the days of her decline. At Saratoga she could play on these familiar strings, although war had dimmed the picture even there and fewer belles paraded on Broadway. It was no wonder that she became at once the most conspicuous figure at the spa.

Things were off and on again between Kate and Sprague. She had been concentrating heavily on Lord Lyons all winter and Sprague was losing hope of capturing her as his bride. Her father was his ally, however, when he could take time from stalking McClellan and meddling in military affairs. Sprague was doing some personal missions for Lincoln that summer.

The war news that reached Kate in Saratoga, both through the papers and her father's letters, was enough to daunt the most persistent hedonist. After the disaster of the Seven Days' Battles, Lincoln moved with decision on the larger front. He turned to General Henry W. Halleck, the lawyer and business man from the West who had done poorly in the field at Corinth in May, but was thought to have administrative ability. Both his men and this particular quality were needed in Washington at the moment.

Kate soon learned that Sprague served as intermediary between Lincoln and Halleck. Early in July the Governor traveled to Corinth with a letter from the President: "I know the object of his visit to you. He has my cheerful consent to go, but not my direction. He wishes to get you and part of your force, one or both, to come here. You already know I should be exceedingly glad of this if in your judgment it could be without endangering positions and operations in the Southwest."

On July 10 General Halleck responded to the President: "Governor Sprague is here. If I were to go to Washington I could advise but one thing—to place all the forces in North Carolina, Virginia and Washington under one head, and hold that head responsible for the result."

The General soon was to regret this ambitious plan when his was the head that suffered. But the upshot of the parleying was that the

President put Halleck in command of all Union armies and ordered McClellan to give up his position south of Richmond to unite with the Federal forces in northern Virginia, under the command of Major General John Pope, who had done well in Missouri. It was Kate's understanding that the Governor had taken the initiative in persuading Lincoln to sanction his trip to Corinth. She could see her father's hand in this. In any event, she felt that her father had triumphed when McClellan was demoted and Halleck took charge. But the change did not lead to sudden victory. Halleck bogged down in red tape, lost heart with the first disaster and wound up by becoming a desk holder with little real authority.

Pope went headlong to defeat after stirring up resentment by a pretentious announcement when he received his appointment. Kate knew him for a pompous young man, slender, with a silky beard, a sharply tilted cap and a fund of stories that greatly amused the President. He had a boastful way that irritated her father, but his hour in the sun was brief. Lee moved north to strike at him before enforcements could arrive. Stonewall Jackson's men destroyed his supply base at Manassas Junction. Pope, as reckless as McClellan was slow, pursued Jackson and found himself face to face with Lee's entire army. Kate learned in Saratoga that another disaster had hit the North with the second Battle of Bull Run. McDowell was among the whipped.

Nettie had joined her by this time, and together they waited for further news from their father. When it came it was black as night. Halleck was disorganized. Pope, Fitz-John Porter, William B. Franklin and McDowell all were generals in disgrace. It was widely believed that McClellan had deliberately failed to back up Pope with supplies. The capital was again shuddering with the thought of invasion. McClellan was so sure the end was in sight that he planned to get his wife's silver out of Washington. Stanton actually was preparing for the fall of the capital, getting papers bundled up, ordering a steamer to remove the President and Cabinet to safety, if need be.

In the midst of it all, Lincoln ordered McClellan reinstated, in spite of Chase's protest that this was "equivalent to giving Washington to the rebels." Kate was almost incredulous when she learned through the papers of the President's move. She waited for her father's more illuminating comments. In spite of all the opposition, Lincoln had said:

"There is no man in the Army, who can man these fortifications and lick these troops of ours into shape half as well as he."

It was obvious that some directing hand was needed as the army rolled back in broken waves into Washington, disheveled, straggling, battered, beaten in spirit, while the ambulances again clogged the roads and drove slowly through the city with the wounded and the dying. Chase wrote to his daughters of the heartbreaking scenes in the hospitals, the chaos in the streets, the hectic passions that raged among the Generals, the mutual recriminations that further shook the confidence of the public and the awful charge of treason that was being leveled —unjustly, he thought—against their good friend McDowell.

Chase wrote that never had the civilians exerted themselves so thoroughly to care for the wounded as under this new onslaught of suffering men. He went personally to the bedside of some of the soldiers he knew. But he reported great deterioration in the fighting forces. The men were demoralized. Desertions were reaching fantastic proportions. Drunkenness prevailed, even on the highest administrative levels. Nothing could persuade him that McClellan might succeed in tightening up the army again or in bringing it out of its slump.

However, by the time Kate and Nettie were back in Washington, Father Abraham's new three hundred thousand were beginning to roll in—raw recruits on which McClellan went to work, marching them with the veterans, no longer worrying about the glitter and the polish, forging them into another army of drilled men, until even Chase admitted that perhaps his enemy had met the immediate need in a moment of chaos. Out of it all came Antietam on a golden September day, with twenty thousand dead and wounded from the North and South. The Union had lost most men but claimed the victory, since Lee's men had been driven out of Maryland. Again McClellan stood still, instead of following.

Radiant with good health after the spa waters and summer sunshine, Kate returned that month to find Washington deep in gloom, rather than exuberant over victory. Chase welcomed his daughters home. Kate thought he had aged in these few months as she watched him pacing up and down in his library, telling them how the President was at last ready to launch his Emancipation Proclamation, now that Antietam had been won. She knew that it had been hanging fire since July and that Seward had argued against its issuance while the North was being defeated. Lincoln had agreed to the postponement and said that when the Confederate troops were driven out of Maryland he would release it. Antietam had supplied the answer.

They all had special interest in the Proclamation. Chase was the known champion of the slave. He gravely told Kate and Nettie what had transpired at the Cabinet meeting, as he entered it in his diary. They had found Lincoln with *Artemus Ward, His Book* in his hands. The author had sent it to him and he found it very funny. He read them a chapter—"Highhanded Outrage at Utica"—which amused them all, except Stanton, who was impatient.

Then the President turned grave, recalled his earlier overtures on the Proclamation, said he had given the matter much thought and believed that the time had come to issue it. "I wish it was a better time," he added. "I wish that we were in a better condition. The action of the army against the rebels has not been quite what I should have best liked but they have been driven out of Maryland, and Pennsylvania is no longer in danger of invasion."

Lincoln told his Cabinet bluntly that he did not wish any advice on the main matter. He already knew their various views and had taken them into account in preparing the document. But he would welcome suggestions on minor points or in matters of expression. Then, perhaps remembering the sentiments of some members of his Cabinet, he added:

I know very well that many others might, in this matter, as in others, do better than I can; and if I was satisfied that the public confidence was more fully possessed by any one of them than by me, and knew of any constitutional way in which he could be put in my place, he should have it. I would gladly yield it to him. But, tho' I believe that I have not so much of the confidence of the people as I had some time since, I do not know that, all things considered, any other person has more; and, however this may be, there is no way in which I can have any other man put where I am. I am here; I must do the best I can, and bear the responsibility of taking the course which I feel I ought to take.

Seward proposed a modification, which was accepted, and Chase said to the President: "The Proclamation does not, indeed, mark out exactly the course I would myself prefer. But I am ready to take it just as it is written, and to stand by it with all my heart."

Chase had often told Kate that one of the causes for failure and delay in the war was the unwillingness "to take any positive ground against slavery and the neglect to make proper use of the Negroes." In the early days of the war, he had held out, along with Simon Cameron, for arming the slaves. He maintained that if the North did not receive them, they would be forced to serve in whatever capacity the rebels pleased. "They dig, they build, they construct, they shoot for the rebels as the rebels require, and we, in a manner, stand guard over them and keep them at that work," he argued.

Kate concurred in this reasoning and she was pleased to hear from the Governor, when he came to call, that he had asked permission to recruit a Negro regiment. He also entertained her with an account of his trip to Altoona, Pennsylvania, to join the other loyal Governors in pledging support anew to President Lincoln and in ratifying the Proclamation.

Sprague was persuaded that the plan for this meeting originated with Lincoln himself and none other. He based this on a dinner table conversation he had at the White House with the President, in which he claimed they discussed the matter in advance. He was never to be shaken in this belief, although he conceded that both Governor Andrew G. Curtin, of Pennsylvania, and Governor John A. Andrew, of Massachusetts, were pivotal figures in bringing it about.

Sprague told Kate with gusto of his journey to Altoona in a boxcar. He and his aide slept on the rough floor, wrapped in their military blankets. When they got hungry, they notified the conductor, who stopped the train near some hospitable farmhouse, where they fortified themselves with food. It took them three days to make the trip, and Southern sympathizers fired on the train several times, but no one was hurt. There was rough talk at the conference about some of the Generals and the conduct of the war, said Sprague. Governors from the loyal Southern states were unable to give their wholehearted support to the Proclamation, but they were willing to support the President's policies.

As she listened to all this, Kate felt she was back in the thick of things. Immediately after the absorbing tale of the Proclamation, her father asked her if she would drive with him next morning to the insane asylum, where the wounded General Joseph Hooker was convalescing from the scars of Antietam.

She was glad to have an immediate task awaiting her, for Kate's conscience was troubling her after her idle summer. The sight of suffering Washington had sobered her. Even before reaching the capital, the newspapers and her father's letters had made her deeply conscious of the nation's ever deepening woes. Stopping off at West Point on her way back from Saratoga, she wrote to Hiram Barney that her trip to the spa had benefited her greatly—"although there has been enough bad news to greet me on my return, to make one almost despair of the future. However, I try to keep up a good heart, and only long to be of some use, in the humble sphere women are allowed to fill, in great crises like the present."

In spite of this touch of humility, neither Barney nor her father underestimated Kate's influence in affairs of state. She might not sew havelocks or comfort a man whose arm had just been cut off, but she could influence Lord Lyons and fight McClellan in her own adroit way. Chase wanted to get her opinion of General Hooker. It would influence his, for he was wavering on Hooker. He felt Joe might be the man to succeed McClellan, but he had not yet made up his mind about him.

Kate arranged a basket of fruit artistically, wore a new bonnet and set off with her father. Hooker was one of the more impressive-looking generals of the Civil War—tall, with wavy blond hair, blue eyes and a high complexion. Kate saw at once that he lived up to his reputation of being a braggart. He greeted her with the gallantry to which she was well accustomed, although unable to rise from his couch because of his injured foot.

The three were an impressive sight to behold as they tore McClellan apart. Hooker said that when the order came to withdraw the army at Richmond, he advised McClellan to disobey and proposed a plan for an advance on Richmond. McClellan ordered him to advance but, before the time for movement came, recalled this command and ordered evacuation instead. Thus, when Hooker expected to march to Richmond, he found himself compelled to fall back to the Chickahominy.

"General," said Chase, "if my advice had been followed, you would have commanded after the retreat to James River, if not before."

"If I had commanded," said Hooker stoutly, "Richmond would have been ours."

He then spoke of Antietam, and expressed his regret that he could not have remained on the field three hours longer, adding: "If I could have done so, our victory would have been complete, for I had already gained enough and seen enough to make the rout of the enemy sure." As it was, they had fought for ten terrible hours on a strung-out front, with 160,000 men in action and miles of artillery.

Chase studied the General's wounded foot and Kate suggested Dr. Foster's Balm for it, but the doctor had other ideas. Kate left the usual impression of intelligence and charm behind her, but on the way home she shrewdly weighed the General's observations. Both found him less gifted with intellect than they had expected, although "quick, clear and active." Chase was relieved to hear him talk as a soldier rather than an aspiring politician. McClellan was already thought to be angling for the presidential nomination in 1864 on the Democratic ticket, and he was openly contemptuous of Lincoln. Chase had no wish to face a soldier candidate.

Kate was thoughtful over Hooker's braggadocio. She suggested that her father take young Garfield with him next day to study the General further. Both Chases valued the opinion of this rising young officer whom they had known in Ohio. "Fighting Joe," on Chase's second visit, became even more emphatic in his denunciation of McClellan. He insisted that he was not fit to lead a great army; that he was timid and hesitant when decision was necessary; that the defeat of the enemy at Antietam should have been final. As it was, it left the inconclusive impression of many other Civil War battles.

When Chase and Garfield returned from their visit to Hooker, the band that had serenaded Lincoln over the Proclamation came playing along the street to Kate's home and the men demanded a speech. She stood by her father's side while he talked briefly. Then they all had a party indoors with refreshments. It seemed to Kate by this time that her father, and her father alone, had pushed through the Emancipation Proclamation freeing three million slaves. He had indeed been one of its most zealous protagonists.

After this, Lincoln's messages to McClellan became faintly sarcastic in tone. Late in October he telegraphed: "I have just read your despatch about sore-tongued and fatigued horses. Will you pardon me for asking what the horses of your army have done since the battle of Antietam that fatigues anything?"

McClellan was relieved of his command early in November, and Kate and her father were chagrined to see Burnside ride into power, although quite reluctantly. They had settled on Hooker, who by this time had recovered from his wound and was back in action. But Fredericksburg was fought and lost early in December, and Burnside came to the capital in great distress, accepting full responsibility for the debacle. His Generals had advised against the advance. Hooker had protested continuing the useless assault. Burnside was more than ready to resign.

Kate watched all these moves with deep personal interest. She had ample opportunity to discuss them with her father, who was laid up with an inflamed foot and spent hours "reading and conversing with Kate and friends." When this busy man had time to pause and think, the Presidency again became the subject of fond contemplation. John Jay, the New York banker, had just written asking if it were true that he had dined with Thurlow Weed in Washington and had avowed himself a candidate for the Presidency, soliciting Weed's support. This, at least, was the tale that Mayor George Opdyke was spreading in New York.

Jay was incredulous. But Kate was not. She thoughtfully studied this letter. She had much to catch up with where her father was concerned, for, when she turned her back on the capital, he was apt to indulge his taste for gentle romance, as well as devious politics. While Kate was in Saratoga, he had had many pleasant drives with Mrs. Douglas, who was just coming out of mourning. He had always liked the sympathetic and intelligent Addie Douglas and it was commented on at once that he should be seen so often in her company. When he found her out some time later, he left a torn greenback with his face on it for a calling card.

But Mrs. Douglas was a minor threat compared with Mrs. C. S. Eastman, a mature beauty who lived in Beverly, Massachusetts, and who wrote quite loving letters to her susceptible father. Kate, who had a free hand with her father's correspondence and helped him often with his letters, had seen and intercepted a few. Occasionally Mrs. Eastman wrote to him in French and this time Kate stumbled on a revealing postscript signed "Carlotta ou, s'il vous plait, Lotta." "Adieu, my dearest cher, Brûlez, s'il vous plait, ce lettre ci parce que j'ai peur que votre sécretaire particulier il trouvera. Encore adieu."

Kate was even more interested in a letter written late in September, voicing Mrs. Eastman's opinion of the Proclamation. Instead of a juicy orange she had found it "dry and tasteless as a pumpkin." It was always good form to belittle Lincoln's achievements to Chase. Kate must have been a little shocked as she read on:

I am quite of your opinion that were you in possession of the reins of government all would be managed well—no anxious Helios would retreat if having given them into your hands. No world would be in flames, and no Eridamus would be immortalized by becoming your grave—but if your fate was like Phaethon's wouldn't I like to become a poplar tree and weep tears of amber for you forever. I would grow very tall and slender with grief, unlike our model Falstaff. . . .

I am so sorry you did not like my French—I fancy it was because it was so poor, not because it lacked warmth—I think the language capable of more ardour than ours—I am more often afraid of saying too warm things and strive to hide feelings on the shady side.

I thought it was quite funny and interesting to write you a little French each day—'twas a test to me in brushing up the dormant lingo, and at the same time keeping up my sweetest of correspondences. . . . but alas I am waked up to the necessity of using a whole stone for one bird—very well, it's a precious, sweet bird and I will even use a big rock if he requires it.

I am full of regrets that you could not get to the seashore this summer but I can well imagine the impossibility in these perilous times. I suppose McClellan is still "meditating with his head on the pot rail." . . .

The weather is still lovely . . . and Mrs. R[antoul] thinks Washington no fitting place for ladies while these times last, but wouldn't I be so happy to be within reach of you once more—but I don't know what the future months will bring about.

Send me a letter here very soon, my dearest friend, just to keep up my spirits and to make the world look sunny—you are my sun and your letters are the little rays—my perihelion is so distant that unless they come often I may get chilly. Adieu, mon cher ami, C.E.

Kate was well aware that a good many women wrote to her father for his autograph for their albums, or else for his portrait. It was a current fad to which even Abraham Lincoln had been known to respond. Chase was always trying new photographers. Kate made a careful study of the results and helped to distribute the portraits where they would be most useful. He was undeniably one of the handsomest men on the national scene and was always gallant to women, however unresponsive to his colleagues.

Among his women correspondents, Lizzie Pike sent him faintly nostalgic letters, suggesting a romance with Chase before her marriage to the newspaperman who was now U. S. Minister at The Hague, and addressed Chase as Commander-in-Chief of Our Armies. As for the others known to Kate—Susan Walker, of Cincinnati, was jealous of Mrs. Eastman; Anna Ella Carroll always approached him with some plea on war or politics; Grace Greenwood, the correspondent, wrote him admiring, but impersonal, letters after he gave her introductions to various celebrities when she went abroad.

Kate was greatly diverted by Grace Greenwood's account of her presentation to Queen Victoria, of supping with Dickens, of meeting Charlotte Cushman and of striking up a shipboard acquaintance with Charles Kean. She longed to go abroad herself as she read of the ball Grace attended at the Tuileries, of her visits to Lake Leman, Pompeii, Pisa, Venice, Vesuvius and the Vatican. But on her return, Grace found Lincoln's levees more to her "plain democratic taste."

"You have less form and more freedom than anywhere else," wrote Grace. "As perpetual motion is the rule, you can break off a conversation and go on with your promenading at your pleasure."

But Kate hankered for a more formal court, the kind that called for queenly rule. She had no intention of letting this opportunity slip, through any feminine machinations around her father's future. She understood the various interests of his correspondents and their modes of approach. The only one who really disturbed her was Mrs. Eastman. She stood in a class by herself and Kate ranged herself firmly against her. But Chase eluded her. She soon realized that her father, like an amorous schoolboy, was carrying on a clandestine correspondence when Carlotta's letters no longer came to the house. Obviously they were going to the Treasury.

However, even Kate could not find fault with her father's taste. Both Mrs. Douglas and Mrs. Eastman were women of her own caliber, intellectually and socially. She feared their encroachments all the more for that, since the thought that she should cease to be hostess to her father, or give up the prospect of presiding at the White House, was unbearable to Kate and made her hesitate over each proposal of marriage that came along.

Kate was not so diffuse or enthusiastic a letter writer as her father, but she, too, went in for literary communications with some of her friends. Sumner constantly fed her interest in the books and writing celebrities of the day. Her father did not approve of the work of Walt Whitman—the lusty red-headed bard now becoming familiar to the Union soldiers—who happened to lodge in a dingy rooming house across the street from the Chase home.

Henry C. Carey, economist and publisher, frequently sent books to Kate and asked for her opinion of them. His Philadelphia firm, Carey, Lea and Carey, published the works of Thomas Carlyle, Washington Irving and Sir Walter Scott in America. He was extremely anti-British himself and his political views were advanced. This was not disconcerting to Kate, who had been listening to extremists from childhood onward.

She thanked Carey for taking "so much pains for my pleasure and amusement" when he sent her his photograph and some quips on "Tardy George," which she immediately sent on to one of McClellan's satellites.

Kate particularly enjoyed Fanny Kemble's *Journal of a Residence in America* that Carey had sent her. She found it interesting to compare it with Pierce Butler's all-revealing statement about Fanny at the time of their divorce. She had little sympathy for Fanny's former husband, who was arrested in Philadelphia in 1861 on a charge of treason but was released a few weeks later. Kate knew that he had lost half a million dollars in the panic of 1857 and had sold his slaves on the block in Savannah to pay his debts, making $300,000 trading in human beings. She held no brief for Butler but had always been fascinated by Fanny. After reading her *Journal* Kate wrote to Carey:

Mrs. Kemble's account of herself in her "Journal" of her younger days, and her husband's account of her in his "Statement" . . . are strongly contradictory. Indeed, when I "look on this picture, then on that" I find it difficult to identify them with the same original. What a lifetime of misery she brought upon herself and friends by her ungoverned and capricious temper. Yet I think I see faults on both sides. Her husband should either use tact or consideration by demanding an "unconditional surrender" of will from a "temperament" that could ill brook such terms. With all her faults I feel for Mrs. K. and am glad I have had an opportunity to read these books, if only for the lesson to every woman they convey. I will return them to you with many thanks as soon as I can do so with safety.

When are you coming to finish your visit with me? Please bear in mind that you will always find the latch string out.

Both Kate and her father heard periodically from their old Columbus friend, William Dean Howells, then living in Venice. He was com-missioned by Chase to buy trinkets and paintings for Kate and Nettie. He had already shipped a stereoscope to Nettie. He forewarned the Chases that his book would be out in New York at Christmas time— "a poem, about half as long as Evangeline" and illustrated by his wife. He foreshadowed his *Venetian Life*, published in 1866, when he wrote:

I am writing in the desultory fashion proper to such work, some sketches of life in Venice, in which I hope really to give an idea of how people live here. Literary travel seldom consents to teach of such small interests as go to form a knowledge of countries, being too generally devoted to experiences of bed bugs, tables d'hôtes, galleries, and so forth; and I think such a book as I propose to myself would have the merit of novelty. But who can tell what a day or a publisher will bring forth?

Like Mrs. Eastman, Howells was scathing about Lincoln's Proclama-tion, writing that it came too late, that its moral effect on a "jaded, suffering and divided people would be null," and that the spirit which would have hailed it a year earlier, and given it vigorous support, was dead. "It cannot recall the wasted lives and treasures which it might have spared before," wrote Howells. "I hope it may be the means of our Salvation."

The President was meeting with abuse on all sides. He was harassed by the Committee on the Conduct of the War. The autumn elections had gone badly for the Republican party. Fredericksburg was another crushing blow. His disaffected generals were as troublesome as the two chief figures in his Cabinet, Seward and Chase. The feeling was spread-ing that changes were imperative.

In his annual message to Congress on December 1, 1862, he said prophetically:

Fellow-citizens, we cannot escape history. We of this Congress and this administration will be remembered in spite of ourselves. No personal significance or insignificance can spare one or another of us. The fiery trial through which we pass will light us down, in honor or dishonor, to the latest generation. . . . We shall nobly save or meanly lose the last, best hope of earth. . . .

The words were poetic, like many of Lincoln's utterances, but even as he spoke a Senate caucus was demanding the dismissal of Seward, largely on the strength of feeling whipped up by Chase. A committee of nine waited on the President and assailed Seward for lukewarmness in the conduct of the war and for lack of interest in the slavery issue. Seward, hearing of this, promptly resigned.

Using his own skilled brand of diplomacy, Lincoln confronted the Cabinet members with the committee and the charges were openly aired. Seward was missing and all took it in good part but Chase, who felt he was being arraigned. Sumner attacked Seward, but Chase squirmed when it came to airing his views on the Secretary of State in this open manner.

At a second meeting with the President, Chase also resigned. He stood with the letter in his hand, and, as Nicolay and Hay later described it, "The President stepped forward and took it with an alacrity that surprised and, it must be said, disappointed Chase."

Lincoln later explained that from the moment he saw Chase holding his resignation, the way was clear to him. He would take both resignations, then ask Chase and Seward to stay on in the Cabinet as a patriotic duty. As he saw it: "Now I can ride; I have got a pumpkin in each end of my bag." He respected the work of both men and did not wish to play favorites.

Thereupon he wrote urgently to Seward and Chase, saying that the public interest did not admit of their resignations. "I therefore have to request that you will resume the duties of your departments respectively." Seward returned at once, but Chase was deeply wounded. He talked it over with Kate, sulking badly, because he had seen the gratification on Lincoln's face as he took his letter from him. However, in the end, with Kate's hearty approval, he returned to his post. He had responded to the phrase in the President's letter involving the public interest. Never had he failed his country. This was the first, but by no means the last, of Chase's resignations—submitted, then withdrawn.

Kate did not wish to see her father out of office at this juncture. When she was certain that he would remain in the Cabinet, she left for New York to bring Nettie home for the Christmas holidays. Nettie was now attending Mrs. Mary Macaulay's school. But Kate fell ill and spent most of her time in bed with a pain in her chest and a swollen face. She had taken cold "from the change of weather and climate, and not being sufficiently warmly dressed."

In spite of her abundant vitality, Kate fell victim to many serious colds, was predisposed to cough, and each occasion alarmed her father. He was always haunted by the specter of her inheritance, and, although his personal life now ran along smoother lines, he never forgot the early years of death and discouragement.

Kate and Nettie returned in time to spread some Christmas cheer around the hospitals. Fredericksburg had brought fresh waves of wounded men into Washington. More than twelve thousand Federal soldiers were casualties in this costly venture by Burnside. They had been badly handled at the battlefield, and by the time they reached Washington, their sufferings were extreme.

Driving through the snowy streets bundled up in furs in a cutter, Kate and Nettie were aware of the constant parade of coffins, of maimed men limping about, of the growing number of women clad in mourning and of the sadness that tinged the faces of many of the passersby. The people were discouraged, dismayed and without faith in their government. They were giving much thought to the kind of care the wounded were receiving, harrowed as they were by tales of neglect, carelessness, inadequacy and the downright torture of wholesale amputation. The entire plan of hospital care was being revised. The Sanitary Commission had developed a system of immediate relief on the battlefield of Antietam. Clara Barton was spreading mercy among the suffering men. Dorothea L. Dix, with her candle and watch, her smooth brown hair and stately bearing, had been working since June, 1861, to get plain women in plain clothes to do sensible nursing in the hospitals. She battled authority at every turn, focused a searchlight on hospital abuses, was a thorn in the flesh of the Medical Bureau, but often seemed an angel of mercy to a wounded man.

Kate saw, on her return, that order was evolving gradually from confusion, and that the Sanitary Commission was pulling all kinds of isolated efforts into focus and achieving centralization. It concentrated on camp sanitation, on suitable food to prevent scurvy, on pavilion hospitals, on properly equipped hospital ships and—in a most effective way—on the distribution of supplies.

This had been one of the great problems from the beginning of the war, when relief societies were formed everywhere and well-intentioned women flooded the railroads with food and clothing, much of it unsuitable, much of it destined to rot before reaching its destination. Now thousands of relief societies sent supplies that were practical to storehouses where they were properly handled and distributed. A relief service worked constantly in the camps and hospitals, and every type of woman—even those who chronically lay on sofas and suffered from the vapors—bestirred themselves to help the Union.

Kate, observing all this, could scarcely ignore the growing tide of helpfulness. She knew that it was scarcely enough for Secretary Chase's daughters to spread largesse only at secondhand. She forced herself to overcome her repugnance and spend more of her time in direct work with the wounded. She found the new pavilion hospitals a great improvement over the early arrangements of which she had caught occasional glimpses.

Kate still shuddered over the drip-drip of cold water on festering wounds, the gangrene and blood poisoning, the amputations and defaced young boys, the terrible smells and sights and groans, the awful silence of the hopeless. But whitewash now freshened up the buildings. There was running water, and instruments were scrubbed and kept in large wooden boxes. Kate came to know when a Minié ball had done its work with a neat round hole or when a splinter of shell had ripped a wound in human flesh.

She had heard many gibes about the useless women in fine clothes who paraded around the beds to the annoyance of the professional workers. But she felt a glow of Christian charity as she wrote letters for dying men, left delicacies beside them, wiped sweat from a soldier's forehead or smiled softly into the tired eyes of pain-racked youths. When she swept away to spend a gay evening with her friends, she left behind her a wake of perfume and the memory of a pale and striking face, screened by a fashionable bonnet.

Sprague sometimes went with her. He was still remembered by the fighting men for his role at the first battle of Bull Run. By this time he was getting desperate about Kate. Her moods about him varied from week to week. Yet her father kept insinuating his cause. She now knew him for a heavy drinker—not an uncommon habit among the men around her—but his behavior was sometimes vulgar in public. Proud Kate was fastidious in her tastes and had been brought up to consider total abstinence a virtue. Chase served wines at his table but deplored the heavy drinking among the ranking officers of the army. Some of his own best friends had lost their status through this habit.

It was plain to Kate that her father, who could do no wrong, was tolerant of Sprague's drinking. As the year ended, she was face to face with the fact that she must finally make up her mind about the Boy Governor. For once Kate was beset by indecision, weighing millions against love. She had other suitors who were handsome, intellectual, high minded, and men of substance. So proud was Kate's demeanor that she repelled intimacies and frightened off the fainthearted. But not Sprague, who approached her with humility but persistence. He knew that he was angling for a jewel. Kate was angling for power. Everyone understood her devotion to her father. No man could reach his standard in Kate's eyes, least of all the intemperate Governor Sprague. John Hay thought so poorly of him that he dismissed him in his diary with the comment: "A small, insignificant youth who bought his place."

Kate, who usually was practical and clearheaded, saw the Governor without illusion. He was no match for her in intellectual vigor or social finesse, but he was openhanded and generoushearted. A faint aura of heroism still hung around him. But his manners declined to a shocking degree when he lost himself in his cups, and Kate had been nurtured on the courtly ways of such men as Sumner, her father and Lord Lyons.

Stronger than all Kate's doubts in the end was her determined ambition to preside with her father in the White House. There was the added pressure of immediate financial embarrassment. As usual, the Chases were up to their ears in debt. They were living on an extravagant scale. Neither father nor daughter showed good sense in this respect. Chase was tired, worn out by a year of terrific responsibility, trying to finance a war that bogged down, with repeated failures for the Union forces. Kate thought that he was aging fast. The next presidential election was approaching, and now, if ever, the time had come to launch a well-organized campaign on his behalf. Such men as Hiram Barney had pushed Sprague's cause. Her father had worked in the background, more subtly but with even greater persuasion. Jay Cooke, too. In the end, hope for the Presidency proved to be the deciding factor. Sprague's cause won.

Later, at the time of her wedding, Henry Adams likened Kate to Jephthah's daughter.

Chapter VIII

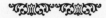

THE COTTON KING

GOVERNOR SPRAGUE took his seat in the Senate in the spring of 1863 and it was noted that Kate appeared in the gallery on his first day in a walking dress of lilac silk, with shaded purple trimmings and a bonnet adorned with wood violets and ties of lilac tulle, a misty drift against her gleaming hair. The sharp-eyed Olivia observed that she was without a single jewel and, as usual, "was the acknowledged queen of fashion and good taste."

But the queen was beset by practical thoughts and was weighing her personal problem. Sprague had now moved into the immediate political picture. He was a Senator with voting power and influence in affairs of state. She had yet to hear him in debate. Kate had friends who were brilliant in this field. Her father did not happen to be one of the elect; she was forced to concede that his public delivery was poor. But he always had something thoughtful and vital to say. Did Sprague? Before long she was to learn that he filled his role in silence. But she had the satisfaction of seeing him become chairman of the Committee on Manufactures.

Kate's engagement was announced in May, just after Hooker's defeat at Chancellorsville. In January the Chase interests had won, and Hooker, the blond giant on the white horse, had received the command of the army, succeeding General Burnside. For a time he stiffened up the morale and raised the Union hopes. The Lincolns stayed at his headquarters for the best part of a week. The President rode at the head of the cavalry, watched the troops parade and felt that he had a sound and fighting army.

"Beware of rashness but with energy and sleepless vigilance go forward and give us victories," Lincoln had advised Hooker, in appointing him to succeed General Burnside.

Kate felt that her father's judgment was vindicated during this interlude of preparation, but Chancellorsville proved to be one of the most conclusive of the Confederate victories. The Union Army, twice as large as Lee's, was badly whipped after three days of fierce fighting. It retreated across the Rappahannock, with a loss of eighteen thousand men. The only consolation for the North was that Stonewall Jackson was out of the running forever. Accidentally shot by his own men, he died eight days later.

Again the transports brought in their freight of the wounded and Washington steeled itself for further endurance. But business was good. War profits were beginning to show. There was much speculation, and people gave parties again and danced and pretended to be merry against an unchanged background of death, suffering, uncertainty and defeat.

Again Kate's father had made a dramatic move on the financial front. Payments in metal currency were suspended in December, 1862. The Treasury was almost depleted. Chase finally listened to the bankers who urged paper money. He disliked the idea as much as Alexander Hamilton did in 1790. But he accepted the inevitable and brought all his weight to bear on his Congressional friends to push through the measure. "Reluctantly, painfully" Sumner backed it in the Senate, arguing that "the medicine of the Constitution must not become its daily bread."

Years later, as Chief Justice of the United States, Chase was to declare the measure unconstitutional, but before the war ended legal-tender notes aggregating $1,250,000,000 had been authorized by Congress, and Chase's greenbacks flooded the country. His own face appeared on the small denominations and President Lincoln's on the larger notes. Kate decided that nothing in her father's career had brought him more generally before the public eye than the much discussed greenbacks.

She was in the limelight herself, following the announcement of her engagement. But right up to the moment of her marriage her father was not completely sure that Kate would go through with it. He told Jay Cooke that he feared she might change her mind. Her friends were thunderstruck when they heard that she finally had accepted the Governor. Waves of gossip were let loose, and there was open talk that Chase would now push harder than ever for the Presidency. Was Kate being sold at the auction block? None who knew her believed that she could be persuaded into doing anything she did not really wish to do. Besides, a great many women considered the Governor attractive.

The Lincolns, the Cabinet members, the Generals, all were vastly interested to learn that their prize belle was marrying millions. Gideon Welles, always a little scathing about Chase, observed: "Few young men have such advantages as he [Sprague], and Miss Kate has talents and ambition sufficient for both."

Years later Henry Villard was to give a realistic view of this marriage in his Memoirs: "Sprague had very limited mental capacity but had reached political distinction at an early age through the influence of real or reputed great wealth. It was at his headquarters that he became acquainted with Kate. She was superior to him in every way and married him for the enjoyment and power of his money."

No one was more convinced than the Governor himself that he was quite unworthy of the honor done him by the Chases, father and daughter. On May 18 he wrote to his friend Hiram Barney: "What shall I say to you? I thank you most heartily for all your kindness to me. The Governor and Miss Katy have consented to take me into their fold. You have fought my battles. Let me be always ready to fight yours, but you don't have them. Please congratulate me."

Barney wrote immediately to Chase, saying how dear to him both Kate and the Governor were, and adding that if daughters had to be given away, it was gratifying to turn them over to the keeping of one who was "all kindness and love," like Sprague.

As soon as he could break away from the muddled Washington scene, Chase went to Rhode Island with Kate to pay formal respects to the Sprague family. They visited Newport and Boston, where Chase was received always with the greatest acclaim and where some preliminary groundwork was laid for his approaching campaign. In Providence a reception was held for them in City Hall, and the Secretary of the Treasury and his daughter were feted by all the local functionaries.

Salmon P. Chase

William Sprague

Kate's prenuptial trip was promptly turned into something of a political jaunt for her father.

When she entered the Sprague kingdom—and kingdom it was, with its well-tilled acres and numerous mills—Kate was well aware of the expansion it implied for her in worldly terms, but she knew little of the family history beyond the fact that four generations of Spragues, including two Governors, had founded and developed one of the greatest manufacturing industries of the era at Cranston, Rhode Island.

She was at once drawn to Fanny Sprague, the Governor's mother, a spirited character who had weathered much, including the murder of her husband Amasa. She was an individualist who did not give a fig for form or convention. Madame Fanny, as she was generally known, came from Groton, Massachusetts. She was said by some to be a cobbler's daughter; by others to be the daughter of wealth. In any event, she was a personality and she recognized in Kate something more than a handsome face and an admirable figure.

Knowing her son as she did, Madame Fanny was to back Kate in many of her marital troubles. In an intimate talk on her first visit, she told her much about the family history. The Governor's great-grandfather had come to Salem from England in the 1620's and had settled eventually in Cranston. There he started a sawmill and gristmill. Before long he added a cotton mill, where the rough fiber was carded and sent out to the farmers' wives and daughters to be woven on old-fashioned looms and bleached with the contents of watering pots. His descendants turned to weaving by water power, and in 1824 began to print indigo blue, the first calico made in America. They built mill after mill in Rhode Island hamlets, until they ruled like feudal lords.

Now, said Madame Fanny, they had more than 100,000 spindles working in their various mills. They wove 800,000, and printed 1,400,000, yards of cotton a week. At the moment they were bringing in French-Canadians to take the place of men going off to war. They had sawmills in Maine, land in Texas for cattle raising and in Kansas for horse breeding. They controlled three national and two savings banks in Providence and a number of commercial companies. In the postwar days they would also have steamboats to bring the cotton bales from New York to Providence, railroads to haul goods to and from their mills and agents in the principal cities in the East.

Amasa, the Governor's brother, showed Kate and her father the mills, the schools for their employees' children, the homes they had built for their workers and the blooded horses that he raised on the company farms. Kate took careful note of the imported carriages, the custom-made harness and the liveried coachmen. She quickly grew to like Amasa. He left most of the business end of the mills to the Governor, while he devoted himself to his horses, to his land, to organizing the Narragansett race track, to founding the horsecar railway in Providence, using his own horses; to building a fine home on a bluff at Cowesett; to having a good time and entertaining others.

He had more of Madame Fanny in him and was quite unlike the Governor. It was from Amasa that Kate heard the curious story of their father's murder. Chase remembered the case quite well, for it was of national interest. Kate was three at the time. The Governor was thirteen, and in the Smithville Seminary in Scituate, when word reached him that his father had been clubbed to death as he crossed the Pocasset brook by a footpath on his own land on a bitterly cold December day. He was a huge man and put up a struggle when his murderer jumped on him from behind a rock.

The crime stirred up Rhode Island, for Amasa Sprague was a power in the state. Four brothers—William, John, Robert and Nicholas S. Gordon—were arrested and charged with the crime. Nicholas had vowed to get even with Sprague, who had sought to withhold their liquor license. Skilled cotton workers of the old school had been imbibing too freely on their premises. When Sprague was unable to buy out the Gordons, he pushed the matter through the Town Council.

John was hung for the crime. He had worn the bloodstained coat found at the scene of the murder. The other brothers had alibis. But the issue was clouded by a deathbed confession, supposedly made by one of the other brothers. Feeling in Rhode Island ran high. The issue became the poor against the rich. It led to the abolition of capital punishment in that state.

On their father's death, Madame Fanny and her husband's brother, William, who took over the mills, decided that the boys had better learn the business from the ground up. Fanny was a mighty power herself, but stayed in the background after the fashion of her generation. Willie was taken out of school and put to work in the factory of the Cranston

Print Works. At first he dealt out supplies; then he graduated to the counting house. At twenty-one his uncle took him into partnership. Five years later, when Uncle William died, a new company, known as A. and W. Sprague and Company, was formed. The partners were the brothers, Amasa and William, along with their cousin, Byron Sprague. By that time they owned nine mills. The business expanded still further under the Governor's shrewd direction. It was booming now, in the midst of the Civil War, and would flourish in the postwar days. It had its own water and gas systems, its fire engine company and its farms where cattle, sheep and poultry were raised, in addition to its great stables and horses.

Chase and Kate toured the valley with Fanny, the Governor and Amasa, and visited all the mills, where the female operatives gazed with curiosity at the beautiful Miss Chase who was about to marry their employer. Amasa gave Kate a bolt of cotton to have some dresses made up and told her that there would be more where that came from! Kate laughed. Amasa had the knack of making one feel happy.

He thought that Willie had found a wonderful bride. Fanny had already decided that Kate had brains and that she would be firm with Willie. This, Fanny believed, was just what her son needed. There were two sisters, Almira and Mary Anna (Mrs. John E. Nichols), sensible, handsome women who were quietly impressed by Kate. All stood a little in awe of the stately Chase. But he unbent as far as he could to meet this warmhearted family halfway.

Altogether, the visit was a success, although Chase left without being able to confirm one report that had troubled him since he had first heard it in 1860—that Sprague had bought the Governorship for $100,000, or thereabouts. As they drove through the streets of Providence behind magnificent horses, Amasa showed Kate the steps that the Governor had once charged up on his white mare. But no one mentioned to Kate the name of Mary Viall, the Governor's discarded sweetheart, a girl of good family who bore his child and was in course of becoming an outcast. Soon she would take to drink, and to following Kate around without her knowledge; to making scathing notes on her conduct; to hexing her and eventually to writing a novel, *The Merchant's Wife*, about their triangle. The Governor must have worried lest her vengeful eyes rest on his future bride as they drove through the streets, for the girl was known to be desperate at the time of his marriage.

Neither Kate nor her father had any idea in the midst of all the feting that the most conservative families of Providence had closed their doors on the Governor for this and other reasons. They were intensely interested in the engagement of this controversial character to the famed Kate Chase, but they had no intention of welcoming her as one of themselves, beautiful though she might be and the daughter of Salmon Portland Chase.

Back in Washington, tension soon began to show between the engaged pair. Kate was utterly exhausted from late nights, a constant round of gayety and the strain of finally making up her mind to marry. Sprague was getting on her nerves. On the last day of May he wrote to her father: "For Katy's sake I think a respite necessary, and have concluded to go home tomorrow." In this same letter, he made it clear to Chase that they expected him to share their ménage after their marriage in November.

"Let me here, my dear Sir, thank you from the bottom of my heart for the treasure you have reared and given to me," the Governor added humbly. "God bear me witness that it will be the object of my life to see that she receives no detriment in my hands. If a life of devotion to her, and to yourself, can make me worthy of it all, I shall deem it well spent."

Kate had arranged it all. They would buy the house they already occupied. They would maintain separate arrangements for carriages, horses and servants. The main financial burden would be borne by the Governor. Chase would board de luxe in the family mansion, paying a fixed sum when in residence, half-price when away. Kate would now not only be her father's hostess, but would have the added prestige of entertaining as a matron and Senator's wife. She had worked it out carefully and Sprague had cheerfully agreed. The only reluctant spirit was the Secretary, who may even have thought of freedom for himself.

Chase replied cordially but pointed out to Sprague that all might not be clear sailing with Kate. He gave his prospective son-in-law a briefing on the high-spirited girl, and Sprague wrote at once in more chastened spirit: "Your council is timely. I do not, however, expect that all will, at all times, run smoothly, but I do expect that so far as human happiness can be arrived at, it can be attained by mutual interests, mutual forbearance and mutual love. It will I think be my fault if such is not the future of your daughter and myself."

A few days later the Governor was urging that Colonel H. T. Sisson —"the most successful recruiting officer I had in this state"—be promoted for gallantry and then be sent to Florida to recruit a brigade of Negroes. His only fault was intemperance, said Sprague, but he had promised to reform. In a burst of realistic self-appraisal, the Governor added: "I deem nearly all our defects occasioned by this practice; and I know that in my own life whatever of improprieties I may be charged with, is from this cause."

It was a plea familiar to Chase. He was badgered for favors by friends and relatives, to whom he was invariably kind, giving loans when in debt himself and helping young cousins and nephews to establish themselves. For Sprague to fall in line was not unexpected, and at the moment he would rather have propitiated his future son-in-law than almost anyone else within his ken.

Liberal flattery usually accompanied the requests for aid, position or patronage that reached him. When Chase wrote kindly to Sprague about Sisson, drawing Stanton into the matter, the Governor promptly replied: "I have no grudge against Mr. Stanton, but I do think he is thoroughly unfitted for his position. We want, my dear sir, men in position who can command other men from *the power* within themselves. You have that power eminently. You have not the weakness of using the force as *some* do, but you step ever steadily onward and upward."

Sprague had joined the parade of hero worshipers and Kate listened with silent approval. One of his good points in her eyes was his genuine devotion to her father. She knew that during her absences they had got on well together and she saw no reason why a joint household should not be equally successful.

Sprague had planned a summer of touring and yachting for Kate and Nettie, bringing the women of his family along and making it a group party. He took Kate north to Troy first to visit the McDowells again. This time, with her suitor in tow, she did not show her boredom, but benefited by the rest and change. Sprague was delighted with the simple life. He liked farms, livestock and hearty cooking. He was glad to see Kate pick up and bloom. She was almost in collapse when they started but soon recovered her vivacity. Her ups and downs that spring suggest considerable mental distress over the decision she had made.

Chase, sweating out a trying summer in Washington, sent them letters that brought war's realities into their peaceful setting. Kate was restless until she heard how her father fared. At the end of June he wrote that things were getting serious again. Lee was expected to try an invasion of Maryland and possibly of Pennsylvania. Some thought he might try to reach the Ohio at Pittsburgh or Wheeling. But he would not get far, wrote Chase optimistically, without feeling Hooker strike him. "If God smiles on active and earnest work on the right side, Lee will never take his army back to Richmond," finished Chase, who had not considered Chancellorsville the end of Hooker.

Four days later he wrote that his protégé had been relieved. And by his own request. Chase was much surprised. No one had thought to inform him, not even Fighting Joe himself. General George Meade had succeeded him.

"I did not hear of it, nor of the appointment of Meade in his place, till Sunday, when at a meeting of the heads, called for a different purpose, having no connection with Hooker's affairs, the President mentioned it to us," Chase wrote to Kate. "I understand that General Meade is preferred by the majority of the officers of the army to anyone except Hooker, and perhaps now to him. . . . I like General Halleck personally, and he seems to have large capacity; but he does not work, work, work, as if he were in earnest."

At last the tide of battle turned in favor of the North when Lee met Meade at Gettysburg. On Independence Day, just as this victory was being celebrated, word reached the capital that Grant had taken Vicksburg after a desperate siege. Five days later Port Hudson, the only remaining Confederate river fort, surrendered and the North rejoiced.

Chase wrote to Kate about Lincoln's carriage being mobbed by the crowd. At last a winner, the President was cheered and extolled. But this brought him no elation. Behind the victory he saw the dead—both of the North and South. "How much more of this killing have we got to stand?" he asked after Gettysburg.

There was little glory in it. Chase wrote again of the city filling up with the wounded, of the churches being turned into hospitals, of the United States Sanitary Commission and the Christian Commission asking for nurses, matrons, lady superintendents, help of all kinds. He urgently advised Kate to decline Hiram Barney's invitation to christen a launch in New York immediately after the two great battles.

Sprague wrote to Barney on Kate's behalf: "It is thought that while the country is contemplating the great destruction of life the name of Chase had better not be known in connection with a circumstance of semi-festivities. You will I know appreciate this old womanly view of Miss Kate and procure some other fair lady to perform the part allotted to her."

Chase wrote of Lincoln's incessant trips to the War Department to talk by telegraph to his generals; of Stanton, brusque, bearded and excitable, comforting the tired President as he flung himself on a worn old couch to snatch a little rest. Often Lincoln worked far into the night, stretching, yawning, looking somber, dropping off to sleep, reading dispatches with open dismay, jesting in homely fashion, looking yellower than usual in the gaslight. Chase joined him at times, to sit stiff and pompous as bad news clattered in.

The President had many dreams and alarms that summer. Early in June he wired to Mrs. Lincoln, who was in Philadelphia with Tad, all her interest in shopping revived: "Think you had better put Tad's pistol away. I had an ugly dream about him." Like all the other small boys in the country, Tad was playing soldiers.

A few days later the President telegraphed her again, saying: "It is a matter of choice with yourself whether you come home. There is no reason why you should not, that did not exist when you went away. As bearing on the question of your coming home I do not think the raid into Pennsylvania amounts to anything at all."

Mrs. Lincoln returned with Tad and rejoined her husband at the Soldiers' Home, where goats grazed that summer under the cedar and poplar trees and Mrs. Keckley helped Mary run her household. But while out driving a few days after Gettysburg, her coachman was thrown to the ground when his seat broke, the horses bolted and Mrs. Lincoln jumped from the carriage. Her head was injured and she was ill for some time. She went to Manchester, New Hampshire, to recuperate, but again Lincoln showed a longing to have his family with him. "The air is so clear and cool and apparently healthy that I would be glad for you to come," he wrote. "Nothing very particular but I would be glad to see you and Tad."

Mary was again shopping, buying the finest lawns and sheer crape veiling for her mourning bonnets. Nothing less than the "very finest and blackest and lightest long crape veil" would do. She also wanted the "genteelest and tastiest" undersleeves and collars in white and black, with cuffs to match. While Mary Todd moved toward half mourning, Kate Chase was preparing her trousseau. Most of it had been ordered in Paris. The purchase price for their Washington mansion was $35,000 and Kate planned $1,400 worth of repairs—the installation of a bathhouse, and fresh paint for the roof and outside woodwork. Potomac water was to be introduced, to be followed by better water from the Great Falls, when that became available. Kate was planning a magnificent season, in which she would work for her father with all the Sprague resources behind her.

She was having a taste of the luxury that lay in store for her as she cruised along the Atlantic coast in a yacht, her pale skin lightly tinged with color, her reddish hair flying out from under her bonnet as light breezes whipped around her. Kate loved the sea and the starlit nights and the songs that Nettie and the other young people sang as they sailed toward Newport. In these surroundings she could forget for hours at a time the young officers who had paid her court, and now were dead, wounded or maimed. Because she was so remote from it all and sailing between sea and sky, she could wipe from her mind the thought of all the bloodshed; the dead horses and bodies of men strewn around Gettysburg; the women who hid in caves in the hills and in cellars during the Siege of Vicksburg; the rats and mules that were eaten in the South.

Before leaving Washington, she had heard that there was not a bonnet left for sale in Richmond and that the girls planned to plait hats when the wheat ripened that year. They used gallnuts filled with crimson sap for ink and, in Mrs. Pryor's words, "there were dandelions and the songs of the birds in the park, but not much else."

Kate must indeed have suffered twinges of conscience from time to time as she followed her pleasurable course, while disorder reigned and the women of the North and South worked and nursed and sorrowed for their dead. The reports turned in by workers for the Sanitary Commission rolled back the curtain to give glimpses of what went on close to the battlefields. Meanwhile, Kate traveled from the Atlantic coast to the mountains, and Sprague wrote cheerfully to Chase on August 20th: "The weather is good, the mountain scenery grand, and the accommodations various. The trip will produce, I think, good results to all interested in the health and happiness of the members of our party."

Chase, bowed down with his political cares, had little time that summer for romantic correspondence and Mrs. Eastman wrote to him rather chidingly from Beverly two weeks after Gettysburg. With Kate's future disposed of, did she hope at this point that their friendship might at last lead to marriage? She fastened quite acutely on the overweening ambition that guided Chase, no less than his daughter. Mrs. Eastman showed deep understanding of the man in most of her letters. On this occasion she wrote:

I have a feeling nowadays that my letters to you give but little satisfaction, as they can do nothing to advance the object for which it seems to me you live—how shall I be frank and perhaps offend you—and tell you I am jealous! And of whom and what? Of your ambition and through that of yourself, for doesn't ambition make the worshipper the god of his own idolatry?

I feel if each of my letters could help you on one step to place and power, what satisfaction they would give, but as they are ineffective they are proportionately stupid, and only your amiability induces you to say they are acceptable. Am I not correct, or am I a little insane?

Is it not better to be frank? I prefer to know the true sentiments of my friends, the true state of everything connected with myself—even the saddest, the most heart breaking calamity—'tis better to suffer acutely for a time than to live on, a martyr to a flattering lie.

Mrs. Eastman was summering pleasantly too in spite of the war. She sketched, read by the sea, looked out from her library window "upon the sails that float along the coast" or gazed at the distant islands "meditating upon the memories"—presumably concerning Chase—"that the murmuring waves recall." She visited the James Russell Lowells and the Theodore Parkers, but found that Dr. Parker was "ennuied away from the excitement of city life."

As the summer wore on, Chase's thoughts were focused quite constantly again on the Presidency. Some of the war tension had eased since Gettysburg and people were spending money. He had bickered all through the spring and summer with the President over army matters and political patronage. He was a thorn in the flesh of all but Stanton. He wrote to the generals as if he were their chief and encouraged their complaints. The same old siren voices were calling him and he soon set forth on a tour of the West with all too palpable motives. His best friends looked with suspicion on this performance, but Kate had urged it.

While in New York she had brought pressure to bear on Horace Greeley, always a variable factor in her father's life. Greeley hearkened carefully to her words, but probably was affected less than most of the men who listened to her. However, on this occasion he took specific note of Chase's aspirations and wrote him a letter on September 29, 1863, that was not too reassuring for Kate when she read it on her return from New England:

I know no man in our country who is in my view better qualified for President than yourself, nor one whom I should more cordially support. Yet I am by nature a devotee of ideas, of principles, of measures, and accustomed to regard man merely as means to ends. It does not seem credible to me that a great man should much care to be or not to be President. Hence Webster was all his voter life one of my deep enigmas. In '60 I heartily supported Judge Bates, with a perfect understanding that there could never be any sympathy or cordiality between us—because I thought him the man of all men best calculated to bridge over our national transition from the side of slavery to that of Liberty without provoking a desperate and bloody Civil War. . . .

You know that our national sky looks darker to me than to most others. I see men intent on what we shall do after 1864. . . . If in 1864 I could make a President (not merely a candidate) you would be my first choice. Yet it may be that I shall see six months hence—what I do not now see—that the national existence and well-being require a concentration of our strength in someone else. In that case I shall put the country first and individual preferences nowhere.

Frankly yours,
[Signed] Horace Greeley

By this time Chase's campaign was well under way and Blair had called his stumping tour at the time of the Vallandigham contest in Ohio an open declaration of war on the President. Others saw it as a smart move by the Secretary of the Treasury. James A. Briggs, a politician of Olean, New York, wrote that another such trip would "put you so far ahead that you would distance the 'Rail Splitter' and the whole 'entry.'" However, Briggs said that he would like to spike the New York Herald in some way. He added, not too subtly: "Bennett is vain and likes to be noticed by decent people, or to have his family noticed. How would it answer to send James Gordon Bennett Jr. an invitation to the approaching wedding? He is, I believe, a likely young man. If advisable it would greatly please the old folks."

A pamphlet, Going Home to Vote, threw the spotlight in an intimate way on Chase's excursion west. John T. Trowbridge, who did Horatio Alger books for boys, wrote a fictionized biography of Chase—The Ferry Boy and Financier—which highlighted his ferry boat runs on the Cuyahoga. Jay Cooke bought a large supply for free distribution and some of the text was printed in the Atlantic Monthly. Cooke inspired another account of Chase's life, which appeared in the American Exchange and Review of Philadelphia and was illustrated with a steel engraving by John Sartain.

Chase's friends were following the line suggested by Kate—that her father must be humanized in the public eye. But before long the Secretary was busily apologizing to the President:

If anybody wants my autograph, and I have time, I give it; if anybody wants to take my daguerrotype-photograph and I have time, I sit for it; if anybody wants to take my life, in the way of a biographical sketch I let him take it; and, if I have time, give such information as is wanted that he may take it more easily. Some friends wanted a sketch prepared, and engaged a gentleman to prepare it. . . . How could I object? He asked for subscriptions and obtained them. How could I control or supervise that? I was very busy with the affairs of my dept. and had no time to look after such matters, even had I been aware of what was being done. If I had been consulted I should certainly have objected to any subscription by Mr. Jay Cooke or his brother, except such a moderate one as any friend might have made. Not that any wrong was intended to be done, but because the act was subject to misconstruction and there are so many to misconstrue.

As her wedding day approached Kate spent little time with Sprague. She pored over papers with her father, discussed the growing strength of his campaign and caught up on the summer's discord with Lincoln. She was disturbed to find how badly the publicity had backfired. But she had laid her plans skillfully. She would come back from her wedding trip the bride of the year. Her father was already none too secretly in the running. Sprague could not only finance a campaign, but as Senator he could give it some political support.

General Jacob D. Cox, writing to Chase from Cincinnati on November 10, summed things up, taking note of Kate's "career": "Permit me to present my most cordial good wishes to your daughter upon her approaching nuptials. It is a great satisfaction to know that this event will not turn her from the brilliant career she has had at the head of your household, but will only continue it at the head of her husband's. May every private and domestic happiness accompany her."

Kate moved in a whirl of excitement at the end. Every day she visited the shops or worked over the detailed arrangements for a wedding that would be smart without being ostentatious. She was feted and dined. Official Washington thought that Sprague was getting a prize, and the gallants, at their army posts, cast affectionate thoughts in Kate's direction as her wedding day drew near. Girls all over the country snatched vicarious excitement from the approaching nuptials.

The President valued Miss Kate and had a warm spot for Sprague, who had been both brave and generous. Mrs. Lincoln alone thought that Miss Chase was the lucky one. She had no intention of going to the wedding. Her dislike for the bride was at its height. She was all too sure that Chase was preparing to ride into the Executive Mansion on the Sprague golden horse. But not if she could help it!

PART TWO

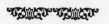

4

Chapter IX

ABE KISSES THE BRIDE

ABRAHAM LINCOLN wore his customary dark look of sorrow as he entered the Chase home to see Kate married to Governor Sprague on the evening of November 12, 1863. He was not in the mood for merriment. The dead of Gettysburg weighed on his spirit. The end of the war was not yet in sight. The people everywhere suffered, and Lincoln's sympathies blanketed both North and South.

He was weary from lack of sleep, from studying maps, from hearing bad news, from conciliating generals and Cabinet officers. Not the least of his worries was Salmon Portland Chase, who greeted him at the entrance as if he, Chase, were God Himself. The President had arrived unattended, but a burst of cheering from the crowd heralded his presence.

Kate, aged twenty-three at the time of her marriage, looked dazzling as she walked in a golden glow of gaslight, flowers scenting the air, with the President, the Cabinet, the diplomats, Senators and Generals looking on. The official set was present without a break in the ranks, save for the Generals in the field and Mrs. Lincoln, whose excuse was that she was still in half mourning.

But the public knew better. The whisper spread that she was snubbing Kate's wedding. The New York *Herald* had gone so far as to suggest that she should have invited Kate to hold her wedding reception in the East Room, so that "in view of a certain possible event she may have an opportunity of judging how its associations suit her."

Deep though they were in the woes of war, spectators jammed the street so that the carriages had difficulty moving through. The gowns, jewels, laces and feathers were a satisfying sight to the avid-minded. So were the uniforms and gold lace of the diplomats, arriving in carriages lined with amber velvet, white satin and other fripperies. McClellan had not been invited, but General Halleck, stout and drooping, slouched in, and then McDowell, somber and dark as the cloud that shadowed his reputation. A string of top-ranking army officers clanked through the doorway along with Senators friendly to Chase.

The crowds hoped to catch a glimpse of Kate in her bridal gown through the windows, but large mirrors had been attached to the window frames to enlarge and enhance the scene within. However, the strains of the Kate Chase Wedding March, played by the Marine Band, reached the street. Joel Benton, young poet and protégé of Horace Greeley, had written special verses for the occasion.

Lincoln studied Kate with mournful appreciation as she marched on her father's arm. They made a stunning pair. Her skin was as white and smooth as the long velvet train of her dress. Her lace veil was held in place by a parure of pearls and diamonds in orange blossom design, the gift of the bridegroom. Her bridesmaids were her sister, sixteen-year-old Nettie; her cousin, Alice Skinner; and Ida Nichols, a niece of the Governor. Bishop William Newton Clarke had come from Rhode Island to perform the ceremony, and her father gravely handed her into the custody of Sprague, who seemed overawed and embarrassed by so priceless a gift.

When the ceremony was over, the President bent from his great height and kissed the bride awkwardly on the cheek. Surely perfidious Kate must have been touched by the kindly spirit of this honest man, knowing the traps that she and her father had laid for him in the coming months.

He had sent her a fan, one of the simplest of her wedding gifts. They represented a fortune in themselves. The bridegroom's business friends in New England, her father's banker allies in New York and Kate's own fashionable coterie had not forgotten her. Forty guests had come from Rhode Island for the wedding, and five hundred guests in all attended the reception. Champagne flowed freely. Toasts were drunk. The cake was a masterpiece of confectionery, since the caterers had outdone themselves for their favorite belle. Two parlors running together were cleared for dancing and hung with the national colors. Kate swept her train over her arm and led the lancers with Richard E. Parsons, who had first introduced her to the Governor in Cleveland. The Marine Band, long familiar with Kate's grace on the dance floor, played as softly and romantically as it could at her wedding.

Chase held stately court with his peers and took pride in his magnificent daughter. Lincoln, who was genuinely fond of Sprague, had a chat with him before returning to the Executive Mansion, lonely, without escort, as he had arrived. Only Sumner was missing, but a letter had just reached Chase in the familiar handwriting on paper with a lemon stripe: "This note will arrive, perhaps, at the wedding of your daughter—for whom be all happiness and love—my benedictions I offer with a warm heart."

Sumner enclosed a note from John Bright, answering his protest about British ships being prepared for hostile expeditions against the Union. War impinged on every front. Chase prayed fervently for the bride, as he had done on the day Kate was born. But this time he was forced to mingle his petitions with prayers for the fate of his country.

He had tried to avoid ostentation in the wedding, but because of Kate's national reputation this had proved impossible, he realized as he studied the newspapers afterward. He suffered as he read a letter from Alexander E. Drake, of Philadelphia, comparing the lot of his children "equally dear to me as is your daughter to you—on a *pallet* on the floor, for God help me, their father, having no bedstead for himself, has none for them." Drake was an army captain and a discarded civil servant, complaining about his pittance of ninety dollars a month and asking for Chase's intercession.

It was an unfortunate moment for display. Strikes were widespread. Machinists and car drivers were demanding better pay. The female operatives in New York, whose interest in clothes had long ago focused their attention on Miss Chase, were on strike because they worked from eleven to sixteen hours a day, making one to three dollars a week, getting fifteen to twenty-five cents a hundred for hoop springs and sixty cents a dozen for finishing shirts. It was a good day when they turned out as many as six.

On the war front, news from the Army of the Potomac was "All Quiet Along the Lines Again," a familiar theme. A few shots had been fired after a body of rebel scouts to the left of Culpeper. The border conspiracy was making headlines. And on the morning of Kate's wedding the New York *Herald* published two attacks on Chase—a news item and an editorial. The first concerned a call made on Lincoln by Francis P. Blair, the elder, in which he told the President that he would be ruined if he "did not at once emancipate himself from the pernicious influence that Chase was exercising over him." He advised him to reorganize the Cabinet and get rid of General Halleck. Chase arrived in the middle of the interview. Some sharp talk was exchanged and he left deeply depressed. Kate did not see the paper until she had left on her wedding trip but her father had told her of the incident.

The editorial did not beat about the bush. It said that Lincoln was understood to be in the field for another term, and it bluntly attacked Chase's "electioneering tour in Ohio and Indiana." It continued:

The Secretary of the Treasury, controlling the financial elements of the country, and the fanatical elements of the Republican party, is beginning to overshadow the President himself; and if the latter would continue to be the master of the situation he must take the bull by the horns and without further loss of time. In other words, he must reorganize his Cabinet, beginning with the removal of Chase, Stanton and Welles, and every other crooked piece of timber, and ending in a New Cabinet which will unanimously and distinctly reflect the policy and the wishes of the President.

Kate left on her wedding trip, heedless of the spate of bills that remained to be paid. She already knew that none of this would matter now, with the Sprague money behind her. But her father eyed them with dismay—carriages, collation, music, bouquets, Tiffany invitation cards, trunks, a platform for the wedding party, flowers and chairs, costing fourteen hundred dollars, even without the trousseau. Kate's wedding dress came from Madame Hermantine du Riez, of the Place Vendôme, Paris. The rest of her trousseau was also imported, except for some things from Arnold Constable and Company in New York. The Chases were already heavily indebted to A. T. Stewart.

Chase was in wretched financial condition himself. At the time of Kate's wedding, his account was overdrawn. It was an anomalous situation that he should be handling the Treasury so efficiently, while his own finances were always in a hopeless muddle. After Kate's departure, he settled down to prepare his annual report. As usual, the Generals were after him for more money. Where was it to be had? His legal-tender notes now flooded the country and a new era of spending had begun. Greenbacks were depreciating and there was wild speculation in gold.

While her father wrestled with his 1863 report, Kate was already moving into her Rhode Island kingdom, where welcoming arrangements had been made for the young couple. Madame Fanny and the bridesmaids traveled north with the bride and groom to continue the festivities. Kate soon felt like a Barnum exhibit. She was used to extravagant effects, but in reasonably good taste. The Sprague arrangements, as her cousin, Alice Skinner, crushingly described them to Uncle Salmon in a letter, resembled preparations for a horse fair. Amasa and his aides had gone the limit at Cranston. Over the gateway on an arch of red, white and blue was strung the message *Welcome* in huge gilt letters on a black background. The house was smothered in flags and bunting. Streamers of red, white and blue trailed from the central tower to each end of the piazza. The porch itself was a canopy of flags, with the emblems of other nations over the doorway.

It was all kindly intentioned but Kate could scarcely conceal her horror. She showed signs of faintness, and when she had her husband alone she ordered him to have the decorations removed. Crestfallen, the gardeners and housemen who had gone to such pains, ripped down their glory. Madame Fanny took Kate's displeasure in good part. Each had the sort of backbone that the Governor lacked and they shared some of the same feeling toward him. Kate's disgust was passed off as fatigue, just as her son's sprees were conveniently labeled dyspepsia.

Madame Fanny was used to those around her doing individualistic things. She could take Kate's displeasure without losing her balance or even feeling resentful. But the Governor and Amasa were taken aback. Kate's next shock was the reception given by the Spragues. Elaborate in all its trappings, the knowing Kate had only to study the five hundred guests to see that something was amiss. They were not the people who had feted the Chases on her earlier visit. It did not take Kate long to see that somehow or other the social pattern was frayed and that the guest list was not what she had come to expect as her due. Officialdom was missing; so were the first families of Providence.

Before long she was to learn that, in spite of their power and fortune, her husband's family was cold-shouldered on Rhode Island. The Governor was regarded as an impulsive and eccentric character, who had been known, when in his cups, to plant his feet on a hostess's damask chair and spit cheerfully at her jeweled vinaigrette. Up to this point Kate had seen him only on his best behavior. At that, she had felt some qualms about his social graces, but war made for rough manners.

However, Sprague was greatly pleased with Kate's reception. All were impressed by his bride after she had decided to be gracious. He wrote to Chase saying that the reception "had passed off quite brilliantly," that Kate was "a little fatigued at first but as progress was made she was herself again." She was now happy, wrote the gay cavalier—"the rightest and wellest one of the party and I cannot but admit that it gives me great happiness and satisfaction in knowing that she fares thus in my hands."

Nettie and the other young people were having a glorious time. So was the good-natured Governor. "One would never grow old if such material always surrounded him," he wrote enthusiastically, adding that Nettie bade fair to eclipse Kate. They all rode around the city with Amasa and toured his splendid stables. They bowled in Byron Sprague's bowling alley and visited the mills. They danced and feasted and made merry from morning till night. It was not so much Kate's honeymoon as a roistering good time for the young people whom Sprague always drew around him.

When the festivities finally were over, the guests scattered and Kate and the Governor journeyed to New York to settle Nettie again in Mrs. Macaulay's school, where she was popular but by no means the student her older sister had been at Miss Haines's. Kate thought that Nettie needed tighter discipline. Her earlier school reports had harped on the theme that she was "gifted with a quick and comprehensive intellect, but was deficient in mental discipline."

Nettie started innumerable projects and finished few. She went from one enthusiasm to another and, in steady Kate's opinion, did not show the necessary perseverance. She was also untidy, preferred sketching to study and lacked strength of purpose and the will to excel. This, clearly, was not her Chase inheritance. When they were together, Kate worked hard over her to make her more industrious. She had rigid ideas of discipline and education for the young. But Chase indulged his second daughter, except for constant admonitions about her handwriting and spelling. He found her blithe spirit a relief from Kate's ambitious exactions and he freely bared his heart to Nettie, not afraid to show her his more human side. Nettie was full of love, sympathy and amiability. She bloomed like a flower, heedless, gay and bright, spreading good cheer. She was also highly intelligent, but she had none of the instinctive Chase drive.

Back in New York, with Nettie mourning her return to school after so much adult gaiety, Kate settled down to sober appraisal of the news, while the Governor went down to the Stock Exchange to do a little business. She picked up the *New York Times* and read a full column on the front page on Edward Everett's speech at the dedication of the National Cemetery at Gettysburg. One paragraph followed, quoting what Abraham Lincoln had to say.

Kate was interested because she felt sure her father must have been there. She learned later that, like most others, he had no particular realization of the majestic words delivered so simply in the high-pitched voice of the President. But Everett, official orator of the occasion, had heard the whisper of history, for he wrote to Lincoln next day: "I should be glad if I could flatter myself that I came as near to the central idea of the occasion in two hours as you did in two minutes."

Ohio was still a focal point of interest for the Chases, so Kate had planned that her wedding trip should take them West. Her looks and possessions were observed all along the route to Cincinnati. The story of her nuptials, her charm and her influence had spread before her, and she traveled in state. Her wardrobe was an impressive one, even by the standards of the day, and Kate did justice to her clothes. She was warmly welcomed both in Cincinnati and Columbus, where Parsons gave a large party for her. She wore her diamond parure and flounces of point lace, also given to her by Sprague. Kate had come back in triumph.

She adroitly turned her wedding tour into something of a campaign trip for her father. She had many allies in Ohio and Chase's able work in the Treasury had not gone unrecognized in the West. The Spragues entertained lavishly all along the line, drawing in the key figures in political circles. It was clear to observers that Mrs. Senator Sprague could do even more for Salmon Portland Chase than Miss Kate and that she was wasting no time about it.

The bridal pair proved to be overpowering to the Chase relatives, whose lives were cast along simpler lines. Kate's cousin, Mrs. Jane Auld, wrote to Uncle Salmon from Loveland on December 7: "We had the pleasure of seeing dear Kate, her husband and some of her beautiful things at Cincinnati. I saw her big trunks and quite despair of her ever coming here. I was delighted to see her looking so well and happy."

But few of the letters of this period suggest real happiness of spirit on Kate's part. She waited anxiously for word from her father, and her thoughts were all on his political future. Sprague remarked on her tenacity and absent-mindedness. The wedding festivities also had put a strain on his naturally convivial spirit. It was difficult for him to stay sober under the least demanding circumstances and now, with the imperious Kate his treasured prize, he was ill at ease and anxious.

Sprague's honeymoon letters to Chase show him holding a jewel that he considered quite too precious for his keeping. Kate was uncommunicative during this period. She had the Governor write the family letters. In one, which she clearly inspired, he questioned Chase as to whom he thought should be the presidential candidate. Kate was already getting her husband into the picture. Chase replied in his usual artful manner:

If I were controlled by merely personal sentiments, I should prefer the re-election of Mr. Lincoln to that of any other man. But I doubt the expediency of re-electing anybody, and I think a man of different qualities from those the President has will be needed for the next four years. I am not anxious to be regarded as that man; and I am quite willing to leave that question to the decision of those who agree in thinking that some such man should be chosen.

Kate reached eagerly for this letter when it arrived. Sprague, replying, said she had become "anxious for intelligence from her father and I turned over to her the ever welcome hand, and waited my turn for the share which fell to me." They had both taken cold, he said. He was over his, but "Katy holds to hers but will relinquish it later—you know she is very tenacious of everything." The good Governor cryptically continued:

I am delighted that you see a bright future for us, as I have known that you trembled a little for that which was yet a solution of that which was to come. We are happy. We feel we base it upon a foundation which will not give way. With God on our side, and the ever watchful eye and council of one so dearly loved, we share with you in feeling that misfortune can never come though trials may.

I am glad you speak so of Katy's anxiety for your future, and I am amply glad to have you speak of your connection with Mr. Lincoln. Could that letter finds its way into print as from you it would rectify the effect of the whole bitter work of Seward, Blair, Lincoln and Co's attack upon you.

The Spragues wound up their wedding trip in New York and took occasion to visit the Rev. Henry Ward Beecher in Brooklyn. Chase had urgently asked Kate to pay this visit. He had already written to Dr. Beecher soliciting an opinion on the Proclamation. Kate arrived just after he had sent off the kind of letter that would give her father small consolation: "I agree with the view which you express of the President's message and proclamation. His mind works in the right direction, but seldom works clearly and cleanly. His bread is of unbolted flour, and much straw too, mixed in the bran, and sometimes gravel stones, yet, on the whole, the loaf will sustain life, tho' it makes eating a difficulty rather than a pleasure."

Beecher, at the time, could give strong support to anyone whose cause he espoused. Kate worked adroitly but persuasively on the famous divine. She was not to know for several years how ill Beecher thought of her father's aspirations to the Presidency.

On her return to Washington, she found to her chagrin that one of her aunts had been trying to persuade Chase to remarry, pointing out "there are so many elegant ladies in, and about Washington—who will make affectionate and excellent wives." She also discovered that he had returned to his correspondence with Miss Susan Walker, who by this time was nursing in a Union camp in the South, and that he was in communication again with the irrepressible Carlotta. One note, which Kate probably never saw, went to Mrs. Eastman while she was on her wedding trip. It made clear that more letters had been intercepted.

"No, indeed, I do not forget you; nor am I likely to forget," he assured Carlotta. "I think of you constantly; and if any feeling is left in me, with the sincerest affection. We have been friends a long time and I hope shall be better friends instead of worse."

But all this dalliance faded into the background as Kate became a stronger factor than ever in her father's life, with a fortune to spend on his furtherance, with added prestige as a matron instead of a maid, with the name of Sprague—still honored—in the background. Far from relinquishing her hold on her father, she was now a strongly creative force shaping his destiny. The Executive Mansion seemed within reach at last.

Kate's own home was in perfect order. Her invitation lists were ready. Her campaign was mapped. She could indulge every whim in perfecting her setting. Her dinners, *matinées dansantes* and receptions that winter became the talk of Washington. They were never showy but always in perfect taste, and sometimes quite original. Kate made clever combinations of guests and sparked up the conversation herself, never missing an opportunity to belittle the Lincolns. She talked finance with the bankers; arts, books, philosophy and the opera with Sumner; military tactics with the generals; farming with a rural Senator. But with any one of them she swooped with deadly effect when a political point was to be scored. Her wit and perception were relished by Henry Villard who was not, however, blind to her calculated tactics when he wrote of this period:

The more sordid pursuit of supporters, the angling for delegates, could be left to the politicians enlisted in the cause. Kate's activities were of a more subtle kind—making friends by the adroit exercise of social flattery. Her receptions and dinners were the great events for Washington; an invitation to her home the most desired. In the critical winter of 1863-4 Mrs. Sprague distributed her favors mainly with one end in view. Any politician from the provinces, irrespective of his standing at home or his personal graces, became the object of her attention—if he was likely to control delegates to the June convention. Her smaller dinner and supper parties were occasions for the discussions, plans, and even plots that formed the necessary prelude to the open contest. Even so strait-laced a Puritan as Lyman Trumbull, after having been admitted to Kate's inner circle on E Street, began to see value in her father as a presidential candidate.

Kate drew in the press on every possible occasion, although Greeley, Villard, Dana, Theodore Tilton and Joseph Medill were variable factors from time to time. William Wales, of the Baltimore *American*, alone stood firm and consistent for her father. Another ally was young Whitelaw Reid, whom they had known in Ohio. He was in and out of their home now as a correspondent in the field. Both Kate and Nettie were fond of Whitelaw, whom Howells was to describe as "a tall graceful youth with an enviable black mustache and imperial, wearing his hair long in the southern fashion, and carrying himself with the native ease which availed him in a worldly progress uninterrupted to the end." He was friend and adviser to Chase, and at times gave him counsel in publicizing his political career.

James Russell Lowell disappointed Kate by coming out strongly for Lincoln in the January issue of the *North American Review*. She expected him to be in her father's camp. Sumner was a pillar of strength for Chase in New England, but Wendell Phillips and William Lloyd Garrison preferred the President to the Secretary of the Treasury. Even Abe's most ruthless critics—Ben Wade, chairman of the Committee on the Conduct of the War, Zack Chandler and William Pitt Fessenden—did not turn to Chase.

For one so discerning, Kate was curiously dense about her father's situation among men of influence. Her vigorous ego, matched only by his, sustained her pride and blinded her to truth and common sense in this one matter. She worshiped her father and believed that the obstacles surrounding him could be overcome by sheer force of will. Chase's friends were well aware that the way to flatter Kate was to compliment her father. She listened avidly to this false undertone, although on the whole she was more realistic than Chase.

The public was preoccupied that winter with the presidential prospects. It was a relief to talk of something besides war. Although Gettysburg had changed the military picture, things still were moving slowly. Criticism flashed out readily and some of the malcontents rallied to Chase, who wrote during January to James A. Hamilton, a political friend in Ohio, acknowledging that he was in the field for the Presidency.

Kate worked particularly hard on the banking interests in New York and Philadelphia through her husband and the Cooke brothers, all men of financial stature and powerful mercantile connections. Chase was respected in this sphere for his conduct of the Treasury. At times it was Kate's pleasure to juggle these men with Senators and army officers. With considerable tact, she drew them all into accord around her dinner table, never failing to pull the strings for her father.

Chase agents drummed up support for him in the South and West. Kate kept close check of every move made by his lieutenants. She followed his correspondence as closely as if she were his private secretary—a function which indeed she sometimes filled. Her ear was ever to the ground for visitors from the outlands who might have influence over delegates. But it took a parson from the fighting front to checkmate the Sprague bounty. Years later Julia B. Foraker, wife of Governor Joseph Benson Foraker, of Ohio, told how the Rev. Granville Moody, of Ripley, Ohio, arrived before breakfast one morning and talked to Chase as he shaved. Chase tried the same direct method he had applied to Schurz.

"A number of my friends are coming to breakfast," he said. "We want to fix a plan for my candidacy. What I'd especially like you to do, Chaplain, is to tell these men exactly how the boys in blue feel about Mr. Lincoln. You have just come from the front. You tell them."

The chaplain did. When asked to say the blessing, he made it long, taking occasion to tell the Lord how completely beloved Abe Lincoln was by the boys in blue. There wasn't anything they wouldn't do for him.

"Moody never mentioned his host's nomination for the Presidency," wrote Mrs. Foraker. "And it was a delicious breakfast, too. Trust Kate Chase to see that her father's board glorified the flesh-pots!"

Chase, in Mrs. Foraker's view, "always appeared like a very great man to whom nothing could be denied." But she thought he never ceased to have "poaching eyes" on the Presidency.

While on her wedding trip, Kate had no particular regret about missing Mrs. Lincoln's New Year's Day reception in 1864, signal that the queen was back in circulation again. But she heard all about it from her father. Mary wore purple silk, trimmed with black velvet and lace, and sported a white plume in her hair. It was a bright sunny day with a sweeping northwest wind. The crowds were so great that the doors were closed every fifteen minutes to relieve the pressure. The visitors passed across a miniature bridge extending from the window of the East Room to the sidewalk. It was remarked that four Negroes "of genteel exterior and with the manners of gentlemen" passed in the line and shook hands with the President, a milestone in White House history.

Mrs. Lincoln started going to the theater again, making up box parties. She insisted on the President taking drives with her from time to time to take his mind off his cares. She gave a reception for Tom Thumb when he married Lavinia Warren, and people flocked to the Executive Mansion to view this curious pair.

Since Willie's death, she had also been hostess to Adelina Patti, who offered to sing to the Lincolns after tea, and had everyone in tears with "The Last Rose of Summer." Slender and young, Patti wore wine-colored silk and a tricorne hat with ostrich plumes. On an earlier visit to Washington, she had been the guest of Mrs. George W. Riggs, wife of the banker who lived in Georgetown and was the partner of William W. Corcoran. This party was gay and spontaneous, with legerdemain and some opera bouffe, whipped up with poker and brass tongs. Patti jumped on a chair and sang thrillingly for the assembled company. She had made her American debut during the Buchanan administration, and Kate had heard her sing, both in New York and Washington.

The echoes of Kate's enhanced social success after her marriage were disquieting to Mrs. Lincoln. But all Washington was gay that winter, and even Secessionist sympathizers were taking the chandeliers out of their wrappings and polishing up their dance floors. The people were dancing mad—not that there was anything much to dance about. Surly General Meade, like all the others, seemed to be standing still. But the ladies who whirled in rich velvets, in tarletan, heavy moirés and stiff brocades, tried not to talk of war and suffering. They knew that the Army of the Potomac lay along the Rappahannock between Washington and the Confederates, and they felt safe, if not victorious.

The Sanitary Fairs were raising huge sums by supplying diversion. The women worked hard in the daytime for the Union cause. The Patent Office and the Enlistment Fund balls were patriotic, and entertaining, too. Willard's and the National Hotel were drawing crowds to their hops. Sentiment had changed. Cabinet officers could now have dancing in their homes as well as dinners. Kate was not criticized for her lavish parties. Gaiety, however forced, had taken the place of gloom. But the wounded still lay in hospitals, and amputees were part of every crowd.

All winter long the tension between Lincoln and Chase was acute. As usual, they were wrangling about patronage. Some of Chase's appointees had turned out badly. Lincoln wrote to his Secretary of the Treasury on February 12 about Barney in New York, some of whose actions he could not altogether approve. Barney was one of Kate's best friends, as well as one of her father's. But ten days later a new barrier lay between them— the Pomeroy Circular, sent to thousands of voters under the Congressional frank. It openly promoted Chase for the Presidency and questioned the administration of Lincoln. It announced the organization of a national committee, with links in all the Union states, to push Chase for the Presidency. It was signed by Senator Samuel C. Pomeroy, of Kansas, as chairman of the group.

The circular was so fantastic that at first it was considered a hoax. Rumors spread that Chase had resigned; that he knew all about it; that he knew nothing about it. Had Kate helped in its initiation? Many insisted that she had. Sprague was known to be one of its backers. Had it been brought to a head during the expensive wedding trip? If so, Kate had gone one better in intrigue than other famous hostesses who had tried to move the political pawns. In any event, the onus of it clung to her and cast a slight shadow over her impeccable reputation.

When the *Daily National Intelligencer* published the text of the circular, the matter had to be faced openly. Chase wrote at once to the President, disavowing it entirely and adding: "You are not responsible for acts not your own; nor will you hold me responsible, except for what I do or say myself. . . . For yourself I cherish sincere respect and esteem and, permit me to add, affection. . . . Great numbers now desire your reelection. Should their wishes be fulfilled by the suffrage of the people, I hope to carry with me into private life the sentiment I now cherish, whole and unimpaired."

The President replied in a temperate and characteristic way, pointing out that he had known about the Pomeroy Circular, even before it became public. He continued:

I have not yet read it, and think I shall not. I was not shocked or surprised by the appearance of the letter, because I had had knowledge of Mr. Pomeroy's committee and of secret issues which I supposed came from it, and of secret agents who I supposed were sent out by it, for several weeks. I have known just as little of these things as my friends have allowed me to know. They bring the documents to me, but I do not read them—they tell me what they think fit to tell me, but I do not inquire for more.

I fully concur with you that neither of us can be justly held responsible for what our respective friends may do without our instigation or countenance; and I assure you, as you assured me, that no assault has been made upon you by my instigation or with my countenance. Whether you shall remain at the head of the Treasury Dept. is a question which I will not allow myself to consider from any standpoint other than my judgment of the public service, and, in that view, I do not perceive occasion for a change.

It is unlikely that Kate appreciated the nobility and tolerance of the President's attitude. Her pride was hurt that the movement, instead of gaining friends and support, should have brought down a storm of criticism, even among Chase's intimates. The opening gun in her father's campaign had misfired badly. However, she concurred in Greeley's advice that Chase should call personally on the President and thresh out the matter face to face. Abe treated him genially and offhandedly, and repeated that one could not be blamed for the faults of one's friends. Chase wrote at once to Hamilton, one of the backers of the circular, announcing that he had no thought of being a presidential candidate. And since Kate, through Sprague, had been dragged into the mess, he warned her to keep clear of political entanglement. Pomeroy in March got up in the Senate and denied that Chase had anything to do with the circular.

Villard wished to publish the correspondence between Lincoln and Chase, and the President again showed his tolerant spirit in his note to Chase, saying that personally he preferred to avoid an unnecessary exhibition—"yet you are at liberty, without in the least offending me, to allow the publication if you choose."

The outcome of the Pomeroy incident was a swift, but decisive, drift to Lincoln. Votes of confidence were passed in various states, and even in Ohio, where despite the efforts made by Parsons and other of Chase's friends to stem the tide, the Republican members of the State Legislature passed a resolution supporting Lincoln. To Kate's great chagrin, Rhode Island also fell into line. The evidence was overwhelming and Chase thought it best to write a public letter of withdrawal.

The relations between him and the President became practically untenable after this. Mrs. Lincoln found the Pomeroy incident a ripe plum for her, justification for all her warnings. She was so angry that she decided not to invite Chase or the Spragues to the next Cabinet dinner. Nicolay, in charge of seating arrangements furnished by the Department of State, saw at once that this was a serious tactical mistake. Chase could not be openly insulted, and Kate was a formidable character to snub. He took issue with Mrs. Lincoln and finally, in his own words, "ordered Rhode Island and Ohio to be included in the list."

"Then there arose such a rampage as the House hadn't seen for a year," wrote Nicolay. But he won his point. However, "having compelled Her Satanic Majesty to invite the Spragues," he was then taboo himself. Mrs. Lincoln decided to drop Nicolay from the seating list. He countered by refusing to help her any further with the dinner arrangements. That left her stranded.

Hay and Nicolay were at times indomitable souls in handling her tempers. They compromised less with her than Stoddard, who felt genuine sympathy for Mrs. Lincoln and thought her much abused. When the charges that she was a spy were at their height, she turned to him on one occasion and cried: "I'm spied on and talked about in my own house—but I can't discharge a servant who is insolent to me for fear of having more vile stories spread about me. How can I be patient when I'm humiliated every day of my life? I'll go mad if I keep on this way— doing nothing—afraid to speak or move. I'm practically a prisoner in this house."

She was angry with Nicolay about the dinner, but since he had won they all sat rather uneasily at the presidential board. Mrs. Lincoln was even more haughty than usual with Kate. But the genial Governor got around her. In her stubborn way she continued to favor Sprague and to think him the generous and unfortunate victim of a scheming pair.

Mrs. Lincoln was just as anxious to see her husband re-elected President as Kate was to have her father hold this office. It had become a mania with Mary Todd for good reasons of her own. She was deeply in debt and dared not tell Lincoln how much she owed. She confided to Mrs. Keckley that the sum was $27,000 and that most of it was owed to Stewart's. Later it developed that it was twice this amount.

"Mr. Lincoln has but little idea of the expense of a woman's wardrobe," said Mrs. Lincoln. "He glances at my rich dresses, and is happy in the belief that the few hundred dollars I obtain from him supply all my wants."

"And Mr. Lincoln does not even suspect how much you owe?" asked Mrs. Keckley.

"God, no! and I would not have him suspect. If he knew that his wife was involved to the extent that she is, the knowledge would drive him mad. . . . If he is re-elected, I can keep him in ignorance of my affairs; but if he is defeated, then the bills will be sent in and he will know all."

Watching the Chases closely at her dinner table, Mrs. Lincoln resented the fact that her husband still confided in his Secretary of the Treasury in spite of all that had happened. But the horsemen who stalked Chase without mercy were the Blairs. He was savagely attacked in the House late in April by Frank P. Blair, the tall, red-headed Congressman from Missouri, who had been a hero since Vicksburg. For two sizzling hours he hammered away at Chase, accusing him of seeking the Presidency, of creating a corrupt political machine in Missouri to further his cause, of treason, of grasping at power and patronage to fight the administration that had given him place, of being no whit better than Jefferson Davis, of being weak in resisting secession.

Chase was in a fury that night and Kate had difficulty calming him down. Usually it was the other way around. All three members of the family were involved. She heard with grief and horror that Blair had called her father a "rowdy" and a "blackguard"; that he charged him with winking at loose living right in the shelter of the Treasury building; that he had helped the Governor get a permit to buy cotton in the South for his Rhode Island mills; and that he was responsible for the Pomeroy Circular.

Her father was deeply embarrassed at the moment over an inquiry he had launched himself, which had resulted in sensational charges on the goings on of some of his Treasury employees and the women clerks. Kate suffered intensely that her lofty-minded father's department should have incurred such ribald comment. Chase was mortified. It was one more worry piled on top of all the others. The President made matters worse by confirming Blair's commission as Major General immediately after his attack on Chase. He later explained that this was accidental and that actually the appointment had been made before the speech was delivered.

The Chase camp retaliated by calling the Blairs "the Maryland serpents." They had long had influence with the President. In the early months of the war, he had often sought the peace of Silver Spring, where the aging Francis Preston Blair worked over his flower beds, read in his library or spun his subtle plots.

Kate never forgave the Blairs. Her noble father! The flippant enjoyed the picture of a whited sepulcher attached unknowingly to a den of sin. The whole performance was excoriating, even in an age of violent abuse. Kate held her head high, kept on with the social round and was observed with admiration as she helped General Grant weave his way through the mazes of a dance he did not understand, when he was put on exhibition in Washington, a soldier with no taste for gallantry.

Grant was now the hero of the hour. His appearance anywhere meant tornadoes of applause. He was followed about and cheered at receptions and serenades. Both Kate and her father thought him a roughhewn hero. But Lincoln and the public were in the mood for a "man of deeds, and not of words." Grant took it all impassively, his square bearded face glum and uncommunicative.

While her father was enduring his ordeal in April, Kate watched a great military parade that revived some of the enthusiasm of the early days of the war. But instead of fresh-faced youths, seasoned men of battle marched in line and five new regiments of Negro troops brought great applause. Grant had quietly ordered the simultaneous advance of all the armies of the Union, and the Army of the Potomac crossed the Rapidan on May 4 to engage in the Battles of the Wilderness and of Spotsylvania, bloody and not overwhelming victories. For three days and nights ambulances streamed through the city in steady sequence. Men and women worked night and day at the wharves, feeding the wounded, moistening dressings, helping in any way they could. Cook-houses and refreshment stands were set up on the route to the hospitals, and sandwiches and coffee were offered to those who could handle them. It was a period of grief and anxiety, with throngs huddling in the streets, looking for relatives, running about a little wildly.

Cold Harbor early in June added to the dreadful casualty lists and loomed up as another disaster. Again the public faced the fact that Richmond still was far away and that the troops were besieging Petersburg instead. Citizens reeled before such carnage, but underlying was the hope that the end might be in sight.

Kate drove through the streets in the early summer hating the name of Blair. But her own troubles inevitably were dimmed by the horror that washed around her and she did what she could to help. Grant, who moved ahead, instead of suffering from McClellan's "slows," was earning the title of butcher, with fifty thousand dead behind him. Lincoln was letting him alone. He felt he had found a man who would fight, and there had to be more bloodshed in order to end bloodshed. But the agony of war, in terms of wounded men, the dead and the dying, was being felt in every corner of the land. Kate sickened over the constant parade of ambulances and coffins.

Relations between the President and her father grew steadily worse. Chase stayed away from Cabinet meetings, sulked, was ill and unhappy. In June the National Union Convention quietly renominated Lincoln in Baltimore and chose Andrew Johnson of Tennessee, a Democrat, as his running mate. The Republican radicals fumed and raged but were helpless in face of this smooth political coup.

Chase had tried Lincoln's endurance to the limit. When another crisis over patronage arose late in June, the Secretary of the Treasury resigned again. This time the President accepted his letter without question. Both Seward and he had played the resignation gambit with such unshakable faith in their own indispensability that it came as a shock to Kate to find her father suddenly out of office.

She studied the President's letter of June 30th with care and noticed that, as usual, this humble man signed himself "Your obedient servant":

Your resignation of the office of Secty. of the Treasury sent me yesterday is accepted. Of all I have said in commendation of your ability and fidelity I have nothing to unsay; and yet you and I have reached a point of mutual embarrassment in our official relations which it seems cannot be overcome or longer sustained consistently with "public service."

The immediate issue was again a patronage appointment. Chase had nominated Maunsell B. Field as Assistant Secretary of the Treasury in New York and Lincoln disapproved his choice. But the clash lay deeper than this. Hay and Nicolay later summed it up, saying that Chase never changed his opinion that a great mistake had been made at Chicago in the nomination of Lincoln. As they saw it, his predominant thought was to counteract, as far as possible, the evil results of that mistake. They added:

He felt himself alone in the Cabinet. He looked upon the President and all his colleagues as his inferiors in capacity, in zeal, in devotion to liberty and the general welfare. He sincerely persuaded himself that every disaster which happened to the country happened because his advice was not followed, and that every piece of good fortune was due to his having been able, from time to time, to rescue the President and the rest of the Cabinet from the consequences of their errors.

He never lost an opportunity for ingratiating himself with the general in favor, or the general in disgrace. He paid equally assiduous homage to the rising and the setting sun. The surest way to his confidence and regard was to approach him with conversation derogatory to Mr. Lincoln.

The President was not unaware of this disposition of his Minister of Finance towards him . . . and it was the lifelong habit of Mr. Lincoln to disregard slights that were personal to himself. He had the greatest respect and admiration for Mr. Chase's capacity; he believed thoroughly in his devotion to the national cause, and seeing every day the proof of his pure and able management of the finances of the Government he steadily refused to consider the question of the Secretary's feelings towards himself.

Chase told Whitelaw Reid that he supposed the root of the matter was a "difficulty of temperament." "The truth is that I have never been able to make a joke out of this war," he added. He had never had any understanding of Lincoln's earthy humor. In fact it had shocked him. Nor had he been able to tolerate levity in the midst of disaster. Like Kate, he was completely and curiously dead to Lincoln's innate greatness.

Two of Lincoln's comments on Chase give clues to the President's conception of his Secretary of the Treasury. "Chase is about one and a half times bigger than any other man that I ever knew," he said on one occasion. And again: "Mr. Chase is a very able man. He is a very ambitious man, and I think on the subject of the presidency a little insane."

Schurz, who admired both men, commented: "The relations between Chase and Lincoln always remained such as will exist between two men who, in their official intercourse, do not personally come near to each other and are not warmed into confidential heartiness."

"So my official life closes," Chase wrote. "I have laid broad foundations. Nothing but wise legislation and especially bold yet judicious provision of taxes, with fair economy in administration and energetic yet prudent military action. . . ."

In the final analysis, Chase seemed somewhat dazed as he initiated his successor, William Pitt Fessenden, into the intricacies of his difficult department. None of his Cabinet colleagues grieved over his departure save the pugnacious Stanton, a hard worker like Chase, an irascible man of violent moods and great drive. But in the long watches of the night, Lincoln had won Stanton's respect and his loyalty, as both men handled the little yellow slips that raised and dashed their hopes.

Many criticized Chase as he stepped out of office. Few but the Blairs questioned his personal integrity. His stature as Secretary of the Treasury during the crucial days of the Civil War grew as time went on and his measures were viewed in perspective. Kate predicted that it would and she was right. But how much had she contributed to this particular moment of mortification? Probably Chase himself did not know, since Kate was extraordinarily reserved about her operations—particularly those of deep significance to her.

Chapter X

MILLIONS TO SPEND

STUNG BY her immediate defeat, Kate proposed a trip to Europe with her father, but Sprague became ill and she joined him in Newport instead. Neither then nor later did she ever acknowledge any connection with the Pomeroy affair, but the impression remained that she and the Governor had much to do with it. In any event, there was no denying that she had been badly worsted at a crucial moment and her father was now out of office, with the war far from won.

Sprague begged Kate not to leave him at this juncture. Before long she got wind of another political move that was brewing and whipped into action without a moment's hesitation. She wrote to her father on July 26: "My husband now that he is so unwell seems to dread the idea of my leaving him and hopes on my account that the trip to Europe is abandoned . . . for this summer. Indeed the feeling seems to be very strong among your friends that you will not leave the country at this time. *They seem to depend upon your aid for the coming Presidential campaign.*"

What did Kate have in mind at this point? Certainly not that he should campaign for the hated Lincoln. The fact was that some of Chase's more persistent backers, encouraged by Kate, were muttering about an independent candidacy. Her father now was free of official strings and could move in any direction. The Wade-Davis Manifesto issued in August, condemning Lincoln's usurpation of power and insisting that Congress was paramount in matters of reconstruction in the

South, indicated the disaffection in the Republican ranks. There were other signs of trouble. An abortive movement in New York was designed to force Lincoln to withdraw and let another candidate run, so as to ensure a Republican victory.

Criticism of the President mounted during July and August as the war news seemed no brighter, and a disastrous and futile attack was made on Petersburg. Not even Farragut's victory in Mobile Bay relieved the tension. The President himself was dubious of re-election.

The Spragues watched each development from their summer home. Kate, deluded as ever, wrote constantly to her father, whipping up his interest. She badgered the most loyal of his political friends and entertained them at the shore. Various names kept cropping up as presidential possibilities—Benjamin F. Butler and General Grant among them. The whispers concerning Chase could barely be heard, except in Kate's vicinity. The idea seemed too improbable even for the retired Treasury head to contemplate. He was weary and a little angry with Kate for meddling behind his back with the Governor. Pressure was being brought to bear on him to swallow his chagrin and, for the sake of the party, campaign for Lincoln. But it was not easy for Chase to move in this direction. For a time he actually considered backing his old enemy McClellan on the Democratic ticket. "At least McClellan is a *gentleman*," he confided to Kate.

Bitter and uncertain about his course, he left the heat and the bloody shambles of Washington and nursed his wounds in the cool air of New England. Kate learned with satisfaction that he was honored in Boston with a dinner at the Union Club. Sumner, Emerson, Longfellow, Lowell and Agassiz were fellow guests. New England never failed to give him his due. But he did not mention to Kate that he then went on to Beverly and visited Mrs. Eastman. She received the dethroned statesman with joy and soothed his hurt spirit with flattering words and her gracious presence. Carlotta cared little for his public life; in fact, she often deplored it. She was interested in Chase the man.

Next he visited his old friend, Robert Rantoul at Salem, hunted with John M. Forbes on Naushon Island, spent a day with John Greenleaf Whittier and was charmed by Lynn, he wrote to Kate, describing the rocky coast, the vesper bell sounding across the water at nightfall and the great gray boulders piled like ramparts against the incoming ocean.

From there he went on to the White Mountains, visited his mother's grave and did some deep soul-searching away from Kate's pervasive influence, out of which came his decision to stand by Lincoln.

With his mind firmly made up, he reached Newport in time to witness a thundering row between Kate and the Governor. For the first time he realized that his beloved daughter was desperately and dangerously unhappy in her marriage. From then on he was to function constantly as peacemaker. His judicial temperament was to help keep some semblance of good relations between the dissolute Sprague and the overbearing Kate. He was also to shut his eyes to a good deal of painful byplay and to sympathize at times with his daughter, at other times with Sprague.

On this occasion the row was so severe that it dampened the spirits of all the Sprague guests. Kate flounced off to bed after venting her rage on the intemperate Governor. Chase took Sprague for a country walk next day and tried to reason with him. They all ended up amicably having a clambake, but without Kate, who refused to appear. Then Nettie and Chase played croquet against Sprague and Claire Albrecht, one of the guests. In the evening they walked along the shore to Point Judith Lighthouse. Still Kate stayed out of sight. Later that week Chase spoke at the Centennial ceremonies in Providence and was feted, with Kate and her husband both in evidence. She had come out of seclusion to see her father publicly honored.

They were now making plans through Amasa to build a summer home of their own. The Spragues had a number of summer places but Kate was envisioning something more splendid. Four more years and Lincoln would be out of the picture. Four more years in which to promote her father.

That autumn Kate, like most of her sisters of the North and South, read with interest of the drowning of Mrs. Greenhow on her way home from Europe. Her ship foundered on a sandbar. She started for shore in a boat which overturned and the story spread that she was sunk by the weight of gold sewn around her waist and destined for the Confederate Army. Jefferson Davis had sent her abroad on a mission, and both Queen Victoria and Napoleon III had received her.

On his return to Washington in September, Chase reluctantly, but on the advice of friends, called on Lincoln. The abortive revolution in the

Republican party had ended and the radicals were sulkily closing ranks behind the President. Montgomery Blair was out of the Cabinet. A group that had nominated Frémont had been drawn back into line. Great Federal victories were in the making. United strength was needed. Troops passing through the capital alternately cheered the waving banners of the Lincoln and McClellan clubs, as the spirit moved them. McClellan was the candidate of peace, backed by pacifists and Copperheads. He stood in curious rivalry to the man who had once been so close to him, who had backed him under terrific fire. McClellan's candidature added spice to a crucial election, but the Union forces were winning at last and Lincoln's star was on the upswing.

He received Chase in a magnanimous spirit, but he did not show great warmth in taking back the black sheep. He saw him twice and the sensitive Chase noted in his diary: "His manner was cordial and so were his words; and I hear of nothing but good will from him. But he is not at all demonstrative, either in speech or manner. I feel that I do not know him. . . . It is my conviction that the cause I love and the general interests of the country will be best promoted by his re-election, and I have resolved to join my efforts to those of almost the whole body of my friends in securing it."

The die was cast. Chase set out for the West to campaign for Lincoln, taking Kate and Nettie with him as far as Cincinnati. Various possibilities were in the air. An ambassadorship. Rewards of one kind or another. Chase was restless and uncertain about his future. He was a hard-working man who could not bear the tedium of empty days. Sumner and he had discussed the Chief Justiceship, should that honored post become available.

Kate entertained elaborately as they traveled west, paying all the bills, throwing the spotlight on her father whenever possible. He spoke in Chillicothe, where he was quite ill; then in Chicago, St. Louis and various points in the Middle West. The fact that he was campaigning for Lincoln gave strength to both men. Though his oratory was not the sort that would move mountains or even capture many votes, the man himself was respected in the West, as in New England. His mere presence was effective.

Kate thought it the most generous thing her father had ever done in his life. She would have advised him against it, but that it brought him before the public and made him better known.

The picture changed abruptly with the death of Chief Justice Roger B. Taney in October at the age of eighty-seven. The weary old judge who had tremblingly sworn Lincoln into office, who would be remembered always for the Dred Scott decision, had been failing visibly. Sumner had been mounting guard for Chase, whom he thought the perfect appointee. He pushed the matter hard in several interviews with the President. Greeley thought it would go to Montgomery Blair. There was much opposition to Chase. But Lincoln, as usual, was fair—and firm.

Finally Lincoln suggested sending for Chase and telling him that he proposed to make him Chief Justice if he could bring himself to give up all thought of the Presidency. He feared that this important post might become another stalking horse for the Chase ambitions. Sumner considered that any such overture would be a mistake. He so advised the President.

"Well, take this card and write on it the name of the man you desire to have appointed," said Lincoln.

Sumner filled in his friend's name and it was promptly confirmed by the Senate. Kate was furious. She could see it only as a move to hamstring her father, to shove him into outer darkness. It was against all precedent for a Chief Justice to aim for the Presidency. For once, she was angry even with Sumner. He had hurried from the Senate Chamber to notify Chase of the appointment. Leaving the library, he met Kate. She shook her finger at him and said in her low musical voice: "And you too, Mr. Sumner! Are you in this business of shelving Papa? But never mind, I will defeat you all."

In this case she would have to defeat her father too, in order to allay her own ambition. The fact of the matter was that Chase was pleased beyond measure with his new appointment. A taste of banishment from the official circle had whetted his appreciation. That night he showed Kate the note he was sending off to Lincoln: "Before I sleep I must thank you for this mark of your confidence, and especially for the manner in which the nomination was made. I will never forget either, and trust you will never regret either. Be assured that I prize your confidence and good-will more than any nomination to office."

Kate thoughtfully read the congratulations that poured in to her father

from all quarters. John Jay summed it up to her satisfaction: "Accept
our heartiest congratulations on the triumph of the great principles involved in your appointment as Chief Justice." Even his enemies thought
that the right place had been found for Chase at last and that now perhaps he would settle in his rightful sphere and stop nagging Lincoln.

All Washington was worrying about General William T. Sherman's
army, which had taken Atlanta in September, then blanked into silence
as it marched toward the sea, leaving a sixty-mile path of waste and destruction behind it. It was December 20 before positive word came
through that the sixty thousand seasoned soldiers had reached Savannah. On Christmas Day the President received the General's message:
"I beg to present to you as a Christmas gift the city of Savannah."

Joy burst forth in the capital. The end seemed in sight at last. Kate
joined the New Year's Eve revelers and danced the night away, then
gave her usual reception after her call on the Lincolns on New Year's
Day. But the hospitals still were crowded. Men suffered and died on the
battlefield. Reconstruction issues were rending the House. The radicals
were demanding suffrage for the Negroes. Stanton's harsh policies were
under attack. Passions flared high in debate.

Lincoln, who had swept into power in November with every state
going Republican but Delaware, Kentucky and New Jersey, looked old
and worried. McClellan was a deflated figure, his portrait labeled, in at
least one instance, "Great Failure of the War." Chase, who had helped
Lincoln and worked for McClellan's undoing, was functioning with
majesty on the bench. Lord Lyons had sailed for England, ill and tired,
but still lighting up with animation when Kate came into a room. Her
old friend Garfield had taken his seat in the House, after winning the
title of Major General for bravery at Chickamauga.

Sherman moved up through South Carolina in February to join forces
with Grant. Charleston soon was evacuated. Fort Sumter was back in
the Union. Federal troops marched into Wilmington. Petersburg was
weakening under siege. Kate's old friend, Mrs. Pryor, watched a "fountain of fire that shot up to heaven, bearing with it the dismembered
bodies of men made in God's own image." She existed on peas, bread
and sorghum, used thorns for pins, made coffee from cotton seeds, chest-
nuts and sweet potatoes. Her tea was brewed from blackberry and sage
leaves, or sassafras root. She wore a belt with three hundred dollars in

gold around her waist and wept as she watched her gallant Roger come home for Christmas through a blinding snowstorm—"this old gray soldier leaning on his sabre."

Soon Roger, who had fired on Fort Sumter, was back in Washington, a prisoner in the gray uniform of the Confederacy, but as proud and defiant as ever. Deserters wandered into Washington in a ceaseless stream. And Sprague, who spent hours tracing military maneuvers on paper, was sure that the southern capital was about to fall.

Kate heard that the ladies of Richmond had sold the last of their beautiful clothes by 1864, that some wore unbleached cotton gowns trimmed with gourd seed buttons, that they mended their fine china with white lead, made shoes for their children from carpeting lined with flannel, paid as much as thirteen hundred dollars for a barrel of flour when they could get it at all, worked in their thirty-five hospitals, spun to clothe the army and sometimes worked in mills.

Until recently they had danced too—at the Thursday night grand hops in the Spotswood Hotel. The rise and fall of the social life had followed the pattern of victory or reverse. But as Mrs. Chesnut observed: "If I laugh at any mortal thing it is that I may not weep." Kate had frequently heard her father deplore the vast numbers of slaves on the Chesnut plantations.

She was severe with her own Negro servants, but they respected her. Her father's coachman in Columbus liked driving Miss Kate as a girl, for she frequently sat with a book in her hand and, as he put it, "spelled it all out to him without looking at the pages." Now, as Mrs. Sprague, she had built up a well-trained staff. She demanded much of them but treated them with justice. However, there were frequent scenes with the Governor which upset the servants, and in the winter of 1864-65, when Kate was expecting a baby and her temper was not of the best, she was guilty of a piece of stark cruelty herself.

She ordered her coachman to report to the butler and assist at one of her evening receptions.

He said that he had been hired as a coachman only.

"Very well," said Kate, green sparks no doubt flicking from her eyes. "You may go."

At eight o'clock she sent him an order to bring horses and brougham to the front door and wait. It was a cold night with sleet falling. The coachman was wrapped in his storm cape, but the hours passed and no one appeared. At midnight one of Kate's servants came out and announced: "You may drive back to the stable. That is what you were hired for."

Although the North was anxious and suffering and the South was in flames and despair, there was a great surge of entertaining as the second Lincoln inaugural approached. For a year there had been lavish spending and the reckless gaiety that goes with war. Mrs. Lincoln was spreading herself anew and had appeared at a reception in a gilt crown that her husband gently made fun of and told her never to wear again. It was a tinsel conceit devised by a Philadelphia milliner. She had ceased to weep so constantly for Willie, although she still consulted the spirits. Her husband was reaping some of the fruits of military victory and was cheered and lauded at last. But his spirit was weary, his heart still anxious, and his face grew ever more brownish and furrowed.

The Executive Mansion, which his wife had furbished up with such high hopes four years earlier, was now in a state of disrepair. Sight-seers had all but torn the furnishings apart. Guards were on duty to offset further vandalism. The President and his family at last had some protection and privacy. Cloakrooms had been installed outside the Blue Room and guests now checked their things. Kate was indignant when she had to line up and wait for service. She had heard that the idea behind it was to make sure no weapons were concealed in any garment. There was fresh concern about the President's life.

The streets were deep in mud, sodden skies were clearing and a gale was dying down, as soldiers and floats, a battalion of Negro troops, companies of local firemen, a series of rousing bands and a straggling string of pedestrians headed toward the Capitol on the morning of inauguration. Washington was tired of parades. They no longer suggested joy —only death. Lincoln had driven to the Capitol earlier by himself to sign bills. Stern as were the problems that lay ahead of him, he was relaxed at last. His wife arrived with a mounted escort.

Kate watched her father's expression with horror as he swore in Andrew Johnson as Vice-President, since all could see and hear that Andy was roaring drunk. He tottered as he mumbled: "I kiss this Book in the face of my nation of the United States." He had given utterance to a speech that had rocked the assembled Republicans with its confusion and self-abasement. Chase was to insist later that Johnson was ill, not drunk. It was a fact that he had just recovered from a serious bout of typhoid. His rugged face looked yellow and worn. His penetrating eyes were sunk deep in hollows above his prominent cheekbones. The President quickly excused him by saying: "I know Andy—he'll be all right—he's no drunkard."

Outdoors the weather had cleared and a great crowd roared a thunder of applause as the War President took his place at the iron stand and spoke briefly, but again with matchless eloquence. What must Kate's thoughts have been as she listened attentively to his phrases: "With malice toward none; with charity for all . . ."

Once again she had to stand by, frozen with displeasure as well as the March wind, and watch Abraham Lincoln sworn in as President of the United States. Once again she had to see Mrs. Lincoln smugly reap the laurels. This time her father administered the oath, with more strength and dignity than Taney had ever been able to summon up. It was her father she watched, not Lincoln, as the President inclined his dark head over the Bible, kissed it at the fifth chapter of Isaiah and started on his second term of office.

Even Chase was impressed by this speech, and Charles Francis Adams, Jr., wrote to his father: "That rail-splitting lawyer is one of the wonders of the day. . . . This inaugural strikes me in its grand simplicity and directness as being for all time the historical keynote of this War; in it a people seemed to speak in the sublimely simple utterance of ruder times. . . . Not a prince or minister in all Europe could have risen to such an equality with the occasion."

Mary Todd's triumph over Kate was complete on the night of the Inaugural Ball. Kate was enceinte and was neither looking nor feeling her best. Mary strutted in a white silk and lace dress, which her enemies said had cost two thousand dollars. She wore a wreath of jessamine and violets in her hair. Her fan was trimmed with ermine and silver spangles. She paraded on the arm of Sumner, who had pulled sharply away from Lincoln on reconstruction policy and was there only by presidential persuasion. But he still was courtly to Mrs. Lincoln.

Kate did not dance, but watched the guests rollick through quadrilles, lancers and polkas, schottisches and the waltz, always her own favorite dance. Ordinarily she danced as she rode—with distinction. The belles had come from all parts of the Union to attend the ball. Some were friends of Kate's from Ohio. Victory was in the air. The people were weary of war. They danced with abandon. Their ruches and their flounces, their tarletans and their delicately tinted silks, their garlands and their fans, swept pass Kate, as she sat holding court with a group of the handsomest men. President and Mrs. Lincoln occupied the blue and gold sofa on a dais in the great hall of the Patent Office, which two years earlier had been a hospital and the scene of most desperate suffering. Their son Robert was in uniform at last, in spite of his mother, and was now on General Grant's staff.

Supper was even more of a shambles than usual. Preparations had been made for four thousand people, but instead of taking it in sequence they all seemed to charge at once. Kate watched the devastation as legs of lamb and sugar admirals were transported into remote corners to be wolfed. The piles of game, oysters, beef and poultry; the symbolic confectionery; the tarts, cakes, ices and jellies disappeared like magic. Glasses were smashed. Frail silks were stained. Food was mashed on the floor and one guest got away with a sugar charger. The scene made Kate slightly ill. It was everything that she didn't like, but the guests seemed to enjoy it. And Father Abraham was pleased to see them happy. His own days were numbered. John Wilkes Booth later boasted that he had attended the inaugural ceremony.

But victory came first. The fall of Petersburg and the capture of Richmond swung the North into one great paean of rejoicing. Eight hundred guns boomed when Richmond fell. Church bells rang. Some of the wounded rose from their beds and ran out of hospitals to swell the crowds that marched to band music, waved flags, shouted "Let Richmond burn!"

Kate drove about in a flag-draped carriage and even her stately father unbent and mixed with the crowds. Stanton was mobbed. The Negroes rejoiced. Mrs. Keckley gave all her sewing girls a holiday and they promptly got "gloriously drunk." By night there was revelry in the streets and many were helplessly drunk. There was solemn thanksgiving among the more thoughtful.

In Richmond itself the city government had dragged hogsheads of liquor from the shops and poured the contents into the gutters. Women and boys rushed with buckets, pails, and pitchers, and even hats and boots, to be filled. Fire swept up Main Street and roared down the side streets, as the tobacco warehouses were burned before the invaders could seize them. A pall of smoke hung over the broad streets and spacious homes of the once beautiful city, which had housed thirty-eight thousand persons at the beginning of the war and now was a devastated shell.

In Washington the excitement was sustained for days. In the middle of it all, Seward jumped from his carriage when his horses bolted. He was badly injured. Lincoln returned to Washington on April 9 from Richmond, visited Seward and, finding him very ill, stretched himself across his bed as he described what he had seen. He knew that the end had come.

Next morning Washington shook to the rattle of guns. Lee had surrendered to Grant at Appomattox. The Civil War was virtually over. Chase led his family in prayer. The relief was almost insupportable. Four days later he made an entry in his diary: "Katie and Nettie went out to the illumination—tired and declined to go." Never had Washington been so resplendent. The Chase daughters rode past the Treasury, their father's old domain, and saw a huge transparent fifty-dollar bond pricked out in lights. Across the way, Jay Cooke's banking house signaled "Glory to God" in static golden stars. The Capitol blazed from dome to portico. The Executive Mansion and the straggling row of buildings that Stanton had needed to run the war, all were hung with flags and spiked with glitter. Every public building shone with victory, and lights blazed in hotels, shops, restaurants, offices and homes. It was the second illumination within a week.

Kate and Nettie did the full parade, heard the bands, watched the fireworks, listened while Andrew Johnson shouted vengeance on Jefferson Davis. Sprague, as usual, was in Rhode Island. Whenever possible he headed for his native state to run his business affairs. Kate preferred to stay in Washington, except for the hot summer months. They saw less and less of each other.

The President made his last address to the people on April 11, reading it from a roll of manuscript as he stood at one of the White House windows. Tad held up the lamp that illumined his furrowed face and lighted the pages as he read. The boy caught each sheet as it fell. Great crowds heard the grave and merciful address. Few appreciated it. But it was the last time most of them were to see Lincoln alive.

On April 14th the President took a long afternoon drive with Mrs. Lincoln, chatted in his office with some friends from Illinois, crossed the wooded lawn through the familiar little gate to the War Department—anxiety allayed at last—and later on prepared to go to Ford's Theater. The Grants had begged off joining the Lincolns on this occasion and the General had gone out of town.

That night was one of terror in the Chase home, as it was for most of official Washington. Kate, too, had gone driving with her father in the afternoon. He had thought of calling on the President to take up the issue of universal suffrage, one that was troubling him greatly. He had been stirred by Lincoln's thoughtful speech. However, he changed his mind and they all retired before ten o'clock, tired out by the excitement of the last week. Soon a servant wakened Chase with the horrifying news that a "gentleman who said the President had been shot, wanted to see him."

Although there had been many threats against Lincoln's life and everyone had been concerned about the way he went around unattended, Chase was completely incredulous at first. But his visitor, an employee of the Treasury Department, had just come from Ford's Theater. He insisted that the report was true, although he lacked precise details. He did not know whether the President was alive or dead.

Three more Treasury men arrived posthaste, confirmed the story and added that Seward, too, had been assassinated and that guards were being placed around the homes of all important officials.

"My first impulse," wrote Chase in his diary, "was to rise immediately and go to the President, whom I could not yet believe to have been fatally wounded. But reflecting that I could not possibly be of any service and should probably be in the way of those who could, I resolved to wait for morning and further intelligence. In a little while the guard came—for it was supposed that I was one of the destined victims—and the heavy tramp-tramp was heard under my windows all night."

By this time Kate and Nettie were fully aroused and neither one slept for the rest of the night. Kate's baby was within a month of being born and her father did not wish her disturbed, but she took an active hand in things at once.

"It was a night of horror," Chase commented. When daylight broke he dressed and went forth. A heavy rain was falling and the sky was somber. He went first to the house across from Ford's Theater where the President had been taken, and at once learned that he was dead. Then he proceeded to Seward's, found guards in front of his home and in the street, but was recognized and passed the barriers without trouble. Indoors he learned that Seward was alive but that his skull had been "penetrated to the brain by what seemed to be a blow from the hammer of a pistol." At this point, none of the facts had been clarified. A knife was the weapon.

He went back to Kate and Nettie "full of horror and sorrow" to tell them the mournful news, then hurried to the Attorney General's office to look up precedents on Zachary Taylor and Millard Fillmore before swearing in Andrew Johnson as President. By this time church bells tolled and mounted men patrolled the streets.

Entering the Kirkwood Hotel, where Johnson was staying and was to be installed, Chase ran head on into the elder Blair and also Montgomery. "I determined I must bury the past," he told Kate later, "and greeted both kindly."

He described the manner in which he had administered the oath, who were present and how he had finished with: "May God guide, support and help you in your arduous duties." After several snatches of talk with Johnson, he decided that he was "thoroughly in earnest and much of the same mind as myself."

Governor Sprague arrived from Rhode Island for the funeral and Kate was one of the seven women present in the darkened East Room during the services for President Lincoln. The others were Mrs. Welles, who had tried to comfort Mrs. Lincoln; Mrs. Stanton; Mrs. John Palmer Usher; Mrs. William Dennison; her daughter; and Nettie. Lincoln that week had foreseen his own death in a dream and now he lay on a catafalque, the victim of an assassin. Johnson solemnly faced the coffin with his hands crossed on his broad chest. General Grant, in full military regalia, stood at the head of the catafalque. Little Tad mourned his kind and gentle father. The heavy scent of flowers, the veiled mirrors, the subdued light reached Kate's consciousness dimly as she bowed her head in prayer.

Upstairs Mrs. Keckley ministered to Mrs. Lincoln, helpless with grief and oblivious to the pageantry of her husband's funeral, to the booming guns, the city draped in crape, the sorrowing people. She was to remain in hysterical collapse for five weeks. Meanwhile the funeral train moved slowly across the country, the nation mourned and even in Richmond, Petersburg and Atlanta, good words were said for Abraham Lincoln. Johnson told Mrs. Lincoln to stay in the White House as long as she wished, but no one could persuade her that the rough diamond from Tennessee had not had a hand in her husband's assassination.

News of the President's death was kept from Seward, but as he convalesced he looked out the window one day, saw the flag at half-mast and knew that Lincoln was dead. Tears ran down his own scarred face for the man he had grown to honor. Both Sumner and Stanton had been at the deathbed and, as Lincoln breathed his last, Stanton said: "He now belongs to the ages."

Late in April Kate was coughing and her father worried about her, as he always did when she was stricken in this way. But he was due to start south with Nettie to survey conditions after the war and form his own conclusions on reconstruction. Whitelaw Reid went with him and sent back dispatches to his paper, the *Cincinnati Gazette*, which were published later as *After the War: A Southern Tour*.

Kate, who would like to have gone on this expedition, awaited the arrival of her first baby at her summer home in Rhode Island. Nettie and her father kept her informed of what they saw along the way and sent her Reid's dispatches. They made a fascinating narrative. Sumner wrote optimistically about this journey to John Bright: "The Chief Justice started yesterday on a visit south and will on his way touch the necessary strings, so far as he can. I anticipate much from this journey."

Next to the assassination of Lincoln, reconstruction policies were the topic of the hour. Sumner still brandished the avenging sword, but Chase's policy was veering closer to Lincoln's. He took careful stock of the closed banks, the blackened chimneys, the ruined gardens and plantations, the Negro schools, the trampled earth and widespread devastation, the inertia of the vanquished people, the little boys playing marbles in the streets with green oranges. In a speech made at Charleston he assured the Negroes that they would have suffrage in the end.

"The country is in such confusion that many seek the safe shelter of the cities, solely from the blind instinct that where there is force there must be protection," wrote Whitelaw Reid. "Such wagons and horses were surely never seen. . . ."

Chase was among the first of a long parade of visitors to gaze at, comment on and appraise the postwar South. Soon tourists would be visiting the battlegrounds, studying the site of General Lee's headquarters, plucking blades of grass from the hollow of a crater, observing where their kin had died, viewing the fortifications, where signs of slaughter still were apparent.

Kate could picture it all as she lay in unwonted idleness for her, counting the days until her child was born. Things went off smoothly. Her son's birth in May was greeted with national publicity and Kate wrote to her father as soon as she could hold a pen, saying that she planned to christen him Salmon Chase Sprague.

Chase responded in his most judicial manner: "It is natural that you should want to name him after me in some way; but my only tolerable name is my surname; and William is not only a better one; but it is the name of one to whom your duties belong, and it was the name of his father, was it not? It should be borne by his first boy. So please consider that case adjudged."

Chase had always disliked the "fishy" name of Salmon and in his youth had thought of changing it. He considered it somehow incompatible with his dignity.

Kate's small son was the fourth William Sprague, and she watched him with interest, curiosity and dawning love. The Governor was equally proud and the infant was set up in state, with his own staff, nurseries and a trust fund. Every advance he made, every new word learned, was recorded in Kate's letters to Grandfather Chase. His christening robe was described in the national press. But if ever a child was ill starred from birth, it was little Willie Sprague.

Chapter XI

POWER THROUGH FASCINATION

IN THE postwar years Kate's social career flowered into full estate. Her clothes and parties outshone those of the Southern hostesses who had held the field before the war. She was compared to Madame de Staël, to Madame Récamier, to Dolly Madison. In actual fact, she was always quite distinctively Kate Chase. Soon her name carried its own enchantment, and any newspaper item concerning her was read attentively by the rest of her sex across the country. Pride was in full possession.

The Chase mansion on E Street had become a salon of some renown. Kate drew in every contemporary figure of consequence except her father's most bitter enemies. Brains, good looks and political acumen were always to be found in her vicinity. She was particularly beloved by the diplomatic corps for her manners and her knowledge of French. Statesmen, jurists, artists, writers, bankers, mingled in her parlors and around her dinner table. Julia Ward Howe gave readings. Sumner orated on poetry and reconstruction. General Grant fumbled uncomfortably around the punch bowl in her library. Garfield spread affability over coffee on the second floor. In a setting of flowers, music, gaslight and candlelight Kate held court. On warm nights she had her guests sup outdoors, sometimes under a pavilion.

By this time her small son was a joy to her and she exhibited him with pride at her *matinées dansantes*. Nettie was now adult and out of school, an attractive and companionable sister. Her father reaped honor instead of abuse in the Chief Justiceship. All went well except with the Governor, whose fortune gilded the setting, eased the financial strain on her father and gave her scope for her political machinations. But Sprague passed more and more of his time in Rhode Island, was an obscure figure in the Senate and rarely appeared at Kate's more formal entertainments. Her father continued to play host, with the dignity that Kate considered essential to her prestige. Too often Sprague had humiliated her in public. But in the postwar period he was adding fast to his millions.

Kate had excellent relations with the quiet, sincere women who now occupied the White House. She looked with approval on Martha Patterson's Spartan and intelligent treatment of the ravished Executive Mansion. Its scars and frayed edges were hidden under fresh linen coverings chosen by the President's elder daughter. An abundance of flowers sweetened up its mustiness until she had time to do it over—intelligently, tastefully, within her budget. It was not the manner in which Kate would have proceeded but she conceded its virtues after Mrs. Lincoln's rule and complimented Mrs. Patterson when the ebony, satin damask, new wallpapers and velvet carpets finally went on display.

Although Martha quietly settled some of her more pretentious visitors by remarking soon after inauguration, "We are plain people from the mountains of East Tennessee, called here for a short time by a national calamity, but we know our position and shall maintain it," Kate was not among those who tried to patronize her. Martha had often visited the White House during President Polk's administration and had a sound pride in it all. She considered it right and proper to don calico in the morning and look after the dairy, attend to her own housekeeping, stay within her budget, behave in a natural way and not truckle to pomp or wealth.

But she was woman enough to note that Kate was appearing around Washington in the winter of 1865 with a *real* diamond of some dimensions in her bonnet. Not that it detracted one whit from Kate's natural charms. As one rhapsodic correspondent for a Chicago newspaper commented: "Not a gown, not a chain, not an ornament ever attracted attention except in so much as it shared her beauty. She had more the air of a great lady than any woman I ever saw. She could make all the actors look like fish women beside her."

Rough-edged Andrew Johnson treated Chief Justice Chase's daughter with considerable respect, as indeed he did her father. Kate was never Senator Sprague's wife; she was always Chase's daughter. And the gentle invalid who had taught her husband to read and write, and now quieted him in his more rambunctious moods with a gentle "Now, Andrew," always welcomed Kate, as she sat in her rocking chair, with her needlework and her books, suffering from the same disease that had killed Kate's mother.

The Chase girls got on equally well with Mary Johnson Stover, the President's second daughter, and were always signally honored at White House functions during the Johnson regime. Kate had no envy of these undemanding women thrust unexpectedly into their conspicuous roles. They were too unlike her, with their simple manners and their high necklines at a time when shoulders were the keynote of fashion. There was no competition, although Kate concluded that tall, fair-haired Mrs. Stover could have been a belle had she wished it or known how to make the most of herself. After Mrs. Lincoln, they seemed like the breath of spring, chilly but fresh.

There was no question but that Kate knew how to make the most of her own quite salient assets. Clothes were arriving in quantity at the Sprague home from Paris in the autumn of 1865, when she paid a brief visit with her father and Nettie to Gibraltar, the island in Lake Erie where Jay Cooke, now internationally known for his financial operations during the Civil War, had built a summer home.

Kate was utterly exhausted after months of gaiety on Rhode Island, and Sprague wrote to her father that he felt she had been "exerting herself too much at tenpins and croquet and perhaps too much bathing." He thought she had better move south as soon as possible. The Cooke invitation was timely. It was their first visit to this newly opened country place where, between 1865 and the Cooke collapse in 1873, a constant stream of important persons came and went. Kate was always glad to see her father relax in the genial presence of Cooke, whose nature was compounded of godliness, good will and guile. At Gibraltar, as at the fifty-two-roomed Cooke mansion outside Philadelphia, prayers and simple enjoyments were mixed quite speciously with high finance.

Kate admired the turreted house and the luxury of its "rustic" rooms. Cooke was starting vineyards on the island. The grapes were ripening and there was a heavy growth of green corn. Her father had given the house his benison with an inscription in the guest book: "Within this house may Christ, our Lord, give peace."

Kate went out fishing with the men, wearing fashionable country garments and discarding her hoop. Her father caught fifteen fish, including some bass, and hooked a muskellunge, which got away when his line broke. Cooke took them all to the little Episcopal Church on Put-in-Bay, which he had helped to finance. Through all their worldly pleasures, regular churchgoing remained the accepted custom for Kate and Nettie, and family prayers were habitual both with the Chases and the Cookes. In moments of stress Kate reverted readily to the faith of her fathers.

They read poetry around a great fire in the evenings and Chase analyzed it in a judicial way. Kate worked up charades. She still leaned to the stage. They all made merry and she observed with satisfaction that her father's wounded spirit was healing, so much so that she began insinuating thoughts about the Presidency again. Clear of the Cabinet and all the criticism that a wartime Secretary of the Treasury was bound to incur, his chances seemed to her to be better than ever. His stock had risen, even though as Lincoln had feared, he was deeply involved in reconstruction issues and was swept readily into political currents outside of his own sphere.

Kate soon was mapping a fresh campaign and Jay Cooke was a powerful ally. She had brushed aside the conception that the Chief Justice should not aspire to the Presidency. There was no law against it. Seeing Jay Cooke's home gave her further ideas for the place she planned to build on Rhode Island. She already previsioned a summer salon, as she saw the subtle work that could be done in the leisurely surroundings of a country setting. How better, for instance, to keep the restless Horace Greeley within sight and sound for a few hours than as a guest in the country? Visits to the seaside had become a fashionable diversion and in the postwar days every whim was humored.

Immediately after Kate's visit to Gibraltar, Sprague wrote to Chase from South Pier: "I have two or three gold operations, one or two oil speculations and Jay Cooke's coal mine on my hands, all proving disastrous. So I am off from mines. I will look over the farm business, and you can do as you like, if I can make a purchase, take it along with me, or not. I do not like the idea of your setting up for yourself. It is far pleasanter for you to be with us, that is, for us, and I should feel pained to see you going away. We will build your apartment at the farm such as will suit you, and hope to keep you.

"Don't fail to be at our cattle show and bring the President with you. It would set the politicians in motion, and to confuse them is about the same as confounding them."

Sprague's "farm" was to turn into Kate's million-dollar mansion, Canonchet. She had already spotted an old farmhouse, well placed on the Sprague properties at Narragansett, that she planned to make the focus of a great summer estate. It was situated in the thousand-acre park that was originally the camping ground of Canonchet, last sachem of the Narragansett Indians. Sprague urged Kate to keep the core of the farmhouse, but he had no forewarning of the edifice she would build around it or the fortune she would squander in the process.

The work went on for years. The ballroom was still unfinished when Kate left the house for the last time. On her trips abroad she studied various architectural effects, then called in builders and architects on her return to realize her whims. The result was a Gothic style mansion four stories high. Its portico, turrets, bay windows and balconies turned out to be a mélange of period and style—French Gothic, a Pompeian court with fountain, Victorian touches and solid American comforts.

Kate kept a staff at work until Rhode Islanders were sure that she planned to make Canonchet the summer White House of the future. She was capricious and exacting in her demands. She would have entire walls ripped out, fixtures pulled apart, rooms demolished or changed in style. She brought a magnificent carved mahogany staircase from Europe, then had it moved several times before she was satisfied that it would do the most for Mrs. Sprague as she made a dazzling appearance from aloft. She brought mantelpieces, paneling, carved woodwork, ornaments, paintings and furniture from Europe to complete the effect.

One wing was set aside for the nurseries. Her father's room was done in deep blue and walnut, and remained untouched after his death. She named bedrooms after her most favored guests—the Chase room, the Greeley room, the Garfield room and so forth. The main salon was octagonal, with a glass dome, heavy blue silk curtains and walls hung with amber velvet. The carpet was a pale Aubusson. Carrara marble busts stood on pedestals in niches around the walls. A Watteau was displayed on a bronze easel. A malachite clock shaped like a pelican dominated the jasper mantelpiece brought from a European palace. Two smaller pelicans in lapis lazuli stood at either side. A full-length Venetian mirror hung where it would best reflect Kate as she sat in her favorite French bergère.

A guest remembered her drifting in, wearing a ruby velvet gown with a fifty-two-inch train, a string of diamonds around her throat, and pausing before this mirror to adjust a white camellia in her bronze hair before sinking into the bergère with the deceptive air of languor that Kate always exuded in contradiction of her dynamic spirit.

The lofty room held many objects of art and this same visitor recalled particularly the Oriental china vases, the gem-studded candlesticks, the unusual arrangement of flowers and a crystal side table which held gold bibelots, a jeweled vinaigrette and a vellum volume of poems. In the fashion of the day, a censer swung with incense in Kate's salon.

The library was a deep-toned room with a bay window over the portico and the dining room at Canonchet, where many significant political parleys were held, was a long, lofty room opening into the conservatory and Pompeian tiled courtyard, where a fountain splashed audibly. The walls were curiously paneled with ebony. Heavy mirrors reflected Kate's elaborate table arrangements and the walls were hung with Murillo copies. The draperies and Japanese screens were a deep red. The crystal chandelier had a hundred individual lights. Kate used both gold and silver dinner services and was particularly proud of her soup bowls, made from the dust of crushed garnets and brought from Persia. Her Negro footmen wore green and yellow livery. For a summer home by the seaside, Canonchet strongly suggested the fleshpots.

It was only getting under way in the winter of 1866 when Nettie brought fresh alarm to her father and Kate by developing typhoid fever for the second time. But she soon recovered and read with interest a letter to her father from Whitelaw Reid, who was all but lost to journalism at this time. He was considering taking over the management of thousands of acres of cotton lands at Natchez.

"If I do," he wrote, "I'll make at once money and health out of it. New Orleans however will still be my headquarters. . . . Rebels are by no means so defiant here as they were in November; and all along the great thoroughfares, Northern men are as safe as in Washington. How it might be, if they were to embark in business away from rivers and railroads, I am not so certain."

Kate and her father had long discussions that winter on reconstruction. Although presumably a detached figure on the bench, Chase's sympathies were running in the old grooves and Kate was always at his elbow, making soundings, suggesting policies. Sumner and Thaddeus Stevens were pounding away for vengeance. Sumner maintained that by the act of secession the Southern states had lost their rights and privileges in the Union. Chase was more temperate, with better understanding of the South.

The North faced difficulties too. The war debt was nearly three billion dollars. Currency, deranged by Chase's frequent issues of greenbacks, was due to get back on a firm basis. When gold was driven from circulation by the legal-tender notes, it became the favorite commodity for speculation on Wall Street. In the spring of 1864, Chase had been authorized to sell surplus gold to check this wild speculation.

Thousands of soldiers were now looking for work. War had swung them out of their normal channels. New machinery had nullified many of their skills. People poured in to Washington from different parts of the country. Freed Negroes lounged about the streets but were not made particularly welcome in the Union that had freed them. Gambling and bawdy houses grew in number. Saloons did a roaring business and new buildings sprang up. People laughed, danced, made love and roistered after the dark days of the war. The spending in the North was fast and furious. Deep silence blanketed the South. Travelers and observers returned with tales of ruin, devastation and apathy.

In February the Marquis de Montholon, French Minister, gave the most magnificent ball of the era in Washington. General Grant was stationed in Washington at the time. The city was filled with army officers, and the staff from a French ship lying at Annapolis made extra dancing partners for the belles of the capital.

The Marquise de Montholon wore a striking dress covered with jeweled fleur-de-lys, ordered from Paris for the occasion. She sported the Order of Napoleon (a de Montholon had been aide-de-camp to Napoleon at Waterloo) and the insignia of the house de Montholon. Kate looked her most brilliant self in a stiff dress of white moiré, striped with green. She wore an antique tiara of emeralds and diamonds and, although many of the women had their hair powdered à la marquise, hers shone in its natural burnished state. The former Mrs. Douglas was present as the bride of General Robert Williams, wearing the white silk with tulle overdress that had been her wedding gown. Strands of pearls circled her dark hair and her white throat. She was one threat removed from the Chase horizon, but Kate liked and admired Addie beyond most of her friends and was happy to see her suitably remarried.

General Grant's favored dancing partner was Clara, the daughter of Senator Ira Harris, the girl who was in the Lincoln box on the night of the President's assassination and whose escort on both occasions was Major Henry R. Rathbone, whom she later married but who went insane. It was widely believed that his mind was affected by the events on the night of Lincoln's death.

The de Montholon party was so crowded that it was five o'clock in the morning before the first cotillion was reached. Dancing continued until breakfast was served, a novelty not yet made popular by custom. It was considered quite remarkable that the men should go on to business without going home, and Kate and many of the other ladies made their round of morning calls in their ball gowns.

Olivia conceded that the Marquis de Montholon's party equaled but was in no way superior to the "same kind of parties given by our accomplished countrywoman, Mrs. Senator Sprague." She quaintly added: "In both cases no expense is spared in the entertainment of guests, and any amount of greenbacks do duty in the shape of costly silks and laces; but I learn that the precious stones are more or less abandoned, since the shoddy and petroleum have learned to shine.'

This was an allusion to the fact that Kate was firmly closing her doors to some of the postwar nouveaux riches, and had stopped decking herself with jewels, except on the most formal occasions, now that the surrounding display had become vulgar and competitive.

Kate haunted the Senate gallery that spring to hear the reconstruction debates. She was as often the observed as the observer. Right after the de Montholon ball, she sat with the widow of Daniel Webster and bowed to Mrs. Julia Dent Grant, who sat in the front row wearing a pink hat, a red plaid scarf and black gloves, along with a heavy plum-colored dress. Ever alert to the political whispers in Washington, Kate had her own favorites on the floor. Senator Sprague, who rarely spoke and often was absent, was not one of them that spring. As Kate galloped past the flowering Judas trees in the Rock Creek region with her father on their evening rides, Chase could see that she was deeply worried, but she held her counsel and did not confide in him.

By Easter it was common gossip that the Sprague marriage had foundered. Throughout the brilliant season, the Governor had rarely been seen with Kate in public. After the last big party of the year, she confused the gossips by packing up and sailing for Europe with Nettie, William and his nurse Maggie. This was the first of many expeditions Kate was to make to Europe in the years to come. At the moment it covered a gaping wound, but not even to her father did proud Kate disclose the depth of the breach that lay between her and the Governor.

Chase and Sprague saw them off on the *Australasia*. Kate parted coldly with her husband but kept up appearances in front of her father. There was a good deal of uneasiness all round and Sprague took his father-in-law to Barnum's to divert him immediately after the ship sailed. They went on to Philadelphia to visit Jay Cooke, while the girls and little Willie sampled some rough ocean travel.

Back in Washington the two men were thrown together and had long discussions on politics. Mrs. Edmund C. Smith, Kate's aged grandmother, supervised the household in her absence, with the help of Mrs. Crawford, the housekeeper. They provided excellently for the two bachelor gentlemen coping with the nation's affairs. A special session of Congress held Sprague in town, and Chase had an opportunity to serve as peacemaker. Although Kate had held her counsel, he had witnessed many angry scenes. He had seen Sprague in ugly and drunken moods. He knew there was gossip and a thousand evidences had reached his sensitive understanding that all was not well between his daughter and her husband.

He was convinced that the temporary separation might help matters. He picked up Sprague at the Capitol every evening and they rode together before dinner. He shepherded his son-in-law around the best parlors, keeping an eye on him for Kate. Chase was always gravely courteous to his son-in-law, whatever the provocation, and the Governor retired with "dyspepsia" when he felt he could not face his majestic father-in-law. Both men waited eagerly for letters from Kate and Nettie. Sprague always enjoyed himself with Nettie. She shared his love of merriment. Both had the easy knack of turning all occasions into a party. Nettie's Ludlow blood gave her an entirely different outlook from Kate, who took life seriously and did not suffer fools gladly. Her letters from Europe were more entertaining than Kate's, with their spontaneous touch and pencil sketches.

Nettie, who had once been strongly drawn to Whitelaw Reid, now was dancing in London ballrooms. Charles Francis Adams, American Ambassador at the time, opened all doors to the Chase girls. They were presented to Queen Victoria, Kate making a striking figure in her satin, lace and feathers. They visited the Houses of Parliament, where Kate had a rewarding talk with John Bright.

On hearing this, Chase wrote back at once: "I am very glad you have seen Mr. Bright and hope you may see more of him. I think him among the foremost of modern men. His work on the Reform bill has proved him a sapient as well as an earnest friend of progress. I wish some of our 'liberals' had his sterling good sense, as well as his zeal. We are all disappointed that the Reform bill did not command a larger majority, but glad that the Ministry does not give up."

Kate reported that she was charmed with Mr. and Mrs. Adams. Her father wrote back that Mrs. Adams had first interested him by the "spunk with which she stood up for her husband when the Boston aristocracy was inclined to frown upon his Free Soil opinions." However, Boston, like all other parts of the country, now gratefully acknowledged Mr. Adams's eminent services in a most difficult post during the war, he added.

The Chief Justice reported that he had just received the engraving of Francis B. Carpenter's painting of the Cabinet gathered around Lincoln for the signing of the Emancipation Proclamation. Kate had been hearing for an entire winter of Carpenter's proprietary interest in Lincoln and his Cabinet and the things the President had made these gentlemen do in order to please the artist. Chase, who was always willing to sit for a portrait, had come to the conclusion that things were getting rather undignified, with all the chitchat and the swapping of stories and the antics they had to go through to please Lincoln. Anything Carpenter wanted was approved by the President, although his Cabinet met at the time with mutual hate and in revolt against him.

Kate was glad now to hear that it had been worth it all. She was sure that none would dignify the painting more than her father.

"It is really very fine," he wrote. "The likenesses are excellent. That of myself would satisfy, I think, even the fastidious exactions of my children. It is almost too large to send abroad—but I am endeavoring to send you a copy."

Early in May Kate and Nettie moved on to Bonn, visiting the Baroness de Gerolt, whom Kate had often entertained in Washington. Her husband, Baron F. de Gerolt, represented Prussia. Wherever she went, she looked up the diplomatic set and was at once feted and entertained. Letters reached Chase and the Governor from Berlin and Frankfurt, from Baden Baden and Vichy, from Florence, Rome and Venice. In Florence they had busts in baroque made by Hiram Powers. Kate was observed at the spas as the fashionably dressed American. As she moved about, she bought glass, china, silver, leather, lace, the fine products of each area. She took note of architectural styles and noble interiors. She studied the castles and the great homes she visited in England. Canonchet later was to bear the imprint of Kate's first trip abroad.

Back in Paris, she was received by the Empress Eugénie, who must have observed Kate's looks and clothes with more than passing interest. She gave M. Worth a large order and he later declared he had never designed gowns for a better figure than Kate's. She was to be one of his favorite customers for years to come, and he kept her measurements on hand. They varied little. Kate had a tiny waist and slender dimensions for her era.

On her return to Britain, she traveled north with Nettie, visiting Edinburgh, North Berwick and reaching Inverness, the capital of the Highlands, where they took a trip to view Culloden, the battle ground of Prince Charlie. Kate had Scottish blood, inherited from her paternal grandmother. Meanwhile a spirited correspondence between father and daughters kept each informed of what the other was doing. Now and again Chase played the schoolmaster with Nettie, scolding her for careless writing and spelling, for dropped commas and loose syntax, but he almost invariably pointed out that her letters were more entertaining than Kate's—a judgment in which the Governor heartily concurred.

At last Kate was irked by these comparisons and wrote quite sharply to her father, saying he was altogether too critical. Chase hastened to assure his daughters that they must console themselves about his criticisms with the thought that "the children of great men! were always liable to them." He reminded Kate and Nettie that it was all prompted by his great love for them and his desire that they should aim at perfection.

After this he adopted a more flattering tone and wrote to the exacting Kate: "You and Nettie write such excellent letters that I begin to think there was a good deal of sense in the remark I once made in answer to somebody who wanted to know my opinion on women's rights, that I was for putting everything in the hands of the women and letting them govern. Certainly I don't see but you and Nettie are as well qualified to take part in affairs as I was at your age."

Chase was an advocate of woman suffrage but Kate kept clear of the feminist movements of her day. Although she wielded great power, she used subtle weapons and deplored bloomerism, open agitation for the vote and all movements that brought her sex into the limelight in a noisy "unladylike" way. She was to sit across the hall from Susan B. Anthony at a political convention in New York in 1868 and disapprove her tactics, while behind the scenes Kate was actually trying to swing the convention for her father! There were times when she was not beset by the larger vision of mankind. Nor was she richly endowed with a sense of humor.

Chase's letters to his daughters often were written in his library early in the morning before he set forth for the Supreme Court. He was usually up at five and on a June morning he described the surrounding scene to his "dear, precious Kate": "The morning air comes in sweetly upon my forehead and the milkman is going by with his car, and one boy is whistling on the pavement, and some birds join their notes from the trees, and a martin puts in his crow, and the newsboy cries 'Da-il-y Chronicle.' "

Kate could picture it all as she walked along the Embankment and studied the House of Commons, comparing this massive pile with the Capitol, which held so much significance for her. She knew that her father, among other things, was worrying over Jefferson Davis, who had been indicted for treason. Like Lincoln he favored tolerance, but he was torn this way and that by his more radical friends and his old sympathies. Sumner was beating the drums for vengeance. It was putting a barrier between them.

Kate felt as her father did. She urged him to keep her informed on every step. The British papers gave little impression of the true picture at home. But Mr. Adams was communicative to the intelligent Kate. He let her use the diplomatic bag for correspondence with her father. Kate greatly enjoyed herself in London, where she met the poets, authors and statesmen of the hour. She shared in the rejoicing when the Atlantic cable was landed at Trinity Bay, and Britain and the United States were thus brought one step closer together.

The Governor moved his part of the household to Narragansett Pier for the hot summer months. Chase sweated on in Washington for a time, lonely now, and suffering from severe toothaches. As soon as he could get away, he headed for New England. Kate then read of fishing parties off the reef of Norman's Woe, of dinner with the William C. Endicotts at Salem, of visiting the Robert Rantouls, of sailing when the weather was fine and of playing bagatelle when it rained. Kate felt Mrs. Eastman in the background again, although he never mentioned her name. Only in his diary did he record the fact that they were having long walks and talks and attending church together and that she drove him to Marblehead in her carriage and there bought a parasol which she paid for "from my portmonie."

Nor did Chase mention to Kate the clouds that were gathering around the name of Chase again. An insidious campaign had been started in the press, which he ascribed to his old enemy, Thurlow Weed. First came reports that he was about to marry a Mrs. E. This seemed to Chase to be impudence on the part of the newspapers, although he conceded that he did not absolutely renounce the idea.

Then, as he visited his birthplace in Vermont, came the flat statement in the World, which often reflected Weed's opinion, that he was "intriguing for the campaign of 1868." More wounding still to his spirit were the questions asked about the enlargement of his fortunes during his years at the Treasury. He answered these so convincingly that his critics soon held their peace. "I believe the country is richer because of my public services," he wrote to a political friend in August. "I am not, and I am glad I am not. Not a cent of public money ever stuck to my hands; nor did I ever make an appointment with any view to private gain. I selected Jay Cooke for the loan agent, because I had tried him in the earliest years among many others. I found him the ablest and most faithful."

Worst of all, Kate's name was being dragged in the mud. Here and there across the country—in Providence, Troy, Washington, Cincinnati and New York—papers published news of an impending divorce. Kate first heard of it when Sprague hurriedly crossed the Atlantic to join her and bring her home. Meanwhile, cold with rage, Chase discussed with his friends the way in which he should stifle these rumors. "Only let not Katie's name be in any way mentioned," he urged his advisers.

Divorce was the symbol of disgrace in 1866. It was unthinkable in relation to proud Kate and an appalling embarrassment for the Chief Justice. He felt that something must be done at once to stem the tide of public gossip. Yet he did not wish to be quoted as "having authorized any notice of so vile a fabrication." He considered collecting all the copies of a Troy paper which had particularly incensed him and having them suppressed.

He took counsel with the Governor, who announced that he would still the talk by going to Europe and bringing home his family. By the end of October retractions appeared in the papers which had first published the report. The Providence *Journal* firmly stated that the story going the rounds about the Spragues was "an unfounded and malicious calumny, without one iota of foundation . . . there is not in the country a man happier or who deserves to be happier in his domestic relations, and nothing has occurred to afford even a pretext for the slanders which have been invented by malice and circulated by scandal." Alarmed and chastened, Sprague greeted Kate with humility for the past and largesse for the future. Willie had thrived in spite of all the traveling. His father adored him and was happy to see him again.

Nettie wished to spend the winter in Dresden and study art and languages. Sprague promptly said he would finance her, but Chase sent a string of objections across the Atlantic. He had heard that Dresden was a damp place where people were apt to get sore throats and lung disorders. He also missed this gay and loving daughter and wanted to have her at home. Moreover, he wrote rather severely to Kate: "Nettie has a charming touch for sketching, and I should be glad to have her cultivate that, as far as possible, but painting involves too much labor and time, for a young lady to expect to make great attainment in it who does not expect to consecrate her life to it, like Rosa Bonheur for example. . . ."

Kate and the Governor stood firmly by Nettie, and the Chief Justice capitulated. Before Kate sailed for home, she remarked, "How like Papa!" as she read his letter of advice to Nettie. He urged her to take regular exercise; to keep her feet dry and warm and her person well protected; to have as little intercourse as possible with people who spoke English, so as to free herself for French and German conversation. His final injunction reminded Kate of countless admonitions she had received while at Miss Haines's: "I don't think you are likely to form any acquaintance which I would not approve, or allow your affections to become engaged to anybody while abroad. I hope you will keep constantly in mind your obligation and privilege as a Christian and avoid all society not of the purest and highest character."

Kate had no fears for Nettie as she sailed home with the Governor and little Willie. Irresponsible though Nettie might be, the more worldly Kate recognized her half sister as a sterling character. She had helped to train and discipline her. Moreover, she had been quite independent herself at a much earlier age than this. Kate was not particularly Victorian in her outlook, even though she would not move a step in public without an escort, a fact which many young embassy aides and gallants in Europe had discovered to their delight.

Kate was much more worried about her father's emotions than she was about Nettie's. In confiding his woe about the publicity their own affairs had had, the Governor told her there had also been newspaper speculation during her absence about the Chief Justice marrying Mrs. Eastman. Kate was furious. It did not cheer her to learn that the perennial bachelor, Charles Sumner, had astounded all his friends in October by marrying Mrs. Alice Hooper, widow of Samuel Sturges Hooper. He was fifty-six and his bride was much his junior. Kate had attended many good parties at the Hooper home, which she greatly admired. She had recently observed Alice in the Senate gallery, hanging on Sumner's words. This, Kate decided, might well influence her father in making a stupid decision about Mrs. Eastman. She had no doubt of the tenacity of this clever woman. And her father was just two years older than Sumner.

But when the *Scotia* docked on a sparkling day in December, Kate was both radiant and serene. She wore the most elegant traveling costume that Worth could conjure up for his new American customer. Her hair, which she had always worn straight and simply parted in the middle, was now differently arranged, with a cluster of curls on her brow after the fashion set by the Empress Eugénie. Chase was not sure that he liked it, having "loved her so long in the old style." And grandmother Smith was bewildered. "Is that really Katie?" she demanded. "How she has changed!"

After studying the reunited pair, the optimistic Chief Justice observed that the Governor was apparently "better contented and happier" than he had ever seen him, and Kate was "more lovely and happy" than he had ever seen *her*.

Happy or not, Kate had returned with a greatly expanded view of the world and her role in it. She had talked to queens and statesmen. She had viewed America through the windows of Europe. She had brought back Parisian fashions, Italian statuary, British customs, china and silver, as well as some markedly extended ambitions of her own.

Chapter XII

ONE STEP FROM THE WHITE HOUSE

KATE HAD arrived in time to sweep with full power into the social season of 1867. Willie had alarmed them all by becoming violently ill the day before Christmas, but by New Year's Day he was better and Kate felt free to leave him with his nurse, don one of her Worth creations and pay her respects to the presidential family.

John Hay, drawn in for a visit by "the beautiful Mrs. Sprague," thought the White House much more "richly and carefully furnished" than in his time, but the visitors not quite up to the old mark—"which itself was not hard to reach." Chase told Kate, after viewing Mrs. Patterson's improvements, that it was now an "elegant mansion fit for a gentleman to live in." The Chases always had a proprietary feeling for the Executive Mansion.

Hay noted Mrs. Sprague's changed appearance with approval. Her trip abroad had given her even more assurance. Her drawl and languid manner were quite pronounced. She was now twenty-seven and every trace of the young girl had been lost in worldly development. He commented on her strong, delicate features, her fine throat, her graceful hands and the remarkable ball she gave that winter. It was known as the Pink Ball, long remembered for its evanescent beauty, with pink hangings, and Kate herself circling in a gown of pale blue silk, draped with pink and festooned with convolvulus blossoms. With this she wore a tiara of diamonds and turquoise. Kate was seen quite often in pink—a misty shade that brought her hair, white skin and hazel eyes into dramatic unison. This and lilac came to be known as her favorite colors. Delicate shades became her coloring best.

"The ladies who danced the cotillion, and many who did not, had their hair powdered à la marquise," wrote Hay. "I have never seen so beautiful and picturesque a roomful."

But he found his hostess most striking of all and observed characteristically, "Chase was always addicted to coups de théâtre." As usual, Kate had made her father the center of the stage. One more year to go before the national conventions!

In February Kate went to Philadelphia to attend a housewarming given by Jay Cooke. The Governor left her there and on his return to Washington reported to her father that the "Cookes outdid all past possibilities of American splendor." Chase had stayed away. The recurrent criticism of his relations with the Cookes worried him. But he made this party the occasion for a little moralizing in his next letter to Nettie. He was keenly aware of the mad pace at which Kate was living, and he wished to impress on his younger daughter the need for simpler ways. "Oh, how I hope you will retain your simplicity of taste! I don't want you to be dowdy or even plain—but simple while elegant. Not expensive—beyond one's moderate means, but at the same time not parsimonious."

There was no use talking to Kate in this vein any longer. She had always been extravagant and now that she knew her resources were unlimited there was no calling a halt. The Governor was becoming slightly cynical about the rapid dispersal of his wealth, in spite of the rate at which his business was expanding. Kate was beginning to cost him a pretty penny. The bills poured in from Paris and Canonchet.

Kate was desperately unhappy in spite of her gay front. She danced, flirted and moved from party to party as if pursued by furies. Sarah and Susie Hoyt, two of Sprague's young nieces, were her guests and they could scarcely keep pace with her. By midwinter the Governor was insisting that she was impairing her health with late nights and too much entertaining. It was invariably after three before she got to bed.

Sprague was suffering frequently from dyspepsia but he sometimes seemed a touching figure to his father-in-law, who could not fail to see that the tension between the young pair was acute again and that the Governor's only family interest lay in little Willie. He wrote to Nettie, who was still abroad, that Kate was looking handsomer than ever, but the Governor was suffering from dyspepsia, adding: "Last night he felt so badly that he could not come down. He takes more to the boy than to anything or anybody else. No woman could have a kinder or more indulgent husband than he has been to Katie. Sometimes I fear she doesn't feel it quite enough; tho' I know that she loves him truly and is proud of him."

Kate was anything but proud of him, and her contempt flashed into full view in public at a dinner that winter. He was seated beside Mrs. Stover and had been drinking freely. This was no novelty to Andrew Johnson's daughter, but Mrs. Stover, noticing Kate's expression across the table, mildly observed: "I would not take more if I were you. There are a pair of bright blue [sic] eyes looking at you."

"Damn them," said Sprague loudly. "They can't see me."

His glass was refilled and he raised it to his lips, then put it down with a bang as Kate leaned forward, gazed haughtily at her husband and remarked quite clearly: "Yes, they can see you, and they are thoroughly ashamed of you."

At this time Kate was angry with her father, too. Quite obviously thinking seriously of marriage, he had invited Mrs. Eastman to stay at their home. Kate had skillfully kept them apart and treated the worldly Mrs. Eastman so coldly that finally she packed up and left before her appointed date, outraged and disgusted by the highhanded behavior of the daughter of the man she loved.

Kate never failed to remind her father that the Sumner union was turning out badly. She had observed Sumner's expression as his wife, in black velvet, with a lace shawl around her shoulders and a flexible golden serpent in her hair, flirted lightly with a Prussian attaché at a reception given by General Grant. Sumner's wife liked parties, but he worked early and late with the intensity of his fanatical nature that could yield nothing. He was fighting the reconstruction battle, along with Thaddeus Stevens, and he had no time for frivolity. Kate was convinced that he had made a great mistake in marrying.

She could picture him in his second-floor study, fingering his intaglios, prizing his Oriental treasures and his rare old books, an expert in the art and literature of his day, a rare conversationalist, courtly on a dance floor in his English evening dress, but always a little aloof, unable to jest or to relax his iron spirit. It would be difficult for him to keep up with Alice Hooper, just as it was inconceivable to Kate that her father should find happiness with Mrs. Eastman.

But the unbending Chief Justice, who bared his heart so freely to his children, wrote rather wistfully to Nettie late in March, showing clearly his own turn of thought: "I saw little of her [Mrs. Eastman]—much less than I wished, for I like her so much, if not better than ever. But for the looks of the thing in an old gentlemen like me, and the feelings of Katie, and I daresay yours too, and some other considerations, who knows that I might not have been tempted to—the consenting! It *is* rather solitary this life that I lead."

But Kate was already on her way to Europe to join Nettie. Having disposed of Mrs. Eastman—she hoped forever—she sailed before the end of March. This time she took a personal maid and Negro servant along, as well as Maggie, Willie's nurse. Sarah, Susie and William Hoyt, her husband's relatives, all saw her off. The Governor, who was concerned at the moment about his own re-election to the Senate, had decided not to accompany her abroad as he had planned.

Kate now knew her way about Europe and her first summer's triumphal tour was improved on. This time she bought more heavily for Canonchet, bringing back paintings, rugs, the fifty thousand dollar carved staircase that was to give her so much trouble, and many objects of art. Nettie trailed along, trying to accustom herself to Kate's mounting extravagance—to six dozen pairs of white kid gloves bought in one order, to twenty-five pairs of French shoes, to lace at forty dollars a yard, to gowns costing hundreds of dollars and jewelry running into the thousands.

While Kate was enjoying her affluence, she heard with interest that Mrs. Lincoln, pressed for money, was trying to sell her clothes in New York with Mrs. Keckley's help. Robert, fresh from Harvard and setting up in law, was shocked. No wonder, Kate reflected, picturing it all—the sable boa, the sixteen dresses and two opera cloaks, the feather cape and real lace shawl. Kate had swung to the top, Mary to the bottom, of the social heap. No one even cared to buy Mary's spent finery. But there was no pity in Kate's heart for the beaten woman. The days of their feud were still fresh and alive in her memory.

Nettie had come into her own property by this time. At last her father had managed to dispose of most of his Cincinnati and Brooklyn holdings and was clear of debt. As Abraham Lincoln had feared, he was busily polishing up the crown again and interfering in affairs of state. By July he was touring with one of his political aides, who was "bent on securing for him the support of all the Pacific states in the next Presidential nomination." Kate read with much satisfaction, and Nettie with affectionate interest, a letter from their father, dated July 11, 1867:

And it does look now that, if there were no military names before the public, the choice of the people might fall upon me. But many seem to think that the nomination of a military candidate is a predestined must, which must take place anyhow, and against which it is useless to make opposition. There are, it is true, many who think otherwise, and who are zealously for me. But there are other non-military men who have also zealous friends—and I can easily see that I am not much more likely to be preferred than I was in 1860 or 1864. So I make myself contented, or try to. . . .

It is true that if it ever came to me I could accomplish, if I had the power, much that would be beneficial to the community and I am not insensible to the distinctions of the Chief Magistery. But if the people don't want my services, I have no right to complain and if the distinctions are not to be mine, I shall, by no means, repine. No man has any claim to such distinctions in a country like ours.

The military man, of course, was General Grant, who was a pervasive and much heralded figure at this time. Neither Kate nor her father discounted the power of a winning General. Wherever he went, he attracted attention as head of the army. He was the "man of destiny" and the "nation's deliverer." But Grant was averse to being a candidate. He had never been a Republican and he had no wish to run, although both parties wooed his favor.

Kate returned from Europe ready to push a strong campaign for her father. She found unbridled passions raging again in the capital. The purchase of Alaska for $7,200,000 from the Russians was labeled "Seward's Folly," but Seward, recovered from his injuries and still serving as Secretary of State, was sure that his icebox held a treasure.

Johnson had tempered his early policy of harshness toward the South and had earned the enmity of the zealots. Thaddeus Stevens, old, ill and weary, was pounding away at the President's policies, while Martha Patterson's husband, David Patterson, sat in the House and heard the abuse heaped on Johnson's head. The magniloquent Sumner thundered imprecations in the Senate. Finally the President's quarrel with the partisan leaders in the House came to a head when he tried to remove Stanton as Secretary of War in favor of General Grant.

The field seemed to be wide open and Kate pushed her Wednesday evening receptions for her father to the limit that winter. Election year had dawned, and she was angling in all directions for support. Olivia, observing her maneuverings, wrote for her Philadelphia paper: "There is only one position at the republican court that this most elegant woman has not attained. She has never reigned at the White House. Every triumph has palled upon her taste. . . ."

The New York *Herald* in January, 1868, viewed Kate as a Madame Récamier, a Madame Roland or Madame Tallien—"the most splendid woman amid the Republican politicians of Washington" and one of the ladies who "had made up the slate for the Presidential programme and chances."

The slate, of course, had her father for the focal point, and Kate flattered herself that his tour of the South immediately after Lincoln's death had consolidated him there. He had been warmly received. Since then he had kept his balance on the tight rope between North and South, but he alienated some of his more radical friends during the impeachment proceedings that spring.

The trial furnished high drama for Kate, to whom politics had become as the breath of life. She walked with her father to the Capitol every day, but he carefully refrained from discussing the issues with his strong-minded daughter. The Senate Chamber had become a court. The black-gowned Chief Justice was the arbiter in a rare and dangerous proceeding, which might help or hurt his own political future.

To Kate, he was the very heart and core of the trial, and she watched him as closely as she did the orators who cast such bitter bread upon the waters. She thought Thaddeus Stevens, one step from death, a terrifying figure as venom spat from his skeleton form, and his worn and furrowed face bespoke his hatred. Toward the end he was carried up the Capitol steps and sustained by brandy. Chase got credit for conducting the trial with fairness, propriety and dignity, although there were many mutterings about the way in which his sympathies lay.

The diplomats turned out in force for so significant an event, and the galleries were crowded over the ten-week period with the ladies of both House and Senate. Olivia pictured the scene as a "real hothouse of rare human exotics and butterflies spreading their crinolines." Time and again she took note of Mrs. Sprague, her poise and her costumes.

In the February snows, she appeared in purple and rich furs. On a March day, she sat in the gallery, "the picture of delicacy and grace, arrayed in silk tinted with the shade of dead forest leaf, with dead gold ornaments to match." On an April day, as spectators sighed and yawned with heaviness, she smiled encouragingly at her father when he had the windows opened to let the spring breezes blow in. Schurz, for the time being working as a journalist; Greeley, who never failed to find out what Kate was thinking; Garfield, Grant, Sherman and Roscoe Conkling were only a few of the men who sought her out and listened to her words of wisdom during these proceedings.

One day she sat beside Mrs. Oakes Ames, of Massachusetts, "old-fashioned in her hospitality, handsome but not elegant." Again she and Nettie were close to Mrs. Benjamin F. Wade, who consistently sat in a front seat, quite obviously expecting soon to preside in the White House. Olivia identified her as "cultured and well-read," a woman who lent herself to good works rather than fashion. Kate must have shuddered as she read the newspaperwoman's comments on her father—"this cold, haughty, handsome face. Not for a moment could one imagine fire coursing along his veins. His lips move, but only inarticulate sounds reach the gallery." It was a fact that even Kate had to strain to catch his rulings, so poor was her father's delivery.

There was oratory enough in the Senate Chamber, however. Kate sat spellbound while William S. Groesbeck, her father's friend from Ohio, closed for the defense, saying: "Kindness, forgiveness, a crime? Kindness a crime? Kindness is statesmanship." She sat through William M. Evarts' speech, lasting fourteen hours and continuing for the better part of four days.

Kate and Nettie sat up with indignation when torrents of applause followed John A. Bingham's speech assailing Johnson, and hisses and laughter greeted her father's command: "Order! Order! If this be repeated the sergeant-at-arms will clear the galleries." When the roars continued and Chase ordered the galleries cleared and offenders arrested, they heard Simon Cameron cry out: "I hope the galleries will not be cleared."

Kate was quite prepared for Sumner's statement: "Andrew Johnson is the impersonation of the tyrannical slave power. In him it lives again. He is the lineal successor of John C. Calhoun and Jefferson Davis; and he gathers about him the same supporters." But before his death this stern warrior conceded that he might have erred in the impeachment issue.

Seward wagered a basket of champagne on an acquittal and Greeley, while the evidence was still being offered, kept battering away editorially: "Impeachment is statesmanship—justice—peace." Johnson, who longed to appear in person but was dissuaded by his counsel, drove out to Pierce's Mill in the Rock Creek region to watch his grandchildren wade in a brook, fish, hunt for bugs and pick wild flowers. He read a little Cato with Eliza, who had perfect faith that he would be acquitted. He asked his secretary to investigate the fate of each man who signed the death warrant of Charles I.

Chase shed the cloak of judicial sanctity when he went home at night and with sundry promptings from Kate continued his ceaseless campaign by correspondence. With the usual backing and filling, he wrote to one man avowing, to another withdrawing, the thought that he was in the field for the Democratic nomination. Time was moving along and he could not wait for the long-drawn-out court proceedings to end. "The subject of the presidency has become distasteful to me," he wrote to Gerrit Smith, a philanthropist associated with Garrison in the Abolitionist movement. "Some will say 'sour grapes' and there may be some ground for the application of the proverb. But I really think that I am not half so ambitious of place as I am represented to be."

At virtually the same time, he sent equivocal letters to other politicians, suggesting encouragement of his cause. After the Johnson verdict, he wrote to August Belmont, his old banking friend in New York, that he did not know whether or not he was a "suitable candidate of any party," but that if his fellow countrymen thought fit "to require such services as I can render, they are without doubt entitled to them."

Five days before the verdict, when the High Court was meeting behind closed doors, Senator B. Henderson, of Missouri, and Senator Reverdy Johnson, of Maryland, dined with Senator Sprague and Chief Justice Chase on E Street. Since much pressure was being brought to bear on doubtful Senators, there was open uproar over this dinner assemblage and Ben Butler shouted at an evening session of the House of Representatives: "We are sold out." Every vote counted at this stage. Senator James W. Grimes, of Iowa, who had suffered a stroke, was carried into the Senate to vote in favor of Johnson.

To Kate's great indignation when she heard about it later, her father was shadowed after this. Detectives trailed his movements. The dinner was interpreted as part of the backstage influence that the Chief Justice was thought to be using on behalf of Johnson, chiefly to checkmate Wade, president pro tempore who, if the accused were impeached, would ride importantly into the presidential picture. It was recalled that shortly before the proceedings started, Johnson and his daughters all dined at the Chase home as Kate's guests.

Sprague's vote, which he had given the President's friends to understand would be cast in Johnson's favor if needed, was never registered, and his name remained on the scroll of the conspiracy. There is no record of Kate's feeling about this. Before the trial ended she was already out of the picture and in deep personal woe. Her trips to the Capitol ended abruptly when she had another blistering row with Sprague. She packed her bags and caught the next train for Narragansett. Chase wrote to her with deep concern on May 10. He mentioned the fact that the final question on the impeachment was ordered for Tuesday. "My own judgment and feeling favor acquittal," he wrote, "but I have no vote and I do not know how the Senate will vote. It seems to me that there is very little balance of probability either way."

The rest of the Chief Justice's letter was one of his veiled appeals to Kate to be tolerant of her husband, who apparently had sinned heinously again. It was not without gentle reproach for her, too, and concern for her health. She had left with a bad cold and he feared that the sea air might be too bracing so early in the year. It was plain from his letter that matters had reached a serious pass between the Spragues:

You must take care of yourself. How I wish you would take a different view of your social duties, & cease exposing yourself, by attending these wretched night parties. You could do so, I think, and lose nothing in any respect.

Most of all I long to see you an earnest Christian woman, not only religious but happy in religion. I realize painfully how far short I come of my own ideal, but I am not on that account the less desirous that you should succeed where I fail. One thing I am sure of, that full faith in Christ is the only thing on earth really worth having, and the only thing that one can carry from earth.

How I do love you, my darling! My whole heart seems to go towards you while I write and tears come into my eyes. How wrong it is for those who love not to express their love. I remember how often you have felt hurt by my apparent indifference to what interested you; and I feel sorry that I ever occasioned any such feelings to you. I see now in your husband something of that which I blame on myself. But I know how things are— and I know how wrong he is. And I am very glad that, while you have sometimes forgotten that the happiness of a wife is most certainly secured by loving submission & loving tact, you generally conquer by sweetness. I never saw him so much affected as by the difference that occurred between you just before you went away. He was almost unmanned—near to tears. I have not thought it best to refer to it; but try to make my society pleasant for him & hope I succeed. You must love away all his rancour— and help yourself to do so by reflecting how generous, self-sacrificing & indulgent a husband he has been to you. How few husbands would consent to such absences; and be at once so liberal and thoughtful. If he was only a true Christian he would be nearly perfect.

Kate was feeling frustrated in all directions. She had missed the denouement, when Johnson was saved by a single vote. She was furiously angry with the Governor, who had again humiliated her in public. On the presidential front, the Republican drift to General Grant was unmistakable and feelers put out for Democratic backing for her father had boomeranged uncomfortably. Late in May Horace Greeley wrote rather chasteningly: "The touching confidence which presupposes that Chief Justice Chase is to be had for the asking would not seem to argue a very high opinion of the integrity of human nature; and we really do not know why the Democracy should have such an opinion."

Whether or not the Democracy had the idea was debatable, but Kate was firmly committed to it and Chase, meeting H. S. Bundy and his daughter, Julia, then a schoolgirl and later to be Mrs. Joseph Benson Foraker, in the Columbus station after the Johnson verdict, told them: "I feel that I am a servant of the people and should they call me to preside for four years over the destiny of our country I doubtless would feel it my duty to comply." His plan at that time was to get the Democratic nomination if possible, and if that failed to run as an independent candidate against Grant. "Of my success," he told Bundy, "there can be no doubt."

But Kate was concerned because, with Lincoln out of the way, another really strong contender had appeared in General Grant to snatch the prize from her patient father. She recognized the fact that the General was an irresistible choice at the moment, although she had little respect for him as a man.

She was now in occupancy at Canonchet and she drew in some of the more powerful political figures as week-end guests. She had to work in new channels with Democratic supporters, and there was little time to be lost, with the convention opening in New York in July. Kate had decided to take personal charge of her father's campaign.

Chase sat in Washington in lofty aloofness as the delegates gathered in New York. Did he really wish Kate to run his campaign, or was it her own mad ambition that drove her into the saddle? When he learned that she had left for New York to attend the convention, he sent her a kindly note, but one of unmistakable warning:

I am afraid, my darling, that you are acting too much the politician. Have a care. Don't do or say anything which may not be proclaimed from the house tops. I am so anxious about you that I cannot help wishing you were in Narragansett or here, where I take all things very quietly, play croquet nearly every evening and sleep as soundly as the heat will let me every night.

Kate ignored the political warning, thanked him for his "dear loving letter" and told him not to worry about her. She felt quite well, didn't cough at all and found perfect rest and quiet at 94 Fifth Avenue. But she had not yet entered the fray. She enclosed a greenback, as she usually did in her letters, and gave him her impressions of the preconvention feeling. Amasa was doing noble duty on his behalf, she said, and they would know that night "which way the cat would jump."

They were settling on Horatio Seymour to nominate Chase. Kate thought the former Governor quite sincere in his intention not to be a candidate himself, although he had been prominently mentioned in this connection. But she knew that he wished to preside at the convention.

Kate told her father frankly that Seymour did not think the convention would go for him—Chase—under any circumstances. She had already heard enough to prepare him for the worst, but did not believe it would come to pass.

"Such men are very rare," she wrote on stationery with the name KATE swung in gold and colored letters from a lion's head. "The popular voice here is all one way, most singularly enthusiastic." Here Kate changed her tack with a note of warning: "I am glad you are not going to be greatly disappointed if the nomination is not for you. I should like to see this bright jewel added to your crown of earthly distinction and I believe it will be. But we can live and be very happy & just as proud of you without it. Will the country do as well?" finished Kate dramatically.

But much water flowed under the dam in the next three days and, wise as Kate was in the ways of politicians, she had her eyes opened to the behind-the-scenes machinations of a political convention. She could not quite invade the smoke-wreathed councils of Tammany Hall, and she had to accept what John D. Van Buren, Chase's campaign manager, told her. He was host to Seymour.

But reporters found Kate herself "active and visibly in charge" at the Chase headquarters in the Clarendon Hotel before the convention opened. It was ninety in the shade. Everyone else was sweating and groaning with the heat. But Kate, in thin muslin, her reddish hair drawn tight back and her bonnet lying on the table beside a pile of papers, was a refreshing sight for the gentlemen of the press, who regarded her presence in this situation as an undoubted novelty. One expressed the view that if she could take the floor, her father would win by acclamation. He considered her equipped with "brains of almost masculine fibre," unlike the foolish Miss Susan B. Anthony, who was determined to present her suffrage petition on this occasion.

But Kate knew little of what was going on behind closed doors; nor were all her father's agents proof against the champagne, beer and guile of the more practiced party leaders. However, she brought her own personal strength to bear on the backsliders until they discovered that the only way to escape her was to absent themselves entirely. Some were getting drunk, running up bills, succumbing to the heat, playing traitor and generally showing an incapacity that infuriated Kate. On the day before the convention opened, she telegraphed urgently to her father warning him about an unfortunate colonel who was "too indiscreet to be trusted in any way." He had disappeared for an entire day, then turned up "still a good deal under the effects of his late intemperance" and was unable to function effectively.

Clearly Kate was working a little beyond her depth in this atmosphere of liquor, secret caucuses and convention rigging. But she wote cheerfully to her father on July 5:

Day before yesterday and today have been as hot as weather can well be, too hot by far, for the warm work on hand here. . . . There is a noble work being done here by your friends. Should success or failure crown their efforts, they will be always proud to have had a hand in it. I will not enter into details, but everything as far as developed looks well—only New York friends inside that close corporation say their action is cautious, those outside say it is timid.

I am so glad that it does not fall to you to bear the burden and heat, and I love to think of you quietly at home, perhaps enjoying a game of croquet or ten pins.

Lovingly your child
[Signed] Kate

The arches of Tammany Hall were festooned with bunting when the convention opened. Flags and shields with the insignia of the states were on display. The speakers stood beneath a turkey-red canopy with a bust of Washington in the background. Kate watched the shifting parade with interest—the placards, the marching delegates, the whirling fans, the maimed veterans of the Civil War, the crowded galleries, the little group of women clustered around Susan B. Anthony, whose memorial on suffrage was greeted with derisive shouts.

Kate sat in the balcony to the left with a group of Chase supporters and away from the "female agitators" on the other side of the hall. The word soon spread on the floor that the striking reddish-haired woman was Mrs. Senator Sprague, hell bent on making her father President. The men in the inner councils were already well aware of it and they studied her with interest, if without alarm. But Kate's work was done in the evenings, when she major-generaled her father's agents. She kept him informed of every move. On the second day of the convention, she wrote to him:

The excitement here is intense. The outside pressure is very great and Chase is the password in the throng gathered about Tammany Hall. [George H.] Pendleton and Johnson have already been put in nomination but no balloting has yet begun. There are various opinions about the duration of the Convention. The feeling improves every hour and there is a growing confidence everywhere that you will ultimately be the choice. There are snares and pitfalls everywhere. Oh, if the convention would only have the courage to do right!

Affectionately and ambitiously for Country—The Democracy & its noblest patriot & statesman.

Your daughter
[Signed] K.C. Sprague

P.S. Your friends suggest that as soon as you see the Platform, which of course you will see tonight in the Press, you send such a telegram as may be advisable & necessary to be read in open convention, addressed to James C. Kennedy, Esq., 94 Fifth Avenue.

Mr. Kennedy is so well known by all the prominent men of the N. Y. delegation, and so entirely commands their confidence that no question will arise as to the authenticity.

K.C. S.

There had been some debate in the inner councils as to whether the platform was broad enough to please the radical Mr. Chase. Kate was alive to the importance of his endorsing it, although she found to her dismay that Van Buren had advised him by telegraph to answer no questions in regard to the platform.

The convention was slow to dance to Kate's tune. It was her understanding that the New York delegation would vote first for Seymour. Then the former Governor would make a speech, declining in favor of Chase. "As New York goes, so goes the convention," Kennedy had assured her. On Wednesday her father received a half vote. That evening Kate, thoroughly aroused and wakening up to the fact that things were not going according to plan, was the central figure at a meeting of the Chase executive committee. She cracked the whip and sent forth a flock of the Chase satellites to circulate at once among the delegations at the various hotels and use every argument to convince them that Chase was the only candidate who could defeat Grant. She primed them with the further thought that her father had telegraphed his approval of the Democratic platform, and that it was strong enough for him to stand upon, should he be nominated.

Had her father's message really come? Had she followed up her letter with a telegram, or did Kate act on her own responsibility in lending her father's approval to the platform?

Next morning a report in the *Tribune* from Washington pictured the Chief Justice as "perfectly tranquil at his home," saying he believed that "any one of the gentlemen whose names had been mentioned would make a good President." By this time there were many in the running.

"I have it on high authority," the correspondent continued, "that Mr. Chase considers the platform framed at New York a pretty good one, but that he does not think that they will make many converts to their party by it."

Meanwhile, Samuel J. Tilden, the shrewd and sagacious scholar of Gramercy Park, had held his own quiet powwow of New York delegates which resulted, in the opinion of many, in the downfall of Chase on this occasion. The evidence was never conclusive but to the day of her death Kate believed that Tilden maneuvered the Seymour nomination and jockeyed her father out of the picture. At all events, she threw in a sharp spear during the Hayes-Tilden impasse of 1876.

After hours of great anxiety for Kate, Ohio, which had backed Pendleton, not her father, threw its support to Seymour on the twenty-second ballot. Kate leaned forward expectantly. At last the moment had come. But had it? Seymour was nominated with an extravagant eulogy. Twice he declined in spite of storms of applause. It became an overwhelming tide. He seemed deeply embarrassed. "Your candidate I cannot be," he insisted. For the third time he rose to refuse, but was buttonholed by one of his intimates. This time he accepted the honor, but with obvious confusion. He was in poor health and no one believed that he had any wish to run against Grant. However, Seymour had received the nomination and Chase's name was not mentioned again, although enthusiastic applause had greeted his half vote earlier in the convention.

Kate sank back in her seat aghast. To add to her humiliation, General Frank P. Blair, her father's old enemy, was nominated for the Vice-Presidency. The victors went off to the Manhattan Club, where Tilden presided over a ratification meeting and Seymour said he had been caught in an "overwhelming tide." Van Buren stayed close to the Manhattan Club and conspicuously avoided Kate.

Chase took the news calmly in Washington, pausing in the middle of a game of croquet to read the telegram. His first and most significant comment was: "How did Katie take it?"

She took it with much less equanimity than her father, although she kept her composure in public. She was so outraged that she decided not to write to him until the following day, to give herself time to study the entire picture and find out where things had gone wrong. Then she poured out her heart and showed her great discomfiture:

New York, 10 July, 1868

My dearest Father:

You have been most cruelly deceived and shamefully used by the man whom you trusted implicitly and the country must suffer for his duplicity. I would not write you yesterday in the excitement of the result of the action of the convention & until I had carefully gone over in my mind all the circumstances that had come under my knowledge of the action of Mr. Van Buren. When I get comfortably settled at Narragansett I will write out a full & detailed history of my knowledge of this matter that cannot fail to convince you of his bad faith. Nothing more would be needed than that since the result of the nomination was announced Mr. Van Buren, though constantly at the Manhattan Club, next door, has not been near me. . . .

Had Mr. Kennedy had the authority to act for you, you would have been as certainly nominated on the wave of the enthusiasm created in the convention by the half vote cast by California day before yesterday—as anything could be. Mr. Van Buren's telegraph to you to answer no questions in regard to the platform was the block he put in the way of your nomination, & when at the critical juncture he was at last found (for he has scarcely been seen in the convention) he refused to take the responsibility of speaking for you, & said he was not authorized. . . . Mr. Tilden and Mr. Seymour have done this work, and Mr. Van Buren has been their tool. This is my honest belief, but I will write it out carefully. Do, dear Father, in the future, be guided by the advice of some of those who are devoted to you, but who are more suspicious, than your own noble heart will allow you to be.

With all this you personally can have nothing to regret. Your friends have worked nobly—& the universal disappointment today is amazing. Not a flag floats nor is the semblance of rejoicing visible anywhere. Your name is the watchword with the people & many have been outraged & deceived. . . . You can form no conception of the depression here.

Your devoted Katie

But another blow awaited Kate. Immediately after the convention, she saw a letter by Dr. Henry Ward Beecher in the New York *Tribune* that hurt her as deeply as Seymour's defection. He bluntly said that he distrusted Chase and considered him a "splendid man to look upon, but a poor man to lean upon." He had felt for years that Chase's ambition was consuming the better elements of his nature, wrote Dr. Beecher, adding: "The seven-fold humiliations and recantations through which Chase was required to go for a Democratic nomination, only to see the smiling Seymour looking benignly down upon his lost estate, has no parallel except in the immortal history of Reinicke Fuchs."

Kate returned to Canonchet, her pride hardening under this added flail. She determined to hold her anger in check and possess her soul in patience. The imponderables had played heavily against her, and she had had a sharp lesson in practical politics. In the past she had always felt that things had been bungled through lack of loyalty on the part of her father's followers. This time, against his advice, she had taken a hand herself and had failed. But it was not Kate's habit to lay waste her spirit in vain regret. She always looked ahead.

The Governor was playing with little Willie on the piazza when she drove up with Amasa. He scarcely noticed the fact that his campaigning wife was home. He was for Grant, the soldier, and for once had failed to uphold the Chase standard. Kate could no longer budge her husband on all-important issues. He, too, had hardened under the lash of her relentless ambition. The Governor was easily reconciled to the thought that Canonchet would not be the summer White House yet awhile.

Chapter XIII

※ⓒ❊ⓒⓡ❊ ❊ⓒ❊ⓒⓡ❊

KATE'S IDOL FADES AWAY

K ATE'S TOUGH political fiber showed in the days following her father's defeat. If her pride had suffered that summer, no one must know it. If her father stuck to his proclaimed intention of renouncing all thought of the Presidency, she must gradually shape his mood again. Kate's own sense of power deadened her to the strength of other men's motives, the irresistible force of the political machine, the public indifference to her father's virtues. She was in no way chastened as she followed the uneven race between Grant and Seymour.

As she lay sunning herself on the beach, clad from head to foot, a thick green veil protecting her delicate complexion from the sun and a parasol tilted overhead, she gave careful thought to the future. She had little doubt that Grant would be elected, but she did not believe that the good General would make a good President. Her father was only sixty. Kate's spirits revived. She sent out telegrams in all directions and filled the house with guests, including friendly politicians of various stripes. She drove the workmen hard at Canonchet. She bowled, danced, bathed and entertained with consuming intensity. Kate was a woman of action.

She also spent some time that summer trying to mend her own domestic fences. Her father's advice to meet rancor with sweetness had made an impression. It was not Kate's practice to be sweet, but it was to be clever. The Canonchet bills were staggering and the Governor, ill that summer and somewhat crotchety, was complaining.

But Canonchet now was a mansion fit for a queen—or a President's daughter.

Kate interested herself in Amasa's operations. He had been a loyal and effective worker throughout the campaign and she valued his good will. He was busy at this time with plans for the great gate of Narragansett Park. He poured money into the race track, the grandstand and everything that had to do with the venture. He consulted Kate about the decorations. His own taste ran to bright red wheels on his buggies and curlicue effects on his barns.

She now talked horses with Amasa instead of politics and she followed the fortunes of Ethan Allen, most famous trotter of his day, with the interest of a true horse lover. He was kept on the Sprague stock farm in Kansas and was much discussed at Canonchet. Kate often took small Willie out to watch Amasa's favorite string teams of six brown and six gray horses that hauled the farm produce in big wagons painted up like circus carryalls. The trotting horses were also a delight to Willie, who liked to be swung on their backs. His mother went riding at every opportunity on Amasa's horses. She had many friendly visits with Madame Fanny, whose hardy wit she enjoyed. Kate was also making friends with summer residents at Narragansett. She had little social contact with the old families of Providence.

Nettie was out West that summer visiting her Ludlow relatives. She was exhibiting a touch of her great-grandmother's pioneering spirit. "When I feel myself beyond civilization a kind of wild delight comes over me, my Indian wakes and gives a war whoop," Nettie wrote. She admired the little frame cottages of St. Paul and the light gray stone, quarried in the neighborhood, that was used in the larger houses. She went to the Falls of Minnehaha, followed the stream through thicket and marsh and found it all romantic. Nettie made sketches on the back of a notebook with a burnt match, since she had neither paper nor pencil with her.

She drove from sunset until dawn across country from the Falls to Stillwater. "Such a drive!" wrote the enthusiastic Nettie. "It was perfectly delightful! First we had the sunset, clear bright, red and gold, then the moon, but it was rather young and went to bed early—but the aurora took its place, and illuminated the whole northern sky. We stopped at midnight at a farmhouse and roused up the people, and the woman soon had a hot supper ready for us. It was rather jolly waiting in the kitchen by the fire, for the night was quite fresh."

Kate took a motherly interest in Nettie's adventures and missed her at Narragansett. Chase, whose health was poor at this time and who saw little of either of his daughters, wrote to Nettie in August that young Whitelaw Reid, who was then editing the Cincinnati *Gazette*, had promised Horace Greeley to go to the New York *Tribune*, "during the rest of the campaign at any rate."

Kate returned to Washington refreshed from her summer by the sea and on better terms with the Governor. She entered at once into the usual round of entertaining. The capital was changing fast. Public lectures, concerts and art gatherings were in high esteem. There was less roistering, gambling and talk of duels, although the sporty establishments run by John Welcher and Sam Ward still drew the bloods and politicians. Wormley's, Willard's, the National and the new Ebbitt had public hops, which attracted large crowds.

The Civil War seemed far away, as one by one the states came back into the fold. Great equipages rattled along the road to Georgetown. Young men appeared in hemstitched shirt fronts and lavender kid gloves. And Olivia sized up the distaff side with her usual sharpened pencil: "The old monarch's dying. Andrew Johnson is passing away. . . . If Madame Pompadour is not here in the flesh, she has bequeathed to this brilliant Republican court her unique taste in the shape of paint-pots, rouge, patches, pointed heels, and frilled petticoats; the dress made with an immense train at the back, but so short in front that it discloses a wealth of airy, fantastic, white muslin; the square-necked waist, so becoming to a queenly neck; the open sleeve so bewitching for a lovely arm."

Not having gone abroad that summer, Mrs. Senator Sprague neverthe-less ordered her winter wardrobe from Worth, and her entry into a Washington parlor was immediately the sign for the other ladies to take stock. They rarely were disappointed. She continued to run her salon as if the Presidency were at stake. She went to the Capitol regularly, kept track of every notable debate and was known to influence opinion. She held court regularly with such men as Garfield, Schurz, Sherman and Conkling, whose oratory was flashing on the Senate like a scimitar thrust.

Grant, too, was always studiously courteous to Mrs. Sprague and counted on her husband as one of his friends. The President-elect, like Lincoln, talked politics with her that winter. He had never forgotten that, on his return to Washington from Appomattox, Kate had insisted that he call first on the Chief Justice, instead of having it the other way around. Noblesse oblige!

Johnson was bitter as he moved out of, and Grant moved into, the Executive Mansion. He refused to share in the inaugural ceremonies and was clearing up his papers while his successor was sworn in. At last, he remarked, he was doing something of which everybody would approve. Kate, for once looking more wistful than proud, watched her father administer the oath and thought how ill he appeared as he did so. She was worried about his health. Grant stood square and impassive in his black dress suit and yellow gloves. His mumbled speech was scarcely heard by the crowd.

The balconies along Pennsylvania Avenue were filled with cheering spectators and the inauguration parade had a gay military touch for the Civil War hero. It was not like the somber Lincoln parades. Handkerchiefs waved, the public hurrahed for the soldier President, the trees "bore human fruit" and spectators clung to fences and monuments. Musket and saber glittered and the plumage of the artillery ran like a crimson thread along the marching lines.

The inaugural ball was held in the newly completed north wing of the Treasury, where temporary balustrades had been festooned with spring greenery, bands played in several of the halls and the tasselated pavements and fluted columns, flecked with gold, were much admired by the public. Kate circled around the Grants, who received on the second floor balcony against panels of Sienese marble. Again it was a jam, and Greeley left quite angry and without his hat.

Mrs. Grant wore her satin, point lace, pearls and diamonds without any affectation, and Kate inevitably compared her with the flamboyant Mary Todd. Like Kate, she was to have her state dresses made in Paris of rich materials, but they were to be worn in the manner of Queen Victoria, where Kate gave hers the Empress Eugénie flourish.

The customs of the new White House occupants became almost as widely publicized as those of the Lincolns. Kate listened attentively and used her eyes. It soon became apparent that there would be little cordiality between the Grants and the Chases. A new era had set in, and Mrs. Grant turned to Mrs. Hamilton Fish for aid and counsel. She inaugurated the custom of having the Cabinet ladies receive with her. She had Tuesday afternoon receptions and the President received the public every other Thursday night in the Blue Parlor. There were many state dinners, with printed menus and excellent fare.

When by themselves the Grants preferred to dine at five. They had an efficient steward, and Kate soon learned that the President's favorite dinner was roast beef, boiled hominy and wheaten bread, followed by strong cigars and coffee. He shocked Lady Thornton, wife of the British Ambassador, by rolling bread crumbs at her table. He played billiards and cribbage and filled the White House stables with horses and colts. He kept a great variety of carriages and his young daughter Nellie took her daily drive in a phaeton drawn by two small ponies.

Before long Grant was in trouble with his appointments. He leaned to generals and millionaires. Conkling, his close friend and champion, boasted to Kate of the way in which he stood up to the President, who was humble and lacking in confidence, although accustomed to commanding soldiers.

That spring the Governor astounded Kate, her father and his fellow Senators by ripping out a series of five speeches so sensational that he was called a madman before he had finished. Had Kate finally stung him to fury and articulation? Had Conkling's flashy oratory stirred him into action? Always surrounded by able and eloquent men, Kate had long deplored her husband's silence in the Senate. He had played a thin role in public life, and his counsel was not sought by the men who circled around her. Only her father, in his courteous way, gave ear to Sprague. In general, he was dismissed as a negligible fellow.

Kate had nipped him savagely in public on one occasion after listening to a debate in which she felt that he should have taken part. Smooth oratory had flowed from Massachusetts. Silence had enfolded Rhode Island. Meeting Kate afterward as she came down from the gallery, Sprague politely inquired if there were anything he could do for her.

"Nothing," she said bitterly, "except to go in there and make a speech, and that you can't do!"

Sprague's sequence of speeches came late in March and early in April, 1869. They were delivered with gesture, fire and fury. All were tied to legislation on loans, the national currency, taxation and other fiscal matters. The Senators sat back amazed, watching Sprague come out of his chronic slouch, throw back his forelock and orate. Instinctively some looked toward the gallery, but Kate was not in view. There was instant speculation as to the part she might have played in this unexpected outburst.

Sprague's was the voice of doom, predicting the financial collapse that soon was to be his own fate. In the light of later events, there was much sound sense in what he had to say, but before he had finished, his house was in flames, his native state was wholeheartedly against him and Kate had turned her back on him.

He attacked the new President, while publicly proclaiming the fact that he had favored him "in opposition to the aspirations of one connected with me by family ties," meaning the sacrosanct Chief Justice Chase. He assailed the framers of the Constitution, the millionaires and monopolists, charged corruption in the Senate and finally he turned on Rhode Island. All the snubs he had received in his native state were summed up in his furious attack on Brown and Ives, woolen manufacturers who were his rivals in New England. The two factions were like the Montagues and Capulets in their bitter feuding and they divided the state into two political camps. Both houses were represented in the Senate. If the Sprague mills were more numerous, Brown and Ives controlled more banking institutions. It was a continual seesaw and one that rankled deeply with Sprague, for Brown and Ives had social standing, too, and he did not. Even Katy had not been able to rectify that. He charged that his colleague, Senator Henry B. Anthony, acted as their tool in attempting to destroy his credit.

The Governor flaunted the story of his own courage at Bull Run, insisting that the other millionaires and also General Burnside, had shown the white feather. He embarked on a self-pitying tale about the mill boy who was at work in his thirteenth year, whose father "died by the assassin's blow and for ten long years that dagger rested in his heart." He showed his own private wounds in saying: "I trust, sir, that hereafter the men occupying a commercial station, such as mine, may not be pointed out with the finger of scorn and derision because of that station."

His resentment of the way his senatorial colleagues had treated him bubbled up in his declaration: "The Senate of the United States may well have misunderstood me. It has always been my nature to hide myself from the public gaze. . . . I am supposed to be rich and I am made the objective point for solutions for employment. . . . Why slur my utterances, why underrate the person who utters them, his arguments, his facts and his position? . . . I advocate a true system of finance based on a great principle . . . the power of the people."

Sprague attacked the monopolies one by one and insisted that lust for money was threatening the economic liberties of the people. There was no justice in the land. "Who that is a poor man dare take one that is rich before any court in it with certainty of impartial justice?" he demanded. "You have lost your commerce. American society today has perhaps less virtue, less morality in it, than any civilized Government in the world. It is the striving of the rich to be richer, and the striving of the poor to imitate the rich; and in that contest virtue is lost."

Appalled by the reports she received on her husband's speeches, Kate arrived in the gallery one April day in time to catch one of the daggers herself. Looking straight in her direction, he attacked the fashionable folk who went to Europe and came back laden with extravagant purchases and the customs of a corrupt civilization. Kate, who was much too haughty to show her feelings as a general rule, was observed to turn scarlet, draw a lace shawl around her shoulders and sail rapidly out, looking so angry that one witness observed: "I believe she's capable of hitting him with the coral stick of her parasol."

Sprague's words had sizzled through the Senate and there were immediate repercussions. Whether or not the Governor aimed this insult at Kate—and later he insisted that this was not his intention—her many gallant friends on the floor were outraged. To some this taunt was worse than the charges of corruption made against themselves.

Sprague walked into an avalanche of praise and condemnation. On the whole he was pleased with the sensation he had produced, and he had sixty thousand copies of his speeches printed for distribution. He became a passing idol of the people. He was serenaded by the workingmen of Washington. The band blared loudly beneath Kate's windows and her father stood beside the Governor looking benevolent, while the younger man made another speech, attacking "money power" and the monopolists. Chase did not seem to be deeply concerned, even though the press denounced his son-in-law, Rhode Island raged and the greatly respected Senator Anthony in a polished speech tore his charges apart. He spoke for the state's business, its soldiers and its war dead. Burnside incompetent? What did Tennessee say to that? It was suggested that Burnside was welcome in Rhode Island homes that Sprague could never enter.

Chase dined with the Henry D. Cookes in Georgetown immediately after the attack on Kate. The guest of honor was General Sherman, who had just been appointed commander-in-chief of the army to succeed Grant. The Cookes were under fire by the old guard at Georgetown for their ostentatious display of wealth. They were looked upon as upstarts with their fleet horses, their footmen, their statuary and Oriental treasures. The story persisted that one batch of roses for a dinner had cost them fifteen hundred dollars.

Caged birds sang in the green drawing room on this occasion. Chase wrote to Kate that there were "wondrous table decorations—a flat star-shaped tray with long single rays lengthwise and double rays crosswise, and beautiful flowers and service." The portly Henry Cooke was as jolly as usual and asked most cordially for Kate.

The following night Chase dined with Attorney General Evarts, who also was honoring General Sherman. President Grant dropped in to smoke a cigar with his war comrade, although this was contrary to form, and "I had a few moments pleasant talk with the President, and was glad to have it in my power to speak very cordially and with entire sincerity of what has thus far been done," Chase wrote with his usual omniscience.

The name Sprague was not mentioned at either of these functions, although it was much in the air for several weeks, and indeed Sumner and Sherman had to act as peacemakers when Senator Joseph C. Abbott, whom Sprague had called a "puppy," threatened to horsewhip him.

Chase professed to be a little puzzled by it all. He had seen the Governor slaving over his speeches. He knew they had been carefully wrought, and he wrote to Nettie from Richmond, where he was holding court, that they were attracting much attention and had given him more reputation for ability as a public man and statesman than anything in his past career. "I don't exactly comprehend his views," Chase commented tolerantly, "but I shall try to make myself acquainted with

them. . . . And all who try to improve the condition of the masse
deserve honor."

A few days later he was not so sure that the Governor's speeches wer
sound. The criticism was becoming deafening. "A man is only a grow
child," he wrote, "and as the child will instinctively pick himself u
when he falls and keep out of the pond when he has once tumbled in
so the man will retrieve his own mishaps and amend his own mistakes.

But the real tussle was with Kate. Outraged, humiliated, she ha
turned on Sprague with flashing temper. An acute crisis had developec
and Sprague had flung a string of accusations at her. He had then broke
into a trunk in her room and taken a sealed package of letters written b
Colonel John Schuyler Crosby, one of the Civil War aides whos
services as courier had attracted the attention of Lincoln.

Chase, who had long been peacemaker but now was unable to silenc
the aroused Governor, wrote her from Richmond on May 4 the pa
ticulars of an interview he had had with her husband. Sprague ha
accused Kate of entering his room when she thought he was away an
searching his pockets. "This matter you had explained to me," wrot
Chase, "and I tried to make the same explanation then but what ha
since occurred made it impossible to get a hearing. He then went on t
say that he could not be controlled by you."

Kate had come to a real crisis in her affairs, and, with the Govern
on the rampage, neither she nor her father knew where it might en
They had lost their grip on the situation. Chase's own health w
poor. He was deeply concerned over the debacle of Kate's marriag
and the storm of publicity that now surrounded her. He had been patc
ing up things for years, but further concealment seemed impossible. Th
fires of hate were burning furiously. Sprague was behaving like a ma
man. The situation was aggravated by the fact that Kate was expectin
another child in October.

The Chief Justice pleaded for mollification. He wrote again to h
"darling Katie":

Your letter by express came to me here by mail from Washington th
morning. I read it with profound interest and the deepest sympathy for yo
It is my firm faith that you have only to carry out the purpose you expres
with patience and perseverance, to win a happy issue. Trust God, have fai
in Christ, accuse none but yourself, cherish every wifely sentiment wheth

now reciprocated or not, have no dispute with your husband, let your conduct be as the day and all will come right. God is trying you severely now. If you take the trials as a loving child of God it will make you better & happier, and bring you nearer to Him where perfect safety is. Don't rebel, or let any impatience be suffered in your thoughts. Make all happy around you. Make Willie happy, & Nettie, and the domestics. Overcome your own temper and be transparently truthful.

My advice to you is not to criticize your husband's public acts even in your thoughts. Of course you say nothing to outsiders except all you can say honestly in agreement and approval. But you may write something else to him, which will do harm rather than good. He cannot take criticism from you now patiently. Let him take his own course—without any words but cheer and support. His own judgment will correct what may prove erroneous.

As I write you he seemed gratified by something you had written; but I found afterwards that there was some admonition in the letter which he did not like, tho he said nothing from which I could infer anything more than this.

He went to N.Y. last Friday by the noon train, and before he went I had a conversation with him. I found him under some excitement. He said he had been sincerely anxious to have peace and good will restored; but could not do anything which was not misinterpreted by you, and that you seemed all the time to be wanting to make up a case against him or defend yourself against him.

Sprague continued to rage both publicly and privately and by midsummer was attacking the "money power" at a Masonic picnic on Rhode Island. The feeling in his native state was bitter and he was beginning to catch its effects financially, as his mercantile and banking friends refused him credit. But money still poured into the walls, furnishings and decorations of Canonchet, and Kate passed another summer by the shore on strained terms with her husband. He rarely appeared at the house except to visit Willie. There were always the other Sprague homes on Rhode Island to stay at and he made many trips to Newport.

In spring Jay Gould had engineered an upward movement in gold but the price soon fell and by autumn some of Sprague's prophecies were already coming true. The gold corner in September led to fantastic gambling. The corruption around President Grant was coming into evidence on all sides. Chase was desperately pressed for money himself.

He had firmly decided to pull away entirely from the Sprague ménage
He could no longer control either Sprague or Katie. In October h
was importuning Flamen Ball in Cincinnati to sell more of his property
He had bought an old house with fifty acres of ground outside Wash
ington for $22,000 cash and could muster only $4,000 toward payment
Kate sold some insurance in order to help him.

This was Edgewood, a fine brick mansion set on a gentle slope wit
a view of the Capitol and the Potomac. It was a century old, its wood
work was solid mahogany and its mantelpieces were made of Italia
marble. He and Kate had often ridden out to look at the place and sh
quite approved his choice.

Kate's first daughter was born in October and she named her Ethe
Her father wrote to her: "I am glad that the baby is a girl. For m
part, I like girls rather better than boys, though I would, I believe, hav
put up with one boy—perhaps two—for the sake of having a brothe
apiece for you & Nettie."

A new hierarchy, social as well as political, had arisen around Gran
Kate observed, as the season of 1869-70 got under way. James G. Blain
Speaker of the House, was drawing the intellectuals to his splendid hom
as Sumner did, but Sumner's sun was setting. He was at odds wit
Grant and would have nothing to do with Hamilton Fish, believin
that he should be Secretary of State himself. His thunder was stilled
his noble head was graying fast, but he still went in for brilliant plaid
(inspired by Queen Victoria and Balmoral), white spats and Englis
evening dress.

Schuyler Colfax, the new Vice-President, witty and well informe
entertained once a week, and Mark Twain was a favorite guest, sportin
a white vest and lavender gloves. Zachariah Chandler gave splendi
parties. Mrs. Fernando Wood dripped diamonds. Mrs. Fish advised an
aided the modest Mrs. Grant. Mrs. John Creswell, wife of the Pos
master General, gave Kate some competition with her grace and goo
looks. But as time went on, the second Mrs. William Worth Belknap
known as "Puss," wife of the Secretary of War, was to contest he
supremacy openly with her Worth gowns, French chef, jewels and high
powered entertainment. Madame Catacazy, wife of the Russian Ministe
shone in the diplomatic set, a tall beautiful blonde much liked b
Kate. She was also on the best of terms with Lady Thornton, of th

British Embassy. The Peruvian Embassy was under discussion for a showy carriage in which a lady swathed in snowy ostrich tips rested against a white satin lining and held a white lap robe over her knees. This struck Kate as being bizarre.

She noted a slight coating of frost in the air that winter where she was concerned and responded by becoming more exclusive and haughty herself. The name Sprague had been under attack and the women correspondents watched her closely. The watchful Olivia pin-pointed an incipient triangle on March 12, 1870, when she wrote:

"Mrs. Sprague is also present, superbly graceful as ever. This elegant woman is not only ornamental but useful to the world. When she is travelling amongst foreign nations her manners reflect honor on the country that gave her birth." At the same time she noted Senator Sprague in a "leaning attitude against the wall," observing: "The golden background helps to make a fitting picture of the young millionaire. His face has a marble pallor which the rosy lights of the chamber cannot dispel." And to complete the implication Olivia observed that a "handsomer man than Conkling is seldom seen on the floor of the Senate."

In the spring of 1870, Olivia was not the only spectator who watched Senator Conkling glance frequently toward the front row seat in the gallery where Kate appeared each day in a succession of effective costumes. On at least one occasion, flowers on his desk were said to have come from her conservatory. That same day Olivia noted Kate's costume. She wore a Worth suit of royal purple velvet with a hat that suggested one large marguerite poised on top of her head, with the leaves bent into bonnet shape. Olivia gushingly observed that on this occasion her eyes "rested upon the most graceful, distinguished and queenly woman that she had ever seen in the Capitol or elsewhere on the face of the globe."

Had Mrs. Lincoln heard the gossip that now raged around Kate? She wrote to her Philadelphia friend, Mrs. J. H. Orne, from Frankfurt on February 18, 1870: "I do not see Mrs. Sprague's name among the gay notices of the winter. Is she in Washington—or South? I hope her truly kind-hearted husband will favor our interests."

Mary was sadly eking out her days in Europe, still dabbling in spiritualism, having occasional "visions" and struggling to exist. No longer could she walk into shops and order clothes at will. But if Kate's name was not in the forefront that winter, it was because she was becoming more selective as she watched the people who circled around Grant. She had not retired from the lists. But she gave card receptions, which limited the entries. Her political salon was as active as ever. She served the finest Roman punch, good wines, discriminating fare, and the food at her table was still spiced with the best of talk.

Kate spent much time with her father that winter. The great man was moving into the shadows. In December he was quite ill, but improved after settling in Edgewood. He attributed this to simpler living, plainer food and the "strong" mile and a half he walked each day to the Capitol. His friends the Cookes were setting up financial houses abroad and he wrote to Henry on December 9, 1870: "I hope that your London House will prove as great a success as your other enterprises. I hear that you design establishing a house in Berlin, and I do not know where else. Jay Cooke and Co. are to be the new Rothschilds. Is it not so?"

Early that summer, returning from a trip West with Nettie and some friends, Chase had a stroke on the train between Niagara and Albany. The Spragues met him in New York and took him to Canonchet, where they nursed him faithfully for months. He had worked extraordinarily hard over a great many years. The reorganization of the Supreme Court between 1865 and 1870 had caused much dissension behind the scenes, although the public was little aware of this until Chase came under heavy fire over his legal-tender decision. He was not old, but he was an exhausted man, and the barely suppressed scandal involving Kate and her husband was the final straw. He was still unhappy about it, and was even more concerned when his son-in-law introduced a resolution in December providing for an investigation of charges made against Sprague himself of illicit trading in cotton in Texas during the war. These rumors had repeatedly come up to plague Chase and the Sprague family, and the Governor had taken the bull by the horns. But the charges were not sustained, and the matter petered out.

All through 1871 Chase's speech was unintelligible. His handwriting —always so illegible that even Lincoln had complained about it—became unreadable and Kate took on the task of writing many of his letters. It was the first break in a lifelong sequence of diary entries and sustained correspondence. He was unable to take up his duties on the Supreme Court bench but stayed on at Canonchet through the winter. Kate and the Governor visited him often, and the Governor gave him massage and was kindly and considerate to him in every way, in spite of his strained relations with Kate.

The season did not flow as smoothly as usual for Kate. She was concerned about her father. Her domestic affairs were not in good repair. She was seen constantly in the Senate gallery, particularly when Conkling was due for one of his oratorical outbursts. She attended the most important parties and gave a few herself. But she did not add her name to the petition handed in to the Senate and signed by a thousand of her countrywomen on behalf of woman suffrage. She was a little dubious about Victoria Woodhull, who had drawn up the memorial. Olivia observed that on the January day in 1871 on which these ladies "blethered the Senatorial dames were unfortunately detained elsewhere."

Kate decidedly was. She had been wary of allying herself with these enterprising females, although she watched them with interest. She had mental reservations about their techniques, but not about their basic convictions. She had taken careful note of Elizabeth Cady Stanton, majestic in her black silk, camel's hair scarf and lilac kid gloves; of Susan B. Anthony, in a black silk dress with velveteen overskirt, fancy basque and her spectacles dangling at the point of her nose; of Olympia Brown, the woman preacher in a suit of blue naval cloth and a basque with "masculine coat-tails." Victoria, on the other hand, was something of a siren, but of dubious repute.

In theory Kate was as strongly on the side of the feminists as her father, but she felt there were better ways of attaining a goal. Chase had written in the previous year to Mrs. Elizabeth Smith Miller, daughter of an old friend:

You will not be mistaken if you believe me heartily desirous of all things which will really improve the condition of woman. Among such things I count the increase of facilities for moral and intellectual culture; ample recognition and full protection to rights of property; and access to, and peaceful security in, all employments for which she is qualified by strength, capacity and integrity. I am also so far in favor of suffrage for women that I should like to see the experiment tried in one or more of the states, and, if found to work well, extended to all. I am sufficiently confident of good results to be willing to vote for it in the state where I reside.

Kate was quite familiar with the group of newspaperwomen and lecturers who haunted the press gallery and whose sympathies were much embroiled with these campaigning women. She was sometimes pleased, occasionally angered and often amused by the constant references to herself by the powerful Mrs. Briggs, who lived in a Queen Anne house known as "Maple Square," used the pen name Olivia and saw a great deal through curious half-closed eyes. She knew Mary Clemmer Ames, who wrote for the New York Independent, as a formidable character who sometimes stabbed her sharply.

Jane Swisshelm defended Kate, as she did Mrs. Lincoln. Kate was also aware of Anna Dickinson, who lectured as well as wrote; Gail Hamilton, invited everywhere by virtue of her friendship with the Blaines; Grace Greenwood, who had long admired Kate's father; and Nellie Hutchinson, the "spicy little reporter of the Tribune," jaunty with gilt cord and gold buttons. These women were always circling about, in and out of the parlors, and Kate made them welcome, as she did the newspapermen. They could usually be found at the White House levees, where Mrs. Grant, wearing heavy brocades and conservative jewels, presided calmly in the blue and gold setting of the Blue Room.

In the spring of 1871, Kate was preparing for Nettie's wedding in March to William Sprague Hoyt, her husband's cousin and a partner in his business. She gave a Valentine Day party and several other brilliant affairs for her half sister. She made all the wedding arrangements and traveled to Canonchet to see if her father were well enough to appear in public. She decided that he was.

But Kate stole the thunder at the wedding when she appeared in a turquoise velvet gown, with a high Elizabethan ruff setting off her radiant hair. Nettie's round face and amiable personality were neutralized by the splendor of her sister. Little Willie was dressed in a black velvet suit. Ethel looked demure in a pink silk frock and small white cape. Both had just recovered from the measles and were not at their best. Bishop Charles P. McIlvaine came from Ohio to conduct the service.

Everyone was shocked by the sight of the Chief Justice, shrunken, gray, only the ghost of his old self and unable to talk clearly. Every feature showed signs of strain. His mouth was slightly twisted. His cheeks fell in pouches. The gloss and glitter of his earlier years had vanished. Chase was ill and everyone could see it. Kate watched him with apprehension. She stood protectively by his side through the three-hour reception held at her home after the wedding. President Grant, General Sherman, the Supreme Court Justices and almost everyone else of high estate were present.

It was a glorious day and refreshments were served outdoors under a pavilion. The flower decorations were carefully thought out by Kate. Champagne flowed freely. Dinner was at seven and, as the bride and groom left, the Governor threw one of Kate's shoes after his old friend Nettie. He was mightily pleased to see her marrying his kinsman.

Bright and early next day, the indefatigable Kate was up to take Minnie Vail and Mary Parker, house guests from Ohio for the wedding, to hear Sumner speak on the San Domingo annexation, a burning issue of the moment. That night they attended a concert.

But Chase failed even more after Nettie's wedding and he spent the summer at mineral springs in Michigan and Wisconsin, taking rubs, walks and therapeutic treatment. He had thought of going abroad with Kate and the Cookes, but his doctors had advised against it. His six-feet-two frame had shrunk to 146 pounds. He was at Magnetic Springs when he heard of Mrs. Jay Cooke's death. A good friend gone from his circle! He visited some of his old friends in Cincinnati while in the West and all were shocked by the wrecked grandeur of Salmon Portland Chase.

Meanwhile, Nettie, touring Wales with her bridegroom, wrote gaily from Conway: "Eating fresh eggs and mutton chops for breakfast—no end of beer and bread and cheese and butter for lunch, and spring lamb for dinner. Will smokes his cigar. I finish up my sketches. Will reads out loud. I continue to sketch. . . . Joyful start for Snowdon, blue sky, lazily sailing white clouds, green fields, skipping lambs, birds singing, streamlets dancing, simply perfect, in short."

Nettie had not changed. Nor had Kate, who also wrote diverting but less spontaneous letters to her father from Narragansett. Her summer salon was in full operation again. Ethel, although only twenty-two

months old, could recite Mother Goose rhymes and had "Goodbye
John" and "Up In a Balloon" quite pat, Kate reported, knowing her
father's devotion to his grandchildren. Willie had received a miniature
mitrailleuse from his Aunt Nettie in Europe. She was saluted by it
every morning and found it "ready cocked and elevated for the purpose
at night, at the foot of Willie's bed, beside my own." Little Willie,
like his father, already liked to play soldiers. Nettie had also remembered
Kate's birthday, to her great delight. "I fear I am a good deal of a
child about such things yet," she wrote revealingly to her father,
"though the yearning for love is hardly one of the childish things one
would wish to put away."

In this letter the child was again the politician. Election year was
approaching and Chase's friends seemed to be working in earnest to
build him up as the only man who could defeat Grant on the second-
term issue. Cassius M. Clay lined up twenty leading Democrats to
stand behind him. The newspapers commented on his restored vigor
and Kate wrote rather guilefully in August, 1871:

You will probably have seen (still I cut it out and send it you) an
article in the N. Y. Herald, advocating a mutual friend of ours for the next
Presidency. If you meet him in your travels advise him not to make too
many speeches or attend too many celebrations of one sort or another but
to devote all his energies for a while to getting quite well, that he may yet
live a long while to gladden the hearts of his children and if need be
serve his country.

Chase had shown more than a flicker of interest when the New York
committee of the Democratic party sent him the financial plank of the
platform for his approval. He had asked to see the rest. Then he worked
out one of his ambiguous pronouncements:

Its first sentence seems to place one in the position of a man desiring
a nomination for the Presidency. I do not desire it. There has been a time
when I did. I may say this frankly, and say just as frankly that I have no
such desire. If those who agree with me in principle think that my nomination will promote the interests of the country, I shall not refuse the use of
my name. But I shall not seek a nomination, nor am I willing to seem to
seek it. This with no trace of disappointed ambition.

At the moment Chase hankered chiefly for the quiet of Edgewood,
which he had grown to love. While he was in the West, Kate had

taken over the remodeling of the house and had changed all his plans
—he now thought for the better. She had knocked out walls to give
him a larger dining room, with a fine outlook, and had made changes
all through the house. The gas was not yet in at Edgewood and there
was trouble with the cistern, but Kate bore down on the workmen, just
as she had done—and still was doing—at Canonchet. In January both
she and her father bought lavishly at the Catacazy sale. The Russian
Embassy was noted for its fine possessions.

The Chief Justice "was liking his country life better and better." He
had returned to the bench but was taking things easy and managed to
complete his four and a half months of court work. He rarely accepted
an evening engagement. When he did, he spent the night at the Sprague
house on E Street. Kate kept a suite waiting for him at all times.

In midwinter both she and Nettie bore daughters. Nettie was very
ill in New York with hers. Her father wrote to her on February 4, 1872:
"If you were only as well favored in this respect as Katie! It seems almost
a pleasure to her to have children." In fact, Chase had gone to court
with no thought that Kate's baby was imminent, to be met at the door
by an attendant who told him that Mrs. Sprague had a new daughter.
She had been with him at Edgewood a few days earlier and he had
scarcely been aware that she was having another baby. He had ceased
worrying over Kate's facile accouchements. She named the new child
Portia, a gesture to her father's role in public life, since he had not
wished her to christen her son Salmon in his honor.

By March political strings were being pulled to build up Chase for
the national convention of the Liberal Republican party to be held in
Cincinnati. By April Kate, back in the running again, and well aware
that she had little time to spare, gave the last and most elaborate
reception she ever attempted for her father. Her good friend Carl
Schurz watched the spectacle with genuine sadness, observing the drag-
ging limbs and impaired speech of the Chief Justice. He wrote later
that Chase's "futile efforts to appear youthfully vigorous and agile"
were pathetically evident.

Schurz took acid note of Kate's part in it: "Gossip had it that the
reception was given for the very purpose of convincing the political
society of Washington that he was physically as fit to be President as
ever. He was indeed a great man: but, like Henry Clay and Daniel

Webster, how much greater and how much more useful would he have been had he been content with his real greatness."

Kate had rigged the occasion to the limit. It was a balmy spring night and refreshments were served outdoors under a pavilion. The caterers had created their most imaginative effects in an era when such conceits flourished. The Cookes had set a standard in this respect that was fantastic. Kate's garden made a decorative background, with lights sparkling, a fountain playing, banks of flowers shedding fragrance, a formal arrangement of the sun with its rays done in tinted blossoms as the central piece and soft music coming from the house. Indoors, innumerable wax candles flickered over silver and crystal, and there were more of Kate's individualistic flower arrangements on stands and tables.

Her father was posed in a shadowy corner, where he greeted his colleagues of the Supreme Court, such Cabinet members as Kate approved, the diplomats, his old friends, editors and political leaders who might pull strings in the presidential race. Ben Perley Poore was there taking notes, along with Don Piatt, the journalist from Cincinnati who had just founded the *Capital* in Washington, a weekly paper dedicated to exposing corruption in office.

Kate moved among them all, stately in turquoise blue satin, with her favorite diamond and turquoise ornaments and a headdress of turquoise with feathers and flowers. An observer, watching her as she stood beside her father, wrote that she was "dressed magnificently and yet so perfectly that the dress seemed rather part of herself than an outside ornament." But Chase tired long before the evening ended. He still had difficulty with his speech, and it was hard for him to sustain a steady flow of conversation.

Kate's last grand gesture for her father failed, like so much else in her life. Far from seeing Chase as fit to run, her guests caught the impression of a broken hulk. Bitterly Kate accepted the inevitable, swung her allegiance to Greeley against Grant and invited him to stay at Canonchet on his tour through New England. She named one of her rooms for him on this occasion and entertained him royally. Chase backed his old friend and occasional tormentor with enthusiasm. "I see no reason," he wrote, "why the first of journalists should not make the best of Presidents; while I think experience has shown that the time for the adoption of the one-term privilege has fully come."

That summer the Spragues worked hard to divert and build up Chase. They had clambakes in the bowling alley. They played croquet, his favorite game. If he expressed the slightest wish to see anyone, Kate sent off a telegram at once and brought in another guest. Since her house was huge, she could do it. They attended a great political ball at Narragansett and her father worked as well as he could for Greeley.

Meanwhile, Conkling campaigned vigorously for the President, making a flashing speech on his behalf in Cooper Institute. On this occasion, he called Greeley "peevish, eccentric, grotesque and harmless, a man of oddities, flattered by many, and most of all by himself." Kate did not agree with him in this, but the men in whom she was interested swung in various directions politically. Conkling also battled with Schurz and Garfield, both of whom she admired.

At the end of November, Kate, Chase and Sprague all were shocked to learn of Greeley's death. His defeat by Grant had shattered him. "He closed his busy and eventful life last evening at ten before 7," Chase wrote in his diary. "The night came and death came with the night. His last intelligible utterance was 'I know that My Redeemer liveth.'"

All three went to New York for his funeral. So did President Grant. Kate watched the crowds weeping. She shed some tears herself, in a quiet way, for the strange and memorable Mr. Greeley, who had moved in and out of her life for years. Another of her friends would now take hold at the *Tribune*—Whitelaw Reid.

The passing of Horace Greeley had a profound effect on Chase, who also had suffered and sweated for the Presidency and never attained it. He returned to Washington in a tired and dispirited mood, but still looked impressive as he led the Supreme Court Justices in the parade past Grant on New Year's Day, 1873. The shutters were closed. Light poured from the glittering chandeliers in the Blue Room. White drugget covered the carpets to preserve them. Mrs. Grant stood a pace behind the President in pearl gray silk with point lace flounces. Lady Thornton made her bow in purple velvet. Kate noticed that the sober-looking Mrs. Conkling was present, wearing black velvet and lace. She rarely appeared in Washington. Undoubtedly she looked at Mrs. Sprague with more than passing interest, too.

That winter Kate spent as much time with her father as she could. She also edged in again on Mrs. Eastman, who was now in Venice, painting and selling her work for philanthropic causes. Several letters had been lost—or diverted by Kate—but one written on February 24, 1873, reached him and was not found by Kate until after his death. In it Carlotta described Venice during the carnival season, a ceremonial mass she had attended, and a regatta on the Lagoon. She went on: "I don't like to have my letters to you lost. To be sure I intend them to be as proper, as if from a lady Abbess to the Pope; but they are intended for your eyes, and none other. I only wish they were more proper, more interesting, more worthy of your excellent replies." She asked him for his latest portrait, saying with gentle raillery: "I suppose it would be proper for a lady Abbess to ask one of the Pope."

But Carlotta's was a lost cause. Chase might sigh over her provocative letters, but Kate was moving imperiously through another brilliant season. In February she attended a ball given by the Cookes in Georgetown. The house of Cooke was about to crash, but no one had any inkling of the ruin in sight. The Grants were there. So was "Puss" Belknap, whose extravagances were pushing her husband toward ruin. But the bell was beginning to clang on the administration scandals. Kate that month was listening to the debate on the Crédit Mobilier case. She coolly turned opera glasses on Oakes Ames when he was publicly censured by vote of the House of Representatives for selling shares of Crédit Mobilier stock to Congressmen in order to forestall investigation. The attempt to impeach Vice-President Schuyler Colfax failed but the mud stuck.

Once again Chase officiated at the swearing in. Grant's second inauguration was held on a bitterly cold day with a gale from the southwest. The soldier was showing some of the scars of office by this time, but still enjoyed his cigars, his smoke-room friends and widespread popularity. The guests shivered and danced in their wraps at the inaugural ball, although canaries sang blithely in the glare of the gas jets. The building was draped with white muslin and an American eagle hung from the center of the ceiling. Mrs. Henry Cooke looked flashy in emerald green satin. Mrs. Fish huddled in ermine, trying to keep warm. The ice cream was frozen solid. Hot coffee and chocolate were served instead of champagne and claret punch.

The dome of the Capitol gleamed like a beacon. Colored lanterns festooned the streets. Candles burned in windows and shops blazed with gaslight. There were fireworks at nine o'clock but the wind blew the showers of colored sparks in all directions. It was a vile night in Kate's opinion and she would not hear of her father going out to Edgewood. He felt far from well after the strain of the inauguration.

Early in May, just after the Supreme Court adjourned for the summer, Chase announced that he was going to New York to visit Nettie. He called on Henry Cooke and Sumner to say good-bye. Sumner noticed that he talked a great deal of the past and, in speaking of his future plans, he added, "if I live." He had already chosen a biographer to write his life history.

Nettie was living at 4 West Thirty-third Street. Her marriage had turned out happily. On Sunday the Hoyts drove with Chase through Central Park. On Monday he walked down Fifth Avenue with Hiram Barney, discussing Charles Francis Adams' oration on Seward, who had recently died. He seemed to Barney to be in good spirits but tired. He said he was going to Colorado Springs, stopping off at Cincinnati —again "if I live."

Kate was in New York, waiting for Sprague to come up from the South. She thought her father looked ghastly. When his servant went into his room on Tuesday morning, he found that the Chief Justice had had another stroke. Dr. John G. Perry was summoned, and Kate, Sprague, Will Hoyt, Nettie, Edwin Hoyt and Barney stayed close to his bedside all that day and the following night. He did not recognize Kate or Nettie again.

He died on May 7 and services were held for him in St. George's Church. The pallbearers in New York, named by Kate, were Hamilton Fish, Gideon Welles, General Sherman, William Cullen Bryant, William M. Evarts, Charles O'Conor, General McDowell, Gerrit Smith, Mayor Havemeyer, Whitelaw Reid, Hiram Barney and John J. Cisco. A floral coronet of white roses on the coffin was Kate's last tribute to her father, king of men. A large cross of white roses and a broken column of japonicas, violets and rosebuds from the other members of the family, lay athwart the crown.

His body was taken to Washington and the Supreme Court Justices gathered at the Capitol at noon on May 13 to honor his memory. He lay in state on the same catafalque that had been used as a bier for Abraham Lincoln. Flags hung at half-mast in the capital. All courts

adjourned. In death Chase got his due. The newspapers ran pages ex
tolling the Chief Justice. For weeks, Kate read enconiums on he
father. They came from President Grant and from Civil War soldier
he had helped, from men and women in various spheres of life, from
foreign governments and from freed slaves. All the abuse was forgotten
The good he did remained. Only the editorial writers recalled his vault
ing ambition.

For days Kate moved about as if stunned, although the thought o
her father's death could not have been strange to her. He was only sixty
five but his decline had been rapid. She did her suffering in private and
held her head proudly during the funeral services. Hours later she wep
as she moved about in his library at Edgewood, seeing the straight
backed chair where he had sat in majesty; the square desk with lamp
suspended over it; the leaning case of law books close to his hand
the mantelpiece, draped and tasseled, with Kate's picture in the center
None understood as well as she the infinite variety of Salmon Portland
Chase—the complexities of his nature, the nobilities and the vanities
But it was Nettie who wept openly and unrestrainedly for the father sh
had loved. He had never been the symbol of ambition to her—only
kind and loving parent.

That autumn Kate's fourth and last child was born, as easily as all th
others. She was named after her mother and, alone among her children
inherited her looks, but with the blankness of an imbecile child. Kitt
was to be carefully tended by her mother for the rest of her life,
gentle child who became tubercular and never developed normall
either mentally or physically.

Chapter XIV

FURIES LET LOOSE ON RHODE ISLAND

ROSCOE CONKLING was offered the Chief Justiceship after Chase's death, but he declined the honor, saying he would gnaw at the chains. He was master of the Republican party in New York State and a powerful figure in the Senate at the time. He was also an increasingly significant force in the life of Kate Chase, who had watched him rise from an obscure place in the House of Representatives to great power in the Grant administration.

He was at odds with many of her most intimate friends. He helped to break Greeley in Republican circles. He clashed violently in debate with Sumner and Schurz. Garfield thought him a great fighter, but "inspired more by his hates than his loves." Conkling admired Grant. Kate did not. He had never been one of her father's worshipers. But he was the man in her life who seemed to be irresistible to Kate. He understood her ambition and shared her iron will. In Conkling, Kate had met her master. And in Kate the shining knight of the Senate had met his peer.

It took years of sharing counsel with Conkling to show Kate where most of her failures lay. She learned all her lessons too late and in her fifties acknowledged to a friend: "I never cared for the opinion or goodwill of people. I ran my head against a stone wall. It did not hurt the wall but it has hurt my head."

Roscoe, whose approach to his fellows was somewhat similar, did not underestimate Kate's gifts; he made use of them. "I know your bright mind will solve this quicker than mine," he was in the habit of saying as he laid a political problem before her. As a master tactician who had suffered defeat himself, he preached cynicism where her deeply religious father had practiced faith.

Gradually Kate's philosophy changed. She became more than ever the intriguer, working quietly and subtly with Conkling on many public issues, as she had worked with her father, but with the added element now of a raging infatuation. In Conkling she found a man of physical magnetism and political capacity. There was no life for Kate without power. She was thirty-three, unhappily married, frustrated in her guiding ambition and the time was ripe for Conkling to become the focus of her drive for power. His pride matched hers. His arrogance was less well concealed. His looks were equally striking. Neither one could be ignored in any gathering. Everyone stared when they walked together into a room, as they did with increasing frequency after 1873, since Kate needed an escort now that her father was gone and Sprague rarely or never appeared with her in public.

Kate and Conkling made an arresting pair, although Greeley had rubbed some of the shine from the Senator with his damning gibe that he was "The Pet of the Petticoats—the darling of the ladies' gallery who could look hyacinthine in just thirty seconds after the appearance of a woman."

Everything about him was picturesque and flamboyant. He was six feet three, broad shouldered, and was apt to strike attitudes when he made a speech. His hair was almost the same color as Kate's—a ripe gold with glints of red, thick and springy, running to a peak on his forehead. Heavy auburn eyebrows jutted over blue-gray eyes and his carefully curled whiskers were unmistakably Titian red. As one observer put it, the general effect of Conkling's head was that of a burning bush. Or perhaps a Venetian doge.

He was something of a dandy, affecting bright ties and fancily patterned waistcoats. He usually wore light trousers and a black cutaway coat, with gaiters buttoned over high boots. Conkling was a mass of contradictions. He carried a pistol but wrote his letters in violet ink. The notes for his most savage speeches were jotted down on pastel-tinted paper, which lay in evidence as he orated. He was arrogant, impressive in debate and a ruthless fighter for any cause he sponsored.

He feared and detested publicity, snubbed the press, preferred the secret caucus, despised back slappers, was aloof and supercilious.

He led the fight for hard money and had often flouted Chase. His bill to prohibit the secret sales of Treasury gold, pushed in the spring of 1869, was bitterly opposed by Jay Cooke. He voted for the conviction of Johnson and he was a bosom friend of General Grant, even to the point of sitting for hours with one of his cigars unlit in his mouth. Conkling hated cigars and particularly Grant's!

But beyond all else he was an orator, and Kate sat spellbound in the gallery listening to the man who could swing a debate as neither her father nor her husband had ever been able to do. Only Sumner matched him, she believed, but in the days of reconstruction the Senator from Massachusetts had been carried so far by vindictiveness that Chase and Kate were unable to follow him. Conkling disliked reformers, but he had the quality of the spellbinder himself. His speeches, delivered with ease and deliberation, were carefully rehearsed before mirrors, on long country walks or rides and, during the seventies, quite often in the presence of Kate, who was critic as well as admirer.

Although he struck attitudes, he used few gestures, had a deep musical voice and a gift for unanswerable invective equal only to that of Thaddeus Stevens. His sarcasm had withering effect and his facts were assembled with legalistic cunning. To some he was an egotistical coxcomb and rogue; to others he was the great statesman and orator of the Grant era. From time to time he loomed up as a presidential possibility, but was too proud to come out in the open and admit that he coveted the honor. Once again Kate was to preside unhappily over this familiar and distracting procedure.

Conkling was tacitly but amicably separated from his sage and patient wife, who lived with their daughter Bessie in a square stone house in Utica, where she devoted herself to her garden and her charities and was described as "composed, gentle and firm." In fact, Sumner, who had discussed poetry with her at a dinner given in honor of Grant before his first inauguration, remarked: "Do you know, she is one of the few women who can talk sense." Kate, in Sumner's opinion, was another. But Conkling went home to vote, corresponded in a friendly way with his wife, and there is much evidence that she accepted his philandering propensities in the spirit of the age.

Kate inherited Edgewood from her father, but before moving in, she took all the children abroad that summer with a retinue now augmented by a German governess and two French maids. On her return her political salon was moved from the house on E Street to the old mansion outside Washington. She enlarged the staff her father had kept and ran Edgewood along the lines of an English country estate, with her butler, Albert Wells, in command. She kept her father's library just as he had left it and when uncertain or troubled, she often sat at his desk and evoked the past.

She had much to be troubled about as 1873 faded into 1874, for the powerful houses of Jay Cooke and Sprague, with which her fortunes were so closely tied, crashed in 1873, with reverberations heard on both sides of the Atlantic. The Cooke collapse was sudden, unexpected and complete. The Sprague decline was more gradual.

Kate was staggered by the news of the Cooke failure. From girlhood she had thought of Jay Cooke as a Croesus of inexhaustible wealth and power. She had innumerable memories of his generosity, of great parties given by Jay and Henry, of her father's devotion to both men, of the role they had played during the Civil War. She was slower to comprehend the extent of the ruin in her own family. The Governor's warnings about expenditure had become repetitious and meaningless, as she poured more thousands into Canonchet; bought more and more Paris clothes and European art treasures; and indulged every whim in entertainment, political promotion for her father, travel and worldly diversion.

Like Chase she had never had a glimmering of common sense where her personal finances were concerned. Bills and debts had been almost an obbligato in her life until she married Sprague. Now she was faced with the same old situation on a much vaster scale and her extravagant tastes had multiplied. She had started things at Canonchet that could not be stopped. Contracts had been signed. Workmen still were busy at the establishment on Rhode Island.

But the well had at last dried up. When she asked her husband for more money, it was not forthcoming. His own affairs were in complete confusion. His speeches had hurt his credit. Many of his investments had turned out badly. Banks refused him credit and he issued notes that he could not meet. Creditors pressed him for the immediate payment

Kate Chase Sprague being entertained in camp by General J. J. Ambercrombie

Roscoe Conkling

of a huge indebtedness. The Sprague empire crumbled by degrees. The mills did not close but hard times had hit the country. For a period the estate was administered by a trustee, Zechariah Chafee, Jr., the reports showing assets of $16,000,000 and debts amounting to $14,000,000. The Governor helped at first to run the mills and thereby had some income. Finally the Spragues went into total bankruptcy. The settlement of the estate hung fire for years, with involved litigation and ultimate shotgun defence of Canonchet by Governor Sprague, who defied all efforts to oust him from the house Kate had built. Eventually it again became legally his by purchase as his fortunes rose to some degree through marriages in his family.

After he left the Senate in 1875, Sprague rarely appeared in Washington. His house on E Street was involved in the litigation. In breaking up his estate, he shipped some of Amasa's fine blooded horses to Kate for herself and the children. By this time her affairs were so complicated that she was getting legal advice from Conkling on how to meet the situation. A depression was on. Banks had crashed. Railroad stocks had toppled. Corruption flourished in the Grant administration.

Although a will made by Chase in 1870 showed that he was leaving an estate valued at $150,000 to be divided equally between his daughters, there was little in the end that was realizable. Most of his investments through Joshua Hanna and Jay Cooke had proved disastrous. Chase had always been careful not to become directly involved with Cooke in financial ventures, although he accepted his advice on some investments. He had repeatedly resisted Jay's efforts to enrich him and said in this connection: "I shall never cease to be glad and grateful that I laid down for myself the rule, after Congress gave me such great powers, enabling me to raise and depress values very largely at my discretion, that I would have nothing to do directly or indirectly with speculations or transactions, in gold or securities of any sort, for my own or anybody's private benefit." In the end he had little to leave but Edgewood.

Sumner died on a March day in 1874 and Kate felt that another close link with the past was gone. Seward, Chase, Sumner—all titans of the Civil War era, all dying within a few months of one another. Two months later she attended the wedding of Nellie Grant, aged nineteen, at the White House. The President's daughter had met Algernon Charles Frederic Sartoris, Fanny Kemble's nephew, on the Scotia returning from Europe. Nellie, a favorite in Washington, was married in the East Room in a bower of flowers and white ribbons, with a marriage bell of white roses swinging over her head. One of the eight bridesmaids in white corded silk with overdresses of illusion was Bessie Conkling, Roscoe's only child, who was later to earn his undying ill will by marrying "beneath her." Thereafter he referred to her always as "Mrs. Conkling's daughter." Actually the youth was well to do, but he was working his way up from the bottom, studying railroads, and he sometimes appeared in greasy overalls.

Even Kate approved Nellie's wedding dress, the magnificent gifts in the library, the banquet held in the State dining room around a bride's cake crowned with a bouquet of white flowers, and Mrs. Grant's mauve silk gown with pansies. Kate was moving further and further away from the White House herself and was snubbing many of the parties given by the Grant satellites, but she preserved the amenities and could find nothing to dislike in Mrs. Grant or Nellie. Both were deferential to her.

To the astonishment of all who knew her, Kate auctioned off many of her father's things in the spring of 1875, two years after his death. This meant throwing open Edgewood to a public horde, who picked over his treasures with unfeeling curiosity. She reserved the best of her father's books and pictures, as well as personal mementos, but much else went under the hammer. His library was not disturbed.

The auction was held on a rainy day. Even Edgewood looked dreary in its framework of bare trees, as strangers and old friends drove up to the doorway over a road boggy with mud. The house faced south and the veranda ran along its entire front. The Capitol could be seen through mist. Upstairs, on the top landing, visitors viewed the painting of Catherine Garniss, Chase's first, and possibly his most beloved, wife. The graceful, clever-looking, but by no means beautiful, woman in amber satin, with a square of embroidery in her hands, had never been anything but an eyesore to Kate, who was said even to have refused her father's official biographer the Garniss letters, lest they diminish her own mother's place in his affections. The Garniss painting, however, was not for sale.

The portrait of Kate's mother in puffed grey satin hung in her bedroom and was viewed with interest by the visiting press. A portrait of Abraham Lincoln attracted attention in Chase's bedroom. His stature grew with time. Between the windows in the back parlor hung a portrait of the Chief Justice, and beneath it on a bracket stood a marble bust of Byron. Kate had always seen a close resemblance between the poet and her father, as he was in his younger days, before his hair receded, leaving a domed forehead. The likeness was marked in the portrait she had chosen to hang close to the bust. Pictures of the Chief Justice dominated every room and a bas-relief of him over the library door attracted the eye at once. The front parlor had a Fra Angelico, a Greuze, a Rosa Bonheur and a picture of William Harvey, discoverer of the circulation of the blood, in an elaborately carved Florentine frame.

None of the pictures was sold, but Oriental vases, French gilt clocks, majolica, marble and bronze busts, cabinets, statuettes and ornaments of all kinds went under the hammer, as well as china, glass and silver. Many of the pieces had been brought from Europe by Kate as gifts for her father. Others showed the Sumner interest in ceramics and Oriental art. Actually, the sale brought little, but it made way for the handsome things that Kate was moving in from her old residence on E Street. She intended to make Edgewood her permanent Washington home, and she brought fresh assets to its wide hall and spacious rooms.

In spite of the decline in the Sprague fortunes, she found it hard to break up the expensive pattern of living she had established for herself. Money melted like snow. She no longer gave large parties, but became more of the intimate sibyl in political councils, making her dinners exclusive affairs. She had fewer politicians to truckle to now that her father was dead. Between 1875 and 1880 her romance with Conkling was at its height and was the talk of Washington. Soon they were asked routinely to the same parties. It would have been difficult for these two conspicuous characters to have concealed their growing infatuation in the gossipy capital. The press correspondents observed the ardor with which they exchanged glances and how frequently Mrs. Sprague was in attendance when Conkling was due to speak. They made merry with Conkling when, seeing that a note was coming down from the gallery, he stood facing the Senate and orating with his hands behind his back, so that the page could slip Kate's message into his waiting palm.

Did she prime him politically now and again, or did the notes contain compliments or affectionate nothings? It is unlikely that seasoned Kate would spend her time sending love messages to a Senator on the floor. But it was a self-evident fact that when his colleagues crowded around him to congratulate him on his spectacular two-day speech on the Electoral Commission bill in January, 1877, it was Kate's approval that he awaited, Kate's message that brightened him up, tired and ill from malaria though he was at the time. She had watched every stage of this mighty effort.

This bill was to have an important bearing on the Hayes-Tilden election dispute. Both sides charged corruption at the polls. Samuel J. Tilden, the Democratic candidate, led Rutherford B. Hayes in the popular vote by 250,000, but Hayes finally was elected by 185 electoral votes to 184 for Tilden. Conkling was one of the five senators who, along with five representatives and five justices of the Supreme Court, were delegated to settle the issue. The uproar surrounding this election almost precipitated another war.

Kate was credited in current gossip, and in print by Alexander K. McClure, a contemporary observer, with having tipped the balance in the defeat of Tilden. According to McClure:

The action of Tilden defeating Chase in the Democratic convention of 1868 had its sequel with mingled romance and reality in the defeat of Tilden for the Presidency in 1877, when the vote of Louisiana was passed upon by the Senate. Kate Chase Sprague was the most brilliant woman in Washington society during the war period, and in every way one of the most attractive.

Her home in Washington was the center of the most accomplished men in public life, and among them was Roscoe Conkling, the ablest of the Republican Senators. The contest for the Presidency before the Electoral Commission in 1876-77 turned on the vote of Louisiana, and it required the approving vote of the Senate to give the electoral vote of that state to Hayes. Had it been given to Tilden, he would have been the President. Many believed that Hayes had not been elected and should not be declared elected, and among those who shared that conviction was Mr. Conkling, altho' he did not publicly express it.

The Senate was carefully canvassed, and enough Republican votes were marshalled to throw the vote of the Senate in favor of Tilden on the Louisiana issue if Conkling would lead in support of that policy, and it was understood that he had agreed to do so. When the crucial time came Conkling did not appear at all, and the anti-Hayes Republicans, being without a leader, fell back to their party lines and gave the vote of the state and the Presidential certificate to Hayes. It is an open secret that Conkling resolved his doubts as urged by Mrs. Sprague, who thereby avenged the defeat of her father in the Democratic nomination of 1868, that had been accomplished by Tilden; and thus Tilden lost the Presidency, to which he had been elected by a popular majority of over 250,000.

Actually, there is no irrefutable evidence that Tilden was responsible for Chase's defeat in 1868, although Kate always insisted that he was. Moreover, George Hoadly, Governor of Ohio and one of Tilden's counsels before the Electoral Commission, sharply denied that she had any part in the overthrow of his client, thereby leaving the question open to debate. Hoadly was a close friend of the Chases and later figured as one of Kate's lawyers in her divorce suit.

But there is no doubt that Kate pulled political strings behind Conkling during this period, in so far as the arrogant Roscoe could be influenced by any other human being. She was known to push certain appointments. And when her financial difficulties became acute and taxes for Edgewood were piling up, Conkling was responsible for legislation that exempted the Chase estate from all taxation, a concession to the eminent role the Chief Justice had played in public affairs. Conkling, however, was only one of a number of prominent men who drove by carriage or galloped out to Edgewood on horseback to consult their oracle about measures under debate. Occasionally he observed Schurz's dark horse along the road.

Kate was in her element in 1876. Conkling was deeply involved in the presidential battle and again she was moving pawns behind the scenes and comforting an ambitious, but ill-starred, warrior. She had been generalissimo for so long that the habit persisted. Conkling was less philosophical than her father. He was also a better fighter and much tougher grained. But his pride also kept him hedging. He was silently and receptively in the field for nomination, where Blaine was out in the open. Neither man won. Rutherford B. Hayes did. It took all Kate's wiles to soothe Conkling, but she was expert at flattering and restoring a disappointed idol.

She followed every move in the long-drawn-out feud between Conk-

ling and Blaine, the man of many gifts and suave tongue who could
do what Conkling never could—forgive an enemy. They had battled
since 1866, first in the House, then in the Senate. Blaine was courteous
to Kate. He had been her guest at Canonchet and on E Street. But,
like Seward, he had watched her clever maneuvers for many years and
was not one of her satellites, although even her father's enemies at
times respected Kate. Blaine regarded her with a particularly wary
eye after she became closely identified with Conkling.

Kate was on friendly terms with Harriet, his quiet and sometimes
frosty-mannered wife from Maine. And she was by no means dead to
the magnetic manner of this robust, courteous and eloquent politician.
She admired his long bearded face, full eyes and the self-possessed and
impartial manner he used in the Speaker's chair. Few matched him
in illustrative oratory, in his lucid way of arguing a point.

But she was in league with the red-headed knight of the same party
to head him off in the 1880 election, and as she became more in-
fatuated with Conkling, her hatred of Blaine grew strong. Years earlier,
on the floor of the House, Blaine had spoken of Conkling's "grandil-
oquent swell, his majestic, supereminent, overpowering, turkey-gobbler
strut." Conkling had never forgotten these insults. The Blaine-Conkling
feud affected all the local and state campaigns and kept the Republican
party stirred up for years, until Conkling finally retired from public life.

He was so flamboyant that he was a natural target for deflation.
George William Curtis, of *Harper's Weekly*, sniped at him for years.
Charles Stanley Reinhart and Thomas Nast flashed ridicule at him
with their pencils. Kate must have suffered over Olivia's jab that he
was the Apollo of the Senate, with "beauty of the aquamarine type."
When Olivia saw him reading a yellow-bound pamphlet, she was sure
he had selected it because the binding matched his hair!

In 1876 there were ninety-two Stock Exchange failures, the country
absorbed half a million new immigrants, inflation was in full play, the
Centennial Exhibition in Philadelphia was drawing crowds and the Cus-
ter massacre had stirred the nation. The carpetbaggers were in full cry in
the South. Corruption in the Grant administration had reached its peak,
but the gay days along the Potomac and at the summer palace in Long
Branch were nearing an end. Scandals had piled up, culminating in the
impeachment of General Belknap and his resignation from office. This

removed "Puss" from Kate's horizon—not that she had ever regarded "Puss" as a serious contender. Grant's private secretary, Orville E. Babcock, accused of implication in the Whisky Ring, was acquitted that same year as a result of Grant's deposition regarding his excellent character.

Kate heard much about the bar pins for wives, the diamond studs for men, the personal gifts and fabulous entertaining in exchange for political favors. She thought that political standards had reached their lowest ebb. She and Conkling frequently discussed the charges of corruption as they came up, but the Senator always defended Grant. He kept his own coattails out of the mud but he stood firmly by the square-jawed, silent President. He had pointed out in his Cooper Institute speech on Grant's behalf that Wellington, Marlborough, Nelson, Cromwell and Fairfax all had accepted favors. But Kate turned up her nose at much that went on around Grant, close as Roscoe was to the picture. She considered the regime loud, vulgar, ostentatious, and corrupt.

Early in 1877, the year of the great railroad strike, Kate went abroad again, and when Conkling crossed later in the summer, ostensibly for his health, there was gossip in Washington that these two boon companions were seeing much of each other in London and Paris. Grant by this time had left for his tour around the world.

In London Conkling admired the pluck with which "high born girls rode without groom or companion through tangled thoroughfares." But the women, the horses and the carriages disappointed him. Mrs. Edwards Pierrepont, wife of the U. S. Minister to Great Britain, drove him through Hyde Park and he was struck by the degree of individual wealth in London.

Was Kate with Conkling when he visited Benjamin Franklin's lodgings, Ben Jonson's house, the palace of Richard III turned coffee house, Oliver Goldsmith's grave? Did she wander through Westminster Abbey with the Senator, view Pitt's monument, which he thought a "poor thing," and hear him remark: "There lies the effigy of that monster Elizabeth?" Did she agree with Conkling when he described the newly erected Albert Monument as "the greatest thing he saw in London"? Was she his guide and companion as he viewed the art treasures of Paris? Their friends in Washington thought so, at any rate, as Conkling's letters detailed his impressions.

Kate was as much at home in British and French circles now as she was in Washington. The diplomatic set made much of her. She appeared regularly on the most exclusive lists, but she no longer ordered gowns by the dozen from Worth. In fact, on each trip abroad she was quietly disposing of her jewels. It was almost impossible now to get money out of the Governor, who was juggling his complicated affairs in Rhode Island with considerable furore.

On his return from Europe, Conkling was welcomed enthusiastically in New York. He was driven like a hero through cheering crowds to the Fifth Avenue Hotel, where Gilmore's band of fifty pieces played Southern melodies on the porch in the late evening and he made a speech about his trip to Europe. Music and fireworks greeted him at Albany, Schenectady, Little Falls and Utica, where his lawn was illuminated with Chinese lanterns and locomotive lamps. It all gave a brisk start to that year's senatorial contest in his native state.

When Kate reached home she was all but thrown from a window. She went straight to Canonchet, where one of her more serious rows with the Governor developed. As she described it later, when she brought suit for divorce, Sprague entered her room at night in a drunken state, seized her bodily, dragged her to the window, which was in an upper story, and attempted to heave her out. But Kate, strong and tall, fought like a wildcat. The Governor was no match for her. He was the one who had to go lurching back, until she was able to push him out and lock the door on him. This was by no means the only occasion on which they battled physically as well as verbally. In her suit she charged that he frequently assaulted her when in his cups and readily became violent.

After this, Kate threw the last shreds of discretion to the winds and did as she liked. Her father had served as a powerful check for her behavior. As long as he lived, he could make her respond to the moral and religious principles he had instilled in his daughters from infancy. Time and again he had kept her home intact by prayer, tact and judicial advice, but nothing could stay the furies gathering around her now.

Kate went about quite openly with Conkling. Her carriage often picked him up at the Capitol. The Senate watched each move with interest, and the gossip became so general that it burst into print through the chatty ladies of the press gallery. One particular episode whipped up a storm of talk in February, 1878. Conkling and Senator Lucius Lamar, an old-time Southern statesman who had supported Jefferson Davis's administration and acted as Confederate commissioner in Europe, clashed over a Mississippi River improvement bill.

The word "liar" flashed between the Senators and Conkling coolly and deliberately observed: "Should the member from Mississippi, except in the presence of the Senate, charge me by intention or otherwise, with falsehood, I would denounce him as a blackguard, as a coward and a liar."

At once there was uproar in the Senate, both on the floor and in the galleries. Kate, beautifully gowned in black embroidered with gold, her white face framed by a black lace bonnet crowned with two rows of roses, shading from pink to fuchsia, sat with her father's old friend, Simon Cameron, and his wife. Cameron rushed downstairs in a state of great excitement as the Senators booed and cheered. The story quickly circulated that Kate, leaning over the railing, deadly pale, had almost fainted. For days there was talk of duels, Southern chivalry and concealed pistols. Conkling was sure his antagonist was going around armed. He was a crack pistol shot himself. The Southern papers made much of the episode.

But in the midst of all the gossip, Kate found an unexpected champion in the vitriolic Mrs. Jane Gray Swisshelm, who wrote vinegary notes from the press gallery. She had also been Mrs. Lincoln's defender. Women came first! On this occasion she insisted that when Kate went into Conkling's office alone she went in on business and "not to make love." Mrs. Swisshelm dismissed the exchange of notes as a common practice in the Senate. Common also were "smiles of approval exchanged." Disposing of Kate's part in the Conkling-Lamar episode, she wrote: "They say she nearly fainted. . . . The day Benton attacked Foote one-fourth of the ladies showed alarm. They say Kate Chase rose, leaned over the gallery with blanched face . . . that she is singled out among others shows the deadly malice, jealousy and hatred of 'petticoat brigadiers' in Washington society."

But in August, 1879, when Kate was in much deeper trouble and all the New York newspapers were on her trail, she gave the *Sun* her own version of this affair:

The story that I almost fainted at the idea of an encounter between Senator Conkling and Senator Lamar is utterly false. I hardly knew of the affair until it was over, and I am certain that I exhibited no more feeling than as a warm personal friend of Senator Conkling. There were others who exhibited far more feeling than I. I sat beside Mrs. Senator Cameron, and believe that Mr. Cameron, in his excitement, rushed down the marble staircase two steps at a time, in order to get on the floor before the trouble was over. The report that I wrote notes to Mr. Conkling on that occasion is a shameless falsehood. I certainly would not do so; obviously, it would be an improper and unladylike action.

The same absolute contradiction is due from me of the stories of my remaining out at late hours and meeting Mr. Conkling at the Capitol. I am compelled to speak plainly of these outrageous slanders, because of their wide publicity—of all the crops of slanders which have sprung up. I loathe to speak of these things, but they have been dwelt upon until, instead of monstrous falsehoods, they appear to the public like admitted facts. At the proper time, and in the proper place, I will show the true character and origin of the persecution. I can honestly say that I want the truth, and every particle of the truth, about this matter to be known at the proper time.

With the Hayes administration, many changes were on the way. The bearded, keen-eyed lawyer from Ohio saw the telephone come into use in the first year of his administration, watched electric light flashing from street lamps and approved the exodus of freed Negroes to the northern states as the period of reconstruction ended and Federal troops left the South. The day of the carpetbagger was over.

Again Kate had a close link with the administration—Carl Schurz was appointed Secretary of the Interior. It had become habitual— Lincoln and her father, Grant and Conkling, Hayes and Schurz. It was widely known that Schurz rode out to Edgewood to read off to Kate the first draft of the Civil Service reform bill, but Kate was skeptical. She had seen too much political corruption to believe that competitive examinations would work.

Lucy Webb Hayes was a new type for the White House and Kate noted her lack of vanities, her brunette good looks, her sturdy competence and crisp ways. She was a college graduate and lived in the same

radition of temperance and family prayers in which Salmon Port-
and Chase had nurtured his daughters. Hayes did not drink, curse or
chew, a change from his predecessor. Mrs. Hayes devoted herself to
charities and church work and shepherded her large family regularly
nto the Red Room for hymns and Stephen Foster ballads. No wine
was served at the White House table and there was little gaiety during
his regime after the bounty of the Grant administration.

But the ebony furniture and satin upholstery received the most
meticulous care from Lucy Hayes. Baskets of flowers and pots of greenery
abounded in the White House. She wore ruby satin at receptions and
offered the tips of her fingers to the passing throng. Some called her
Lemonade Lucy but the public as a whole approved her. They rejoiced in her silver wedding anniversary. She revived Mrs. Lincoln's
custom, abandoned by Mrs. Grant, of separating the sheep from the
goats by having official and very important persons come in through a
separate entrance. Mrs. Grant had thought this invidious.

Prosperity returned to the United States with the Hayes administration. The Civil War was truly over. But in 1879 a worn and aging
woman arrived from Europe, after a stay in Pau and Nice. This was
Mrs. Lincoln, who had gone abroad after a year passed in a mental
institution. When she stepped ashore, she thought the crowd had gathered for her—an echo of the past. But a policeman put his hand on the
shoulder of the "little old woman with a wrinkled face and streaks
of white in her hair" and moved her aside to let the real star step
into her carriage—Sarah Bernhardt.

Mrs. Lincoln was on her way back to spend the rest of her troubled
days at the home of her sister, Mrs. Ninian Edwards, in Springfield,
where she would die obscurely in the summer of 1882. But however
deep her misery that summer, she had no cause to envy Kate, who
was heading straight for public disaster.

Chapter XV

᪐᪐᪐᪐ ᪐᪐᪐᪐

A SHOTGUN FOR ROSCOE CONKLING

THE EXPLOSION that had long been brewing in the Sprague family came to a head in the summer of 1879, when the Governor ran amuck and Rhode Island sizzled with the scandal. His jealousy had reached a peak of frenzy that could no longer be controlled, and Kate had lost the guidance of her father. Canonchet was like a castle besieged and the name Sprague flashed into the headlines. A shotgun raid, Kate under lock and key, her flight with her children and the final separation of the Spragues made a chain of news events that Conkling's strategic efforts in New York could not wholly suppress.

Early in the summer there were preliminary skirmishes over a German tutor, George Linck, whom Kate had engaged for the summer at fifty dollars a month to teach Willie and Ethel some German. Sprague adored Willie but paid little attention to the girls. He thought that Kate was too severe with their son and was making him study unduly hard at the expense of his health. She had kept him in a German boarding school for a year. Kate, on the other hand, felt that the Governor was indulgent and was spoiling the boy. He encouraged him to play with guns. He was always pleasure-bent with Willie, taking him away from classes to attend the races, to ride or to shoot. Kate was applying her father's standards to the upbringing of her children, both in their education and behavior. But she wished them to have fun, too.

"Willie proved a good boy, attentive and willing to study—we walked, talked, bathed, fished and had our meals together," Linck reported from Canonchet, where he had gone with the boy ahead of Kate, who was to follow with her daughters and staff.

But when Sprague found Linck at Canonchet, he greeted him with hostility, asked him what business he had being there, ordered him off the premises and took Willie to Newport to watch the races. Linck reported all this to Kate, who wrote at once to the Governor, asking him to return Willie to Linck's custody and saying that this would be a condition of her remaining at Narragansett that summer. She had received permission from Zechariah Chafee, the trustee, to occupy Canonchet for the time being. It no longer belonged unencumbered to the Spragues.

In the meantime Linck packed his bags and returned to New York, but when he reported to Kate at the Hotel Westminster she insisted firmly that he must travel back with her and the girls and take over Willie's care. Returning with the rest of Kate's retinue, they all stopped off at Watch Hill, Rhode Island. The Governor met them there. When he saw Linck, he brandished his walking stick at him and used abusive language. But Kate urged the tutor to go on with them to Canonchet.

Linck's reappearance at the house led to more excitement on the part of Sprague, who by this time seemed to be jealous of Linck, as well as annoyed by his role of tutor to the children. Linck later told of threats on his life, of the Governor pushing him around as he got into a buggy to leave, then running off to get a shotgun and pursuing him in another carriage with a fast mare. He caught up with Linck at a wine house, but the woman who ran it hid Linck in the kitchen and eventually he got away.

Excitement over this occurrence was only twenty-four hours cold when Conkling visited Canonchet in the absence of the Governor, who ostensibly had gone to Portland but was later thought to have set a trap for Kate. Conkling was cruising on a yacht off Newport and Kate met him at Narragansett Pier. Throop Martin, of Auburn, New York, and his wife and daughter, good friends of Conkling's, were staying with Kate at the time. So was Emma Fosdick, of Cincinnati, one of her most intimate friends.

But the Governor returned unexpectedly at three in the morning two nights later and threw the household at Canonchet into an uproar. The first version of the story to get into circulation was that a faithful servant warned Kate of his arrival and Conkling hopped through a window, leaving all his belongings behind him. He went to the home of friends nearby, but was back sartorially perfect on the piazza in the morning when Sprague at last caught up with him.

After prowling in the grounds for a time with his shotgun, the Governor alarmed Miss Martin, when she ran into him later that morning, with the somber announcement that there was going to be a tragedy at the house. She hastily went off to order a barouche so that her father might be removed from so hectic a place.

When Sprague reached the piazza, Conkling was sitting on a lounge running through the newspapers and Kate was conversing with him at a window. When Conkling saw the gun he rose hurriedly.

"Are you armed, sir?" the Governor inquired politely.

"No, I am not," said Conkling.

"Then I give you five minutes to get off these premises. If you are not away I will fire at you."

Kate then entered the picture and, as she later described the scene to reporters:

"Mr. Conkling walked straight across the room to where I stood and said: 'Mrs. Sprague, your husband is very much excited, and I think it better for all of us if I should withdraw. If my departure puts you in any danger, so say, and I will stay, whatever the consequences.' He spoke in a very calm voice although I know he must have been very excited. I told him not to mind me, but that if Mr. Sprague was in a passion, it would be useless to argue with him, and might only lead to violence."

Conkling was about to leave when the carryall arrived for Mr. Martin, and Kate asked him to help the aged and feeble gentleman to get down stairs, which he did. As Kate later told the press, the Governor stood about fifty feet off on the edge of the piazza, "eyeing us in a desperate sort of way. I knew I had done nothing wrong, and I tried to be as calm as I could."

Meanwhile Ethel put her arm around Conkling and begged him

not to go, but Kate said firmly: "No, Ethel, Mr. Conkling will go, but no one shall hurt either him or us."

Sprague said nothing as Conkling left, but as soon as he was out of the house, he started in pursuit. He finally caught up with him at Billingtons, a restaurant where Conkling had just ordered some steamed clams. A scene was staged there that made local history.

After their departure, Willie reported to Kate that his father had gone off in the buggy with his shotgun. He had asked him for some caps, having none himself, but the boy had thought it better not to give them to his father.

"Mamma," he said. "Papa's gun is loaded with three slugs and if he shoots anyone he will kill them sure."

"I have reason to be grateful that no one was murdered," Kate commented at this point in her story.

But there was more to come. The Governor returned to Canonchet and drove Kate out. By noon she had left for Providence with her daughters. She returned with a lawyer and stayed at first with the same friends who were supposed to have harbored Conkling in his embarrassment. Then she moved to Tower House.

Her lawyer went to Canonchet to get their clothing, but was denied admission. Kate had been driven away with nothing but what she was wearing. Sprague called to see her at the hotel and they had another violent scene.

"Your man got away pretty quick that time, didn't he?" said the Governor.

Kate was silent.

"Where is that five thousand dollars you got recently?" he demanded. "I suppose you have squandered it all. Do you intend to come back to Canonchet?"

"I fear for my life if I do," said Kate quietly.

"I never harmed anyone, and you are safe," the Governor assured her. He seemed to be in a sober mood.

Kate began to talk quietly about the children, striving to keep her temper. Willie was still at Canonchet. Now Sprague demanded that she give him the custody of the girls, too. It was later reported that Kate used some hot words at this stage, as well as the Governor. But in the end her lawyer advised her to surrender the children temporarily

to her husband. She acquiesced against her will and Sprague drove off
with Ethel, Portia and Kitty, but by evening Kate was frantic with
anxiety, not knowing what might happen to them. She swallowed her
pride and drove over to Canonchet. Silence then enfolded the house.
No visitors were admitted. Bells were not answered. Notes were not
delivered.

The story soon spread that Kate was prisoner in the fine home she
had built on the shore. Miss Fosdick, who had stayed often at Canonchet and knew the neighboring families, managed to get notes out by
a maid, which established the fact that Kate was indeed under duress.
By this time the story had broken into print in Boston, Providence,
Washington, Cincinnati and New York, and with thundering repercussions. A bartender at Billingtons had telegraphed a scrappy but
sensational account of the night's events to a New York paper. Conkling's political enemies made the most of it. He was promoting a third
term for Grant at the time and was fighting Blaine, as usual. The
story of his embarrassment spread like wildfire in the political clubs.

Attempts were made at Narragansett to confuse the issue by shifting
the emphasis from Conkling to Linck. The Senator was accused of
being party to this deceit, although Kate vehemently denied this when
she was able finally to have her say. The same shotgun elements had
entered into both cases. They had occurred within a day of each
other. But this effort to save Conkling's skin did not work.

One sensation followed another so rapidly and the stories were so
conflicting that it was not until Kate finally sent for a reporter from
the Sun and talked to him at length, that any clear-cut picture
emerged. The Governor, naturally inclined to be voluble, was advised
by his lawyers to say nothing. Conkling, always hostile to the press,
kept silent, but pulled strings assiduously when he got back to New
York to squash a public airing of the incident.

Kate, however, was the one who in her desperation talked with
some abandon. After her stormy interview with Sprague at the Tower
House, she wrote a so-called "private" letter that promptly appeared
in the Providence Journal. This soon became quite the most public
letter of the day, appearing in the New York Tribune on August 15,
1879, and also clear across the country. It infuriated the Governor

still further, for in it she washed some very dirty linen in a way that her father never would have approved:

As you must have surmised, Governor Sprague's dissolute life and dissipated habits have long ago interrupted our marital relations, though I have striven hard, through untold humiliation and pain, to hide from the world, for my children's sake, the true condition of a blighted, miserable domestic life.

About a year ago, even this poor semblance abruptly culminated, after a disgraceful orgy and arrest at Nantasket Beach, with the circumstances of which many people in Rhode Island are not unfamiliar. I then sought, with my little girls, the neighborhood of old friends and the shelter of my honored father's former home. There, dwelling almost within the shadow of his tomb, I felt more secure, less unprotected. Here kindly sympathy sought me out, and though covert malice pointed some censorious comments, relief came, and our circumscribed means were adequate to our simple and quiet mode of life.

Kate then said that the Governor had contributed nothing to the family support for the last six months, that when she had mentioned unpaid bills he had told her to "look to her powerful Washington friends for aid." His "causeless and shameful persecution of the children's teacher" was due to his unwillingness "to be subjected to the restraint at the table, and in the household observances, of the constant presence of a gentleman." The attempt to implicate Mr. Conkling in this matter was "too absurd" since he and Linck had never met or even seen each other. And, added Kate, "Mr. Conkling was of course as unconscious as I that Governor Sprague sought occasion to enact the tragic role of the injured husband."

Kate's "private letter" put Sprague on the defensive, so that when the *Sun* reporter insisted on seeing her, he finally gained entry to Canonchet on August 16. The Governor was surrounded by lawyers when the interviewer was ushered in. At first he refused to let him see Kate. Finally he took the reporter into a retiring room and there fervently denied that his wife was a prisoner. She came and went as she liked, saw the children and had daily contact with her maid and the governess, Sprague insisted. He merely hoped to keep her quiet and composed for a few days, "and beyond the reach of distracting influences, so as to induce a frame of mind in which she might come to some under-

standing about her future relations with him." He was perfectly willing
for her to see anyone she wished, but he could not consent to her "keeping up a private correspondence with the persons whose object was to
destroy the peace and honor of his family."

At this point the reporter did some persuasive talking to Sprague,
who was back in his sober senses and also was in quite a predicament.
Finally the Governor called in his nephew, Arthur Watson, and said:
"Take this gentleman to Mrs. Sprague."

He was led up the great winding staircase of mahogany that Kate
had brought from Italy, and was ushered into a room on the second
floor, "half parlor, half library, with a bay window, looking out on the
lawn." Kate sat in an armchair close to a table. She was white as marble
when she rose to receive her two guests. But she was quite calm. Once
or twice the reporter noticed a slight trembling of the lips, but she held
her head proudly and had perfect command of the situation. Her
visitor was impressed with her "native eloquence and grace, which
would make a powerful impression on the most obdurate." He thought
her language clear and well chosen and her poise most admirable.

Kate first denied that at her Tower House meeting with Sprague she
had accused him of lying or had made the "verbal attacks upon him
which I have been represented as doing." On the contrary, she "bore
with meekness the unmanly sneers and reproaches that he showered
on me, not responding save when my children's relations to me were
touched upon."

He had accused her of trying to poison Willie's mind against him
through Linck, Kate charged. For thirteen years her life had been a
"constant burden and drag upon her." Mr. Conkling had now been
drawn into the case without a particle of excuse. She had known him for
years, as she had known scores of other public men through her father
and husband. The immediate trouble, she insisted, developed from a
business transaction over the pasturing of the horses Sprague had sent
from Rhode Island to her home. There had been some question about
where to keep them. Conkling had introduced her to the farmer who
pastured his own horse. The farmer billed the Governor for this service
but no payment was forthcoming until "I began to feel scandalized,"
said Kate. The farmer appealed to Conkling and threatened to sue
him, "having by his introduction to my husband become the surety of
the payment."

According to Kate, Conkling wrote to Sprague at this juncture, pointing out that he could not be expected to pay any lady's bills, least of all a married lady's, and that it would be an insult to Mrs. Sprague to propose it, but that he, Conkling, would gladly give Sprague the money to meet the bill and let him repay it whenever he could.

Kate was indignant and chided her husband for allowing the Senator to make such an offer. She said she would sell anything she had to raise the money rather than accept such assistance. "And yet this petty, contemptible squabble was the commencement of all my husband's jealousy of Mr. Conkling," Kate continued. But even after this he still sought Conkling's legal advice over his troubles with his creditors. "There was perfect and entire cordiality between them then, although these scandals, it is now charged, had been known in Washington for years," Kate went on earnestly.

"There is not a word of truth in all of these atrocious reports," she added emphatically. "Mr. Conkling never paid me any attention that a wife could not honorably receive from her husband's friend, and it is false to say otherwise." Her husband was "simply worked upon by his business troubles, which had been culminating for years, and by his indulgence in strong drink." He regarded everyone, no matter how honorable, who was a friend of hers, as an interloper and intriguer against him. His jealousy and hatred of Professor Linck showed the workings of monomania, said Kate. He had even written a letter to a friend of hers saying that he did not care about Senator Conkling, but that he was determined to kill both him and Professor Linck. He was just as mad on the subject of Professor Linck as in the case of Mr. Conkling—"as indeed he would be jealous of anyone else whom he fancied my friend."

"How did Mr. Conkling venture to come to Canonchet under the circumstances?" the *Sun* reporter interrupted Kate's smooth narrative to ask.

At this point she gave an involved explanation of the Governor's troubles with Chafee, the trustee, and said that she had invited Conkling to visit them and give legal advice on how best to handle the negotiations. He intended to stay until the Governor returned and then to discuss it with him, said Kate. He occupied a room on the third floor on the Wednesday and Thursday nights preceding the trouble, she continued. On the Friday morning she was told "to her surprise" when she appeared for breakfast that the Governor had come home suddenly at three in the morning and had left again.

"I paid no attention to this, as his movements were erratic," Kate commented. "He comes in on me like a ghost in the middle of the night, and at the most unseasonable hours, and hurries away in the same disquieting manner. I had learned to be used to these freaks, but I thought no more of it, and busied myself about my household affairs, while Senator Conkling took a seat on the lounge, and was looking over the newspapers."

At this point Kate gave her version of the scene on the piazza before Sprague chased Conkling to Billingtons. Although she had had her say and her story was read with much interest in New York and Washington, she still remained a prisoner for several days, watching for a chance to escape. The servants were sympathetic to her rather than to the Governor.

On the last day of April, with the help of her lawyers, she left with her three daughters and their nurse as Sprague drowsed on the piazza. They slipped down the back stairway and hurried to a carriage that waited some distance from the house. Kate and the nurse carried their clothes over their arms and Gaius Smith, who handled freight and baggage at the Narragansett depot of the old Pier Railroad, gave her a trunk to pack her things. He was a great admirer of Kate and had handled her luxurious luggage for many seasons.

They had to seize the moment when it came. Usually after lunch the Governor went to the beach to bathe. But this afternoon he stayed on the porch and fell asleep. He knew nothing of Kate's escape until a gardener told him of it. At once he sprang to life and, without waiting for his shotgun, set off in pursuit of Kate and their daughters. He was determined not to lose the girls. He raced his buggy first to the Pier station, then to Kingston, hoping to catch up with the train and thinking she must be heading for Providence. Smith had helped Kate again by misleading Sprague. She was moving in the other direction—to Wickford and then on to the shore, where she was picked up by a yacht and taken eventually to Boston.

A gay season was at its height. Excursion trains from Boston and Providence had brought in a crowd of more than eight thousand persons for the yacht races at Newport. It was a scene in which she would once have had a stellar part. The autumn trotting season was about to open at Narragansett, but Sprague entries were no longer on the cards. Grant had just been welcomed in San Francisco at the close of his trip around the world. It was a moment of national huzzas, but not for Kate, who was lost to view on the rescuing yacht until late September, when she turned up at Edgewood with her daughters and was again quoted in the newspapers as denying all the charges made against her.

The publicity by this time would have made any but the boldest spirit quail. The Cincinnati *Commercial* pinned down several uncomfortable aspects of the situation for Kate in her native state, commenting editorially:

There is a good deal of levity about Senator Conkling's law business at Narragansett Pier, and a disposition to charge that it was touching the Senator that the ex-Senator's excitement arose to a pitch beyond control. As to the relations between Senator Conkling and Mrs. Sprague at Washington during the recent sessions of Congress, they were certainly not such that either party cared to conceal them, for their friendly intimacy was very conspicuous and the talk of the town. . . . While Mrs. Sprague was in Europe, her little property was almost confiscated by taxation and assessment, and Senator Conkling was of essential service in procuring an Act of Congress to afford relief. If Mr. Conkling and Mrs. Sprague had not been celebrities, and living separate from their companions, we presume they might have found each other's society congenial without arousing the country on the subject. It was no doubt an imprudence in them to brave public opinion which is quick to condemn, but they may have been unaware of the attention they were attracting. When the war of words took place between Conkling and Lamar, the former if he had read the Southern papers, would soon have seen enough to convince him that only the most urgent law business should take him near R.I. during the vacation, for he couldn't go there without bringing a swarm of insects with stings about the ears. However, he made his appearance at Providence as the guest of Senator Anthony, an old friend, and then was so unfortunate as to be at Senator Sprague's house when the Senator was in a state of artificial excitement, and betook himself to firearms. It is lucky for the Senator that his career was not terminated by a shot then and there, and his composure in partaking of clams and spurning all communications with the press is to be commended. The Senator has reached years of discretion, and has had a warning, a very loud one. He should wind up his legal business with the Spragues, and if he must go to a watering place, try Long Branch.

Kate needed all her pride that winter to face the storm of gossip that surrounded her. The years of whispering, the press gallery innuendos, the smoke-room talk took on shape and form. She did not withdraw from the social round, but she looked the saddened woman of thirty-nine that she was. She still held court at Edgewood for men of affairs. She still sat in the gallery when a debate that interested her was in progress. But there is no evidence that she had any further communication with Conkling. Olivia watched them both carefully on the last day of March, 1880, as Kate sat in the gallery and Conkling, "more winning in personal appearance than of yore," took the floor.

But no sign of recognition passed between them, no glances were exchanged, no notes were relayed from gallery to floor. The women who sat near Kate, and Conkling's fellow Senators—all of whom were alive to the situation—cast covert glances in their direction. But Conkling was as pompous as ever, Kate as composed. To Olivia she looked "cold, stately and statuesque as a lily, or a bit of marble in human form." Heavily fringed waxen lids screened her sorrowful eyes as she "seemed as much alone as Cleopatra in her barge floating down the dusky Nile."

On this occasion Kate wore a blue turban with a bird's wing and a dark dress almost severe in its simplicity, touched up by a scarf of scarlet silk at her throat. She was still the glamorous Kate Chase with the pride to assert her will. But it was only pride that sustained her at this point, for official Washington had decided that Roscoe had coldly turned his back on Kate and allowed her to face the situation alone. His embarrassment was intense. He had been made to look ridiculous. His political enemies had a field day.

The only indication that Conkling tried to help her at all was the Governor's statement to the Sun reporter, while Kate was still a prisoner, that he was merely trying to keep her from receiving messages from "those who would destroy his home." It is altogether likely that Roscoe may have tried to steer her course by note at this crucial point, both for her sake and his own. He was an able lawyer. But hating the press as he did, it is unlikely that he would have advised her to talk to reporters. This was a decision she must have made by herself, or on the advice of the lawyer she got for herself after Sprague had driven her from Canonchet. Kate had known too many able newspapermen to have any fear of the press, but she could scarcely have foreseen the effect her story would create as it appeared across the country. When applied to the known facts in the case, it was received with much skepticism.

Later Judge Hoadly moved into the picture and threw a protecting screen of silence and discretion around the daughter of his old friend, Salmon Portland Chase. By the time her suit came to trial, she did not lack for expert legal advice. As usual, Kate gave no further indication of what she thought or felt, once she had had her say in the newspapers, unwittingly exposing the weak points in her own position.

In any event, her friendship with Roscoe came to an abrupt end. From meeting nearly every day, they had no contact so far as anyone could learn. Close watch was kept on them when Kate appeared at the Capitol, but these two proud characters acted as if they had never known each other. Hostesses who had frequently brought them together were careful not to invite them to the same affairs. When a package of papers from Conkling arrived at Edgewood while Kate was abroad, the report spread that the Senator was returning her love letters.

He was as buoyant and self-confident as usual when he took his place in the Senate again. Affairs of the heart were not new to Roscoe. He was popular with women, and none knew how much he was moved by Kate, although he found her a brilliant companion. Her friends were convinced, however, that she was deeply in love with him. The more understanding remembered that her life with Sprague was one of great infelicity and that the gay belle of the Civil War had sobered into a grave and sometimes unhappy woman after her marriage. Her intimates thought that her high-paced round of pleasure was designed to offset the emptiness and grief of her domestic life. She had bloomed again with Conkling and it was common talk that they were well suited to each other—both proud, ambitious, heady characters who snatched what they wanted from life. Up to the time of her divorce, Kate had cared nothing for the opinion of other people. But she was to learn that convention had the power to destroy.

Two weeks after her first public encounter with Conkling in the highly charged setting of the Senate, she invited the newspaperwomen to a luncheon at Edgewood. By this time she recognized the need for friendly support by the press in her approaching divorce battle. She had no intention of discussing her marital difficulties with them but she told them she had no objection to comment on this function, provided they treated her justly and in the spirit of courtesy. Olivia, true to herself, laid it on thick. She described every spoon and fork and gold salt cellar on Kate's table, the Gobelin tapestry on the wall, the screens, the paintings, the Parisian clock with musical chimes, the Persian rugs and the soup bowls brought on the backs of mules from Persia and made from the dust of crushed garnets—the rest of the set that she had at Canonchet. "During the greenback regency a few found their way to the table of an exalted official, and in this way they became heirlooms in a distinguished family," Olivia commented.

Kate made conversation by telling their history as the newspaper-women ate their soup and nibbled at Havenner's cream biscuits and French bread. The oyster patties were served on Sèvres plates, hand painted with such historic figures as Napoleon and Lafayette. The sweetbreads came on plates specially designed by Kate for her father, with bouquets of flowers representing the states he particularly loved— the mayflower for Massachusetts, red clover for Vermont, the scarlet carnation for Ohio. The Virginia mountain lamb with green peas from Florida appeared on another set of distinctive pattern and dessert came on majolica.

A Negro butler and a footman waited on Kate and her guests in the beautifully appointed room. The flower arrangement evoked much comment. Kate always arranged her own flowers, except for her biggest parties, when she had professional aid. Her guests were impressed by everything they saw, including their hostess, and Olivia sentimentally recalled watching young Sprague camping in the market place with his men at the outbreak of the Civil War. She remembered him drinking water from a tin cup, eating baker's bread and cold meat with his regiment and sleeping on the ground. But the Governor's name was not mentioned at Kate's table. He was present like a shadow, however, for she had engineered the affair, knowing that she soon would embark on the major mess of a sensational divorce suit. But she held off for the summer of 1880, so as not to embarrass Conkling, who was a key figure at the Republican convention in June. His friends had urged him to run on his own account, but he discouraged all such talk while Grant had a chance.

Kate must have followed with interest the accounts of Roscoe's dramatic speech, delivered standing on a press table, with his left thumb hooked in his waistcoat pocket—a characteristic gesture—and his sonorous voice booming out the lines that rocked the convention:

> When asked what state he hails from,
> Our sole reply shall be,
> He comes from Appomattox
> And its famous apple-tree.

However, this did not gain the nomination for Grant. The party was badly split between the Stalwarts, who were the Republican Old Guard led by Conkling, and the Half-Breeds, who leaned to Blaine. Neither side would yield, so Garfield emerged as the dark horse and winner. He was a Half-Breed. To conciliate the other faction, Chester A. Arthur, an uncompromising Stalwart, became the candidate for the Vice-Presidency.

Kate sat back at Edgewood, apprehensively watching the storms that roared around Conkling when Charles J. Guiteau shot Garfield four months after his inauguration. At the time the tragedy was attributed to the bad blood between the Stalwarts and Half-Breeds, which he had done much to foment.

As Garfield lay dying, Conkling, who had proudly resigned his seat over the new President's policies, took storms of abuse. John Hay wrote to Whitelaw Reid, then in Europe: "Roscoe is finished. That Olympian brow will never again garner up the thousands of yore. . . . The whole thing has been a freak of insanity on the part of a man who has lost sight of his true relations with the rest of the world. It was the logical result of the personality of Conkling and the workings of the boss system."

Kate sorrowed over Garfield, too. Again two men she admired had locked in deadly conflict. She had often disagreed with Garfield politically, particularly when he stood by the irreconcilable Ben Wade on the conduct of the war and by Thaddeus Stevens on reconstruction. But she had many genial memories of Garfield the man—more than six feet tall, broad and hearty, with keen gray eyes, a vigorous growth of chestnut hair and wide forehead. His healthy and cheerful bearing did not suggest the indigestion from which he constantly suffered and which Kate catered to when he was her guest. She had become

good friends with his wife too, as she was with the correct and slightly
stiff Mrs. Schurz.

She had always enjoyed her country gallops with Garfield, their long
discussions on the Victorian poets, their dinner table conversations in
Columbus and Washington and at Canonchet. There was a certain innocence about him, she felt, as well as an insatiable thirst for knowledge. She had known him as teacher, state senator and major general;
as lawyer, congressman and senator and had never ceased to like
him, although she had seen less of him in recent years. With his
slouch hat and informal ways, Garfield had all the geniality that her
father lacked. She had watched his conversion to Lincoln with interest.
Like other men she had known, he had shifted from contempt to
ultimate admiration. She had seen some signs of this even in her
father, but Kate had never compromised on her own account.

She was on good terms, too, with the man who succeeded Garfield in the White House—Chet Arthur, another lawyer six feet tall,
quiet, polished, rather dudish, like his friend Conkling, and fond of
wide-brimmed white beaver hats. He, too, had often driven out to
Edgewood to seek political counsel from the daughter of Salmon Portland Chase. But by the time he became President, Kate was publicly
involved in her sensational divorce suit.

The charges she brought against Sprague were the talk of Capitol
Hill. Many observers thought that Conkling's romance with Kate was
one of the elements that contributed to the fall of the mighty Senator.
When he ran for re-election, he was defeated and retired forever from
the Washington scene.

Chapter XVI

※ᎶᎯᏘᎶᏙ™ᎶᎯᏘᎶᏙᎥ

KATE FACES DIVORCE

IN THE spring of 1881 the various forms of torture that Kate claimed to have suffered during her married life were spread on the record in Washington County, Rhode Island, where she filed suit for divorce during the February term. Summed up in concise legal paragraphs, it was a staggering review of the abuse, violence, infidelity and intemperance that had been whispered about for years. Sprague promptly entered a cross-suit on the simple charge of infidelity.

Kate charged repeated violence against her person, threats, habitual intemperance, abusive language in public and private and destruction of furniture in their home. She not only cited the occasion in 1877 on which the Governor tried to throw her from a window, but she mentioned another ocasion when he collected bedding and furniture in the night time and made a bonfire of it.

She accused him of unfaithfulness on many occasions, of annoying servants and guests, of falsely accusing her of gross improprieties with other men, of holding her incommunicado at Canonchet, of threatening her life and of interrupting letters from her counsel. Kate charged that, after driving her away from Canonchet, he refused to let her have her clothing or personal property, including portraits of her parents. She also claimed that he had refused to contribute to the family support since 1879, when the period of trusteeship for the estate ended.

Another one of her charges touched a dark area in Kate's life. She was an affectionate and conscientious mother where the actual care of her children was concerned, but she had lost her only son completely to the Governor. For a time she kept him in a boarding school in Germany, fearing for his father's influence over him, but, when Willie returned, his father indulged him more than ever and weaned him away from Kate.

In her divorce suit she stated the issue bluntly. She charged that, since her departure from Canonchet, Sprague had made it a "place of resort for persons of vicious reputation and bad character, consorting with them in revelry and drunkenness, and has allowed the only son of your petitioner, William Sprague, Jr., to consort and associate with persons of bad character and to become addicted to bad habits and idleness, withholding from him all educational advantages, thereby tending to corrupt his morals and vitiate his future life."

At the time Kate, then aged forty-one, brought suit for divorce, Willie was fifteen, Ethel was eleven, Portia was nine and Kitty seven. She asked specifically for the resumption of her maiden name. The Conkling incident was not alluded to in Kate's suit, but the threats made to Professor Linck were. Whether Conkling advised her secretly at any point in the divorce proceedings is an open question. It was a humiliating period for the proud house of Chase, but her father's old friend, Judge Hoadly, helped Kate through the long-drawn-out litigation. Finally she modified her original charges to nonsupport and desertion. Sprague withdrew his countersuit. He obtained custody of Willie, she of their three daughters. The financial settlement was to depend on the final disposition of the Sprague estate, still in heavy litigation.

By legal decree Kate walked forth again as Mrs. Kate Chase, no longer Mrs. William Sprague. In actual fact, she had never ceased to be Kate Chase to the public and her intimate friends. Her maiden name was as much a part of her as the tilt of her chin. It was 1882 before she obtained her divorce and she had already started on a new life. But not a happy one.

She went abroad with her daughters as soon as she was free. For the next few years she spent little time at Edgewood, but she kept in touch with the American political scene from force of habit and was at home before the election of 1884, when Blaine finally was nominated. His enemies had fastened on Arthur for re-election, the ticket was again split and Grover Cleveland, a Democrat, rode into power. Years earlier

Kate had helped Conkling to whip up some of the feeling that culminated in this disaster for the Republican party. And Chet Arthur,
seeking renomination, was said to have sought Kate's advice on political
tactics, but again she stood behind a loser.

When Kate attended a debate now, she was usually accompanied
by one or all of her daughters. Ethel and Portia were in school in
Washington. Kitty was cared for at home. Kate was still closely observed
by commentators when she appeared on Capitol Hill. But the memory
of her distinguished father was fading. This was the decade in which
Nettie died too, leaving another scar in Kate's life. Olivia took note
of her social decline:

History is full of martyred women who have been used to crush ob-
noxious men. When Catherine Chase Sprague was the daughter of the
Chief Justice and the wife of a U.S. Senator she appeared in the social
heavens with the calmness and precision of a fixed star. Sunshine friends
have deserted her, but the star does not waver in its course. It is the same
haughty Catherine, despoiled of her throne, as true a woman today as when
surrounded by her fawning flatterers. It is the flatterers of the Tuileries
that have changed, and not the Empress Eugénie.

There was no one to take Kate's place in the dull and solid eighties.
Mrs. Arthur died just before her husband took office as President and
his hostess was his sister, Mrs. Mary Arthur McElroy, who presided
with quiet good taste. The center of gaiety was shifting to New York,
where the great fortunes amassed by the mining and railroad pioneers
were now showing up in ostentatious living. Fifth Avenue was pushing
north with a series of impressive homes. Art treasures from Europe were
being assembled in their interiors.

East and West were drawn closer together in President Arthur's
time by the completion of the Northern Pacific, the Southern Pacific
and the Atchison, Topeka and Santa Fe Railways. Transportation as a
whole was on the move. The Brooklyn Bridge was a nascent wonder.
Horsecar lines now operated in the main streets and the elevated
railways were sustaining their rattling cars in downtown New York.
Electric power plants were opened to provide current for incandescent
and arc lights on streets and in homes. Trains had comfortable sleeping
cars. Refrigerator cars were in use for the transportation of perishables.
Transatlantic liners were becoming faster and more luxurious.

Kate was struck by the rapid changes in New York after each trip she made to Europe. She had always found it a delight to sojourn abroad and after her divorce she learned that she could breathe more freely in the continental setting. She had been badly wounded socially, although she was too proud to show her scars.

Conkling by this time had opened a law office at the corner of Wall Street and Broadway. He had moved from the Fifth Avenue Hotel to West Twenty-ninth Street and he was rarely seen at Harvey's or his other old haunts. Among his first clients were Jay Gould and Thomas A. Edison. In the summer of 1883 he and Mrs. Conkling toured the Yellowstone region, just opening to the public, in Henry Villard's private car. He had been trying to patch things up with his wife, who had proved difficult about Kate's divorce. Her usual discretion had failed and he had been forced to write chidingly to her while the case was pending:

Do you not think it better to abstain with acquaintances from discussing family affairs of a private nature? Your habit was not to do so, and any modification of it has not, I think, been for the better. . . . We understand some affairs quite differently, and unless one-sided statements are allowed to go without comment we may get into the predicament of contradicting each other. I suggest this for your consideration only.

By this time Kate's way of living had changed radically. When she traveled, it was no longer in the fashion of her more prosperous days. She had ceased to be one of Worth's favored customers. Though her figure was still unmarred, she could no longer pay her bills. She did not haunt the same hotels, dine so extravagantly, attend the races or live in the American tradition abroad. Each season saw a fresh influx of the newly rich. Kate regarded them with the feeling of an alien looking on. She took a villa outside Fontainebleau, entered Ethel in a finishing school and had a governess for Portia and Kitty. She was determined that the girls should speak languages fluently and for a time she kept Ethel in a school in Leipzig, studying German. Ethel was a clever, amiable girl, who reminded her often of the open-hearted Nettie. Portia looked extraordinarily like her father and was a quiet and reserved child.

The lovely Madame Sprague still was noticed when she drove abroad. She was now in her early forties. Her red-gold hair was fading to a colorless ash. Kate watched its radiance go with great rapidity during these years. Her large, languid eyes, which had seen so much, looked tired now. Her mouth had lost the curve of youth. But her bearing was still unique and her clothes quite noticeable for their style. She had taken up the craze for black that developed during the Grant administration, but Kate in a black satin dress with a white satin bonnet made it smart instead of Victorian.

She had fewer costumes now. She was selling both clothes and jewels to give her daughters the kind of education she wished for them. Her bridal parure, which had cost fifty thousand dollars, was the first to go; then her diamond and emerald tiara, her pearls and her numerous diamond rings, necklaces, earrings and pins. The gems that had dazzled Washington brought shockingly little, considering their cost.

Kate's girls grew up with simpler tastes. Ethel was a good student. She also longed to act, a taste encouraged by Kate, who took her behind the scenes to visit Ellen Terry on one of their trips to London. Kate hoped that her daughters would make good marriages, for her resources were dwindling fast and she saw no prospect of better things in the future. She still had friends in London but her story had followed her across the Atlantic and there was a visible drawing away of skirts in Victorian drawing rooms from a notorious divorcee. She was no longer at home in court circles, although welcomed by the artistic set, in which she had many friends. But Kate was never a bohemian at heart. Like her father, she had a strong and constant sense of form and her interests were chiefly political. Her old friend, John Bright, was fighting Gladstone's Home Rule policy, but she no longer sent in her card at the House of Commons. What was there to say? The days when she and Nettie had dined with him and talked about Lincoln and the Civil War seemed aeons away. She observed the visiting Americans, some of whom had once been her friends, some of whom still were. But the diplomatic set had changed. New administrations brought new ministers. The goddess had fallen from grace, except for those who still felt her charm.

Kate felt more at ease in Paris. Time and again she took Ethel to see Sarah Bernhardt, then at the height of her fame, or Réjane, whom they often saw in the Bois in a phaeton driven by white mules. Watching Ethel's excitement over Bernhardt in La Dame aux Camélias, Kate relived the theatrical longings of her Columbus days and encouraged the thought that Ethel might go on the stage. The outcome was that Ethel attended a dramatic school in New York for a year and eventually toured with Richard Mansfield.

In 1886 Kate traveled back to America for the removal of her father's body from Oakhill Cemetery in Washington to Spring Grove Cemetery outside Cincinnati. The state with which he was most closely identified had asked that this be done and Kate wished it. The Government provided a special train for the occasion. Once again she moved in the midst of officialdom, attended a commemorative ceremony in the Music Hall of Cincinnati and heard her idol extolled. She was again the Chief Justice's daughter, honored and observed.

Governor Joseph Benson Foraker and Judge Hoadly, old friends of her father and champions of Kate through her divorce suit, were the principal speakers. The Governor said that "not since Washington had America produced a public man the superior of Mr. Chase in the matter of an exemplary private life." Judge Hoadly called him a "walking arsenal of the law of liberty."

Kate listened attentively to the review of her father's career. His creation of a currency which answered all the vast requirements of the Civil War. His projection of the national banking system. His opposition to the Kansas-Nebraska bill. His decorum at the Johnson trial. His stand on reconstruction and Jefferson Davis. His support of radical causes although a conservative at heart. His will power "dominating and indomitable, yielding to no man and to no force." His upright character. His sincerity, zeal and ability. A painstaking lawyer, a careful Senator, a hardworking Secretary, a thoughtful Justice. . . .

The sentences flowed like balm into Kate's consciousness as she sat, pale as marble, listening to these tributes. Only she—now that Nettie was dead—could testify to his tenderness in the home, to his virtues as a father.

Later Kate stood tall, slim and a little apart, in the cemetery where she soon would lie herself—on a sloping hillside, with cypresses in the distance, a lily-padded lake, and headstones marking many of the graves. Near her father's were others of significance to Kate—the resting place of Alexander McGuffey and of Israel Ludlow, Nettie's great-grandfather; of General Joe Hooker, whom she had known so well, buried beneath a heavy red sarcophagus; of the parents of Ulysses S. Grant; and of Fanny Wright, her likeness in profile, with her long ringlets carved in stone.

Did Kate prevision how it would be when her time came? Spring Grove must have saddened her. She drove through the streets of Cincinnati heavily veiled in black, but all knew that the queen had come home to bury her father. Julia Bundy Foraker, who was welcomed to Washington as a bride by Kate in 1870, entertained her in Columbus, although Lucy Hayes was sharply disapproving, considering Kate a disgraced woman.

As Mrs. Foraker told it, she ran into Mrs. Hayes in a friend's house just before Kate's arrival. Lucy drew her aside, "My dear," she said gently. "I have just heard that you are to entertain Mrs. X. Why should it be you? We must not judge her. Let the Lord do that. But I think . . . in your position . . . to countenance even the appearance of evil is a mistake."

"She spaced the words a little," commented Mrs. Foraker. "That was all. She drifted away with a faint rustle of black silk, a faint fragrance of tea-rose. We did not speak of it again."

However, outraged and unhappy that anyone should scorn Kate, Mrs. Foraker blanketed her with warmth and hospitality, recalling many happy encounters with her father and telling her how he had discussed Robert Browning with her in a railway station when she was quite a young girl. They laughed together over Julia's trousseau, which she had worn with such pride in Washington—a Metternich green corded silk with fifteen yards of material, a white llama shawl, a carriage dress of wine-colored surah, an apple-green calling costume and a Balmoral plaid costume.

Julia, the bride, was dazzled by Kate and her wonderful clothes at that time, and later she wrote of her: "She was a woman of extraordinary fascination, beauty and distinction. She was cultivated to her finger tips, had the manners that come from exquisite breeding and a charming heart, and had been, all through her father's public career, a daughter of whom any man would have been extravagantly proud. . . ."

Julia was happy to welcome her to Columbus, but there were many in the capital who recalled Kate's reckless behavior as Governor's daughter. Cold stares reminded her that no longer was she the inviolable social figure who had enjoyed eminence for so long. The men of Columbus were just as interested in Kate's visit as their wives and daughters, Mrs. Foraker observed. Perhaps more so.

Some time after this trip to Ohio, Kate picked up a newspaper and sadly saw that some of the paintings she had bought for Canonchet had been auctioned off on two March days in 1887. Each one brought back its own memory of the gay circumstances under which she had bought it. Corot's "In the Garden," Émile Vernet's "French Village," a miniature by Eugène Isabey, a pastoral scene by Constant Troyon, "Black Sheep" by Auguste Bonheur, brother of Rosa Bonheur, whom she had met in various salons; Théodore Rousseau's "Rocks at Fontainebleau," a landscape by Gustave Courbet and "The Landing Place" by Jules Dupré, who, like Rousseau, was a member of the Barbizon School.

Strange events had transpired at Canonchet in the five years since Kate obtained her divorce. She heard with grief from time to time of her son's life in the house that the Governor had rechristened "Woman's Folly." She had grown hopeless over Willie and was not surprised to learn that he had changed from a bright and happy boy into a moody youth. The Governor alternately pampered and terrorized him. And Kate knew beyond doubt that Willie had turned against her. This was one of the bitterest facts she had to face in the dissolution of her realm.

Willie and his father had become the guardians by gunfire of Canonchet. The feud over property rights lasted for years and they defended it time and again as if it were a fortress. Guns were a commonplace to the martial-spirited Governor. He proudly showed off his racks of pistols and shotguns to all his visitors and, as he grew older and less angry, he even indicated the one he had used in the pursuit of Roscoe Conkling.

In the year of the Sprague divorce, Canonchet finally was sold by Zechariah Chafee, the trustee, to Francis J. Moulton, of Brooklyn. The Governor had exhausted the last legal device to hold the property. When the new owner and trustee arrived to take possession, they found Canonchet defended in medieval style. The Governor, with the military spirit aflame, had drilled a local corps to defend the property. He was the General. Willie was the Captain. The grounds were ringed with workmen and servants armed with guns. A code of signals had been set up.

The press was on the scene to report the battle. Canonchet was again in the public eye as a center of irrational proceedings. Kate read with horror that when the new owners arrived they found Willie on a gray horse mounting guard with a club. He had a pistol in his pocket. "I have orders not to let any person enter these grounds," he said.

A housemaid armed with a gun guarded the nearest entrance and Generalissimo Sprague patrolled the parapet, brandishing a pistol, while his sentinels paced the property boundaries. In the end the invaders retired, alive but worried. Possession was still nine-tenths of the law and the Governor settled back to doze on the piazza. Litigation started all over again, with Sprague sitting tight until his fortunes improved, and he was able to put up a $62,500 mortgage on the property.

In the year of his divorce, Sprague had married a Virginia beauty named Inez Weed Calvert, whose husband had recently died in Cincinnati. Her seventeen-year-old sister, Avice Weed, no less beguiling in looks, joined them at Canonchet and within a year was married to young Willie. Avice made Kate a grandmother by bearing a little girl, whom they named Inez. Kate was at Edgewood in 1890 when word reached her that Willie had killed himself in the West. Bitter and disillusioned, he had left Canonchet, angry with his father, penniless and with no capacity to earn a living. For a time he worked as a locomotive engineer, then went to Denver in quest of a newspaper job which he found on his arrival to be nonexistent. The boy whose birth was publicized as an event of national importance, whose christening robe and early progress were described in minutiae in the papers, killed himself in a hotel room, leaving a note which made no mention of Kate, but made clear the fact that he felt his father had betrayed him.

Willie's body was brought home and he was buried in the Sprague mausoleum at Swan Point Cemetery outside Providence. On an October day, with tinted light streaming through the stained glass windows, Kate stood at the head of her son's coffin while the funeral service was read in St. Peters-by-the-Sea, where his christening had taken place twenty-five years earlier.

Inez and Avice, on one side of the church with the Governor, must have stared with curiosity at the proud figure whose pallor and fine features were discernible through sheer veiling. It was noted that not once did Kate look toward them or the Governor and he made no attempt to approach her when the service was over, unhappy man that he must have been that day. Once Kate had hoped that Willie would be an architect. Above all, she had hoped that he would be a man of character, a worthy grandson for Salmon Portland Chase. It had all come to this! Kate left the church with Ethel, a sorrowing woman, curious glances focused on her from all directions.

She still had friends at Narragansett and before returning to Washington she heard a great deal about the Weed sisters and the changes they had wrought at Canonchet. There was much entertaining, as there had been in her own time, but it was of a different order. Young people came and went. There were tales of revelry. The fifty by thirty-six foot ballroom, started by Kate but never finished, had been turned into a music room, where the elder Mrs. Sprague gave musicales and sang. Murals representing music, sculpture, poetry and painting now adorned the walls. "The Incarnation of Music" hung over the mantelpiece. Kate heard with chilly indifference that a painting of Sprague on a white horse hung in the library.

The sober elegance Kate had imparted to the house was livened up by such fleshly touches as murals of "Venus Taking a Sun Bath," "Psyche at the Brook," "Love Asleep" and "Love Awake" in her old boudoir. Over the bay window were little cupids and Kate's bathroom was now an ocean scene in pink and blue, with mermaids sporting in the water and a cupid riding a dolphin. The Pompeian court had rocks, plants and running streams. All was light, gay and suited to the temperament of the new occupants. But Kate was relieved to hear that her father's room, with its great black walnut bedstead and massive desk, blue curtains and carpet, had been left untouched. The Governor still honored Chase, in spite of everything.

Kate did not see the high towers and massive wings of Canonchet on this occasion. It had been nothing but a heartbreak to her, but by this time the Governor had come to love it. "Here in the quiet, after the heat of the day, I find bliss," he remarked in one of his more expansive moments.

Kate had not seen how weary, sad and dissolute he looked, more drooping even than of old, his large grey eyes still showing the faithful-dog look that had endeared him to many in his younger days. Neither one could foresee that Willie's widow would marry two rich men in succession, buy back Canonchet for her sister and brother-in-law, only to have it burn down in 1909. Sprague, trying to save his papers, was rescued with considerable difficulty by his coachman, but he was to outlive Kate by sixteen years.

He died in Paris in 1915 at the age of eighty-seven, after turning his apartment in the Rue de la Pompe into a convalescent hospital for the wounded of all nationalities in the First World War. He was a soldier to the last and wished to be taken out to see a battle. When the fiacre in which he was driving to get to the sea coast was pursued by a German plane, the old Civil War hero took out an American flag and draped it on top of the cab. When he died his body was shipped home and a state funeral was held for him in Providence, followed by simpler services in St. Peters-by-the-Sea. A Governor's salute of seventeen guns was fired over his grave at Swan Point Cemetery. He died with more public honor than Kate and in good health to the end. He had climbed the Washington Monument at the age of seventy and had appeared on the Senate floor, a ghost from the past.

Inez lived to be seventy-eight and died at Narragansett in 1938 with the reputation of being a philanthropist. But the strain of tragedy ran on in the family with divorces, suicides, fortunes found and lost and heartbreaks of various kinds. The Governor always insisted that Kate was the "wellspring of much of the Sprague disaster."

If she was, she paid for it in her declining years, as she saw one figure after another pass into the shadows. Two years before Willie's suicide, Conkling died as a result of exposure in the great blizzard of 1888. He had become rich again through his law practice, but he stayed aloof from his old companions and was seen only rarely around the Fifth Avenue Hotel, the Union League Club or at the bar of the Hoffman House. In 1885 his old friend Grant, who had fallen on evil days, had died of cancer of the throat.

Conkling was in poor health, weary and bitterly disillusioned himself when the great blizzard buried New York in snow. The wind reached a velocity of fifty-seven miles an hour and snowdrifts banked the streets. There were no cabs to be had, so Conkling set out to walk from his office downtown to his home on West Twenty-ninth Street. At Union Square he could barely shoulder his way through the snow and was walled in for twenty minutes in a snowbank. He fell flat on his face when he reached the New York Club at Twenty-fifth Street. He was covered with ice and in a state of collapse. It had taken him three hours to make the journey.

He developed a bad cold soon afterward. His ears became infected, he had a brain abscess and he wrote to August Belmont describing the "darkness and disorder" he suffered and the "limitless agony" of the passing days. He died a week later.

Madame Chase at Fontainebleau must have read with some sadness Robert G. Ingersoll's tribute to Conkling before the New York Legislature:

Imperious man. He battled for a nation's life—for the rights of slaves, the dignity of labor, and the liberty of all. . . . He had the tastes of a prince, the fortune of a peasant, and yet he never swerved. . . . He was an orator—earnest, logical, intense and picturesque. He filled the stage. He satisfied the eye—the audience was his. He had that indefinable thing called presence. . . . He believed in the royalty of man, in the sovereignty of the citizen and in the matchless greatness of this Republic. . . . He was of the classic mould—a figure from the antique world. He had the pose of the great statues—the pride and bearing of the intellectual Greek, of the conquering Roman, and he stood in the wide free air, as though within his veins there flowed the blood of a hundred kings.

With the death of Conkling, many who had been their friends paused to wonder what had become of Kate Chase. The calm and kindly Frances Folsom Cleveland was now mistress of the White House. She had married Grover Cleveland in the Blue Room and was entertaining brilliantly. Kate's name meant little in official circles any longer, but she caught the echoes in her exile. She saw that Worth was dressing Mrs. William Astor and had made one of his creations for her for the Centennial Ball of 1889. She hurried home to adorn this function and Kate read later of the blaze of diamonds she wore and the cascades of roses on her white satin and point d'esprit. The Vanderbilts and Fishes had houses in the capital as well as in New York. The Gay Nineties were about to dawn.

Kate had sold the last of her jewels. She could no longer afford her villa at Fontainebleau. For the last time in her life, she crossed the Atlantic—not to attend the Centennial Ball, but to appear shortly at the funeral of her suicide son. Penniless, worn, with three daughters to support, she turned, as always, to the solace of Edgewood.

Chapter XVII

FAREWELL TO THE CAPITOL

KATE ENTERED the 1890's in the shadow of her own depression. She was now fifty. She had swung from the heights to the depths. Nothing remained to her but Edgewood and it was mortgaged to the limit. Bit by bit she had sold her best possessions—her silver, her Sèvres china, her Persian soup bowls, her Venetian glass, her paintings, her tapestries and Oriental rugs, her gold bibelots and objects of art and the best of her mahogany, ebony and rosewood.

Her earlier sale of her father's things was minor compared with the gradual disposition of her own treasures—quietly, without a line of publicity. Her jewels, her furs, her laces and most of her dresses, except those that were too outmoded, went with none of the furore that had attended Mrs. Lincoln's attempts to sell her finery. Kate still kept some of her crinoline gowns from the Civil War days, reminders of the most special occasions. Her girls were dressed for years with the materials from their mother's choice wardrobe.

Edgewood stood like a half-empty shell, its tall cool rooms barren of comfort. The curtains she had kept were faded and worn. The once polished floors were covered with dust and odd bits of carpeting. Few pieces of furniture remained, although a Madame Récamier sofa, an Empire desk and some French period chairs were faint reminders of the days when Kate held court and men of affairs came and went, seeking her advice, basking in the glow of her intelligent response and feminine charm. Her father's portrait was everywhere, even in a crystal paper weight that rested always on her desk.

Her years abroad, the scandal that had dusted her wings, the death of many of her friends, had alienated Kate from her American background. The fact that she was penniless made her shun her former haunts. Her face was habitually sorrowful now, although her head was carried at the old proud tilt. She was living in the past and had small capacity to cope with the present. The broad acres of Edgewood, like the house, had deteriorated. There had been little planting for years, but Kate, desperate for ready cash, decided that she must turn this land to account. She kept chickens and ran a dairy for a time, with a man to help her milk the cows. She opened a little shop in a suburb of Washington and sold milk and eggs. Few who bought from her knew that the tall woman with the striking eyes and fading hair was the great belle of the Civil War. But Kate bogged down again in her accounts. She could never make ends meet. She gave up the shop and found a new way to peddle her wares.

All that remained of the carriages and splendid horses once at her disposal was a broken-down basket phaeton and one aged mare. When down to her last penny, she loaded the carriage with milk and eggs and headed for the outskirts of Washington with her wares. A trip into town involved a plumed hat and white kid gloes, whether to pay a call or peddle eggs. Once she had bought her gloves six dozen pairs at a time and had been outdone in this respect only by Mary Todd, who was known to have ordered three hundred pairs in four months. Kate still had a few, soiled, but of the finest quality. She donned them to cover her coarsened hands, perhaps to remind herself that eggs could be peddled with style. She drove her rickety phaeton with the dash she had once shown with blooded horses.

When this grim expediency yielded little, Portia and Ethel went off to fend for themselves. Ethel went touring with Richard Mansfield. Portia worked for a time in the Treasury Department, where the name Chase still had a magic sound. She married a man named Whitney and after his death went to Narragansett to live with her father's family. There she married Frank Browning in 1914, making her home on Rhode Island until her death in 1932. But Portia's eventual affluence came too late to be of any help to her mother.

Until the girls left, Kate had done what she could to support them. Her venture into business was for their sake. Now she was left to her own resources, with Kitty to care for and two dogs—a collie and Chiffon, the terrier. Kitty's health declined rapidly in her twenties. Her mother kept her in bed much of the time, fed her milk and eggs from the farm and tried to divert the bewildered but sweet-natured daughter who had never matured mentally. At times she hemorrhaged badly and one winter night, when Edgewood was blanketed with a heavy fall of snow, Kate ploughed her way out to the road and fired a pistol to attract the attention of a neighbor, so that he could summon a doctor.

The house was always cold in winter. They had no money for fuel. For a time they had no food, except the produce of the farm. Kate's beautiful hands became rougher and more chapped, as she washed dishes, fed the chickens and scrubbed floors. By and by she didn't bother to scrub or clean, and Edgewood became dirty, as well as dilapidated. The grand stairway, which had been the setting for so many gala scenes, was thick with dust. The chandeliers had lost all glitter, since no one washed their prisms. Kate had always been a capable housekeeper. She knew how to cook and order. She had managed well though extravagantly, but her reputation had rested largely on her skill in directing servants.

Only one room was well cared for now—her father's library. It was dusted every day and when Kate found life unbearable, as she frequently did in the nineties, she seated herself at his desk, tried to forget the present and conjure up the past. As things got worse, she lived more and more in the past, until again she saw herself walking down the stairway in a Worth gown to set forth for an evening's gaiety in the capital. Her dining room reminded her of dinner parties with Sumner, Greeley, Garfield and Schurz in passionate debate and her father judicially smoothing them down. Wherever she turned in the house, she found echoes of the past. On warm evenings she sat on the veranda, gazing toward the Capitol, dreaming no doubt of her days of triumph.

As Edgewood ran down, so did Kate. She ceased to cherish her looks or even to care how she dressed, unless she knew that someone was coming. Occasionally a Senator or old friend would remember her existence and pay her a formal call. Then she would drag out some bit of faded finery, but the old air of grooming was gone, the consciousness of the fitness of things. After a few such experiences, none called but neighbors who tried to help her, and Kate sorrowfully told a distant cousin from the West who visited her while passing through Washington: "Once, great statesmen found their way to my door, proud of my acquaintance; now, none but the poor and lonely seek me out. I am as though already dead."

At long intervals she made forays into the capital in her battered phaeton, wearing her purple-plumed hat and white kid gloves, driving past the White House with a thousand memories and lost ambitions, slowing up to look with haunted eyes at the house on E Street, the scene of her proudest moments. There the radicals had gathered in the days of the Civil War. There they had plotted against Lincoln, made pawns of Generals, worked out campaign plans and schemed to make her father President. There they had celebrated Gettysburg and the end of the war. Such parties! Such high emotions! Such grief, excitement and romance!

Looking at the built-up city and handsome streets, Kate recalled the mud of the Civil War days and the tricks they had played with their hoops to keep their silks out of the dirt. She observed the marble mansions, the long vistas, the tree-lined streets that had taken the place of the shabby, rowdy town of 1861, with its ring of lit-up encampments at night. Little but the Capitol, the White House and the Smithsonian remained as they had been. The Washington Monument now gave drama to the scene. The Library of Congress was nearing completion.

She never went near the Capitol now, although she followed the political news in the papers and still had decided views on all public issues. No one sought her advice. She had been abroad during most of the first Cleveland term and for the first two years of Benjamin Harrison's administration. Blaine was functioning ably as Secretary of State when she returned from Europe. But he would never be President now. He died in 1893, soon after the deaths of three of his children.

Another brilliant figure gone and one of significance to Kate. Both Chet Arthur, her friend and Tilden, her foe, had died in 1886. One by one the warriors had fallen, but for Kate the mighty oak that mattered was Roscoe Conkling. Schurz now lived in New York and had become a figure in journalism. Hay and Nicolay had completed their biography of Abraham Lincoln in 1890, with many sharp allusions to Salmon Portland Chase. Cleveland was back in power in 1893. Everyone was going to Chicago for the World's Fair and making merry. But a year ater the Pullman Company strike tied up railroads all over the country, and Cleveland sent troops to Chicago to protect the mails and federal property.

In the following year Edgewood was threatened with foreclosure. A depression had set in after the panic of 1893. The estate was so involved that Kate could not sell it. Nor could she borrow, or mortgage it further. Desperate, she dipped into her wardrobe for the best of her finery and set off West to see what Ohio would do to save the home of its illustrious son, Salmon Portland Chase.

William McKinley was governor at the time. He had reason to know Kate well. During his long stretch in Congress, he had watched her as a social leader and also as a divorcee, and although he was not among those who consulted her politically he never failed to treat her with kindness and courtesy. McKinley was dignified and serious and in some ways reminded Kate of her father. He was heading for the Presidency when she went west. He and the Dresden-like Ida Saxton, whom he had first seen through the cashier's cage of her father's bank in Canton, entertained her handsomely. Kate had heard much about the frail and delicate woman who had never recovered from the deaths of her two children and on whom McKinley lavished endless time and devotion. She seemed like a girl in a flounced dress of sprigged challie. Mrs. McKinley must have looked at Kate with some amazement, too. As they all drove through the streets of Columbus, the daughters of the men she had danced with in the 1850's saw an old beldame with weary, half-closed eyes and uncurled feathers. Was this Kate Chase? The older ladies of Columbus observed that she was sliding downhill fast. Her decline had been rapid since her last visit for her father's reburial ceremonies.

But they all observed that Kate still held her head at a haughty angle. Those who talked to her said she hadn't lost her pride, even though she had lost all else. She still made others feel like lesser mortals. There was little McKinley could do for Kate financially, but she rounded up $5,000 in Columbus and Cincinnati. She firmly believed that she could get $100,000 for her father's estate. With the house sold, she planned to take Kitty back to Europe to live. In France she would be one of many faded belles with long histories behind them. She would not stand apart. In Washington it hurt her to be within range of the Capitol, yet not of it; to be cut off from the social and political life on which she had thrived and triumphed.

Kate still did not think in terms of pennies, but of fortunes, even when she could barely buy a loaf for Kitty. She knew this to be her weakness, but it was like a tide in her veins, an inheritance that she could not stem. She had her father's generosity to an unrealistic degree. When hard-pressed themselves they gave loans to others, helped friends and relatives and squandered largesse with no thought of the future. Kate had acquired a reputation in the large European hotels for her lavish tipping and for the boxes of gowns, hats, shoes, gloves and flowers that came pouring in while she was in residence. Madame Chase was almost as conspicuous as a spendthrift actress. It was remarked that she even sent back her lacy stockings from Washington to Paris to be rewoven at a fantastic price when there were snags or runs. But that was long ago.

Kate had no compunction now about accepting money from the State of Ohio, but it was only a drop in the bucket in holding Edgewood and again she faced an emergency. A purchaser on whom she had counted died suddenly, leaving her with the problem still unsolved. At last she decided to go after money where it was amassed in the greatest quantities and where again her father's reputation might help her—on Wall Street. Kate had come to know the financial district well during the Civil War. Not only had she accompanied Chase when he arranged the first big banking loan, but she had gone with him to New York on numerous other occasions and had often dined with the most prominent bankers of the day. She frequently entertained them in E Street.

Kate recalled how Attorney General William M. Evarts, in his eulogy of her father delivered before the alumni of Dartmouth a year after his death, had said: "The management of the finances of the Civil War was the marvel of Europe and the admiration of our own people. Whether the genius of Hamilton dealing with great difficulties and with small resources, transcended that of Chase meeting the largest exigencies with great resources, is an unprofitable speculation. They stand together in the judgment of their countrymen, the great financiers of our history."

No one had ever attempted to deny that Chase had been both able and successful in his efforts to finance the Civil War.

As Kate assembled the best of her outmoded things, she could summon up memories of bankers she had known both well and long. Jay Cooke was out of the picture, although he was slowly recouping his fortunes with mining investments in Utah. Henry Villard, her old journalist friend, had become a financier and was president of the Northern Pacific Railroad. Collis P. Huntington, who had often dined at her home and whose lobbying activities she had watched in the 1870's, was president of the Southern Pacific Railroad. Seth Low, another old-time friend, was president of Columbia University. Levi P. Morton was in the House of Representatives during the era of Kate's divorce. He had been kind to her in Paris when he was Minister to France between 1881 and 1885. All these men had been witness to Kate's great days and to her decline and fall.

She made her final effort to project her charm when she visited New York in the summer of 1895 to raise money for Edgewood. She also sought to conceal the ravages of time before tackling her banker friends. The faded mirrors of Edgewood must have dismayed her, for she decided on a blond transformation she had bought in Paris to cover the remains of her once glorious hair. In so doing Kate surrendered one of her chief natural beauties and became something of a fright. She applied heavy make-up and rouge to the skin that had been famed for its marble pallor. During her years abroad she had become addicted to heavy maquillage. There was nothing much she could do about her eyes. Their hazel depths were lifeless now. The lids were red-rimmed, swollen and half closed. Kate was only fifty-five, but she had done a wealth of living and, in recent years, had shed many tears.

Did Kate know that she looked bedizened as she haunted the downtown offices of the financiers, or had she become myopic and lost her famed sense of form and good taste? Her clothes were all of the past, out of fashion and somehow grotesque. She was heavily scented, decked with dashes of lace, her white kid gloves were slightly soiled and little of the old Kate emerged except the musical voice, the vivid spray of thought, the turn of wit, the bearing that she would have until death.

Kate still talked a little grandly and hid her misery behind a mask of pride. But warm-hearted Henry Villard was both touched and perceptive. He was shocked by the sight of her but still was captivated by Kate. When she summoned him to the modest hotel at which she was staying, she seemed upset because she had been represented in the press as begging money for Edgewood.

He wrote to his wife, Fanny Garrison Villard, from his home at Dobbs Ferry on August 6, 1895:

My call on Mrs. Kate Chase was quite pleasant. Not having seen her in over thirty years, it gave me quite a shock at first to be received by an aged woman with hardly any traces of her former beauty. But she is still very intelligent, vivacious & determined as of old and very ladylike withal. You would feel interested at once in her I am sure. The newspaper misrepresented her mission, as she wants no money by way of a gift, but as a loan on good security. She asked me for nothing but advice.

Villard went to work for Kate. The summer was nearly over and the bankers were returning to their desks after trips abroad and long stays in the country. During the autumn of 1895, Kate was seen often in the Wall Street region, looking as flashy as Hetty Green was sombre. There were many calls, broken appointments, excuses, chilly secretaries, as her mission became known. The sympathetic Villard spared her what he could and went after the bankers himself. It was none too easy. Kate's reputation had been greatly impaired by scandal. The drawing rooms of the nineties did not open readily to her and Villard asked his wife to invite her to Dobbs Ferry, which she was happy to do. Fanny knew that Salmon Portland Chase, like her father, William Lloyd Garrison, had been a good fighter for the Negro.

On September 15 she wrote to her brother, Francis Jackson Garrison, saying that Kate was arriving to spend the day with them. "I have not seen her since 1866 in Washington and now she is an elderly woman," Mrs. Villard wrote. "Harry has been kind to her and she is very grateful.

Kate had first known Villard as one of the group of young correspondents covering the Civil War who were in and out of her home when they came back weary from the battle fronts. She had always welcomed them and fed them well. Villard had worked with such intensity that he had made himself ill in the field. When he first brought his young bride to Washington from New England, she was at once received into the official set and Kate was the great star wheeling in that firmament. She was kind to Fanny, as she almost invariably was to the wives of the rising young men who gathered around her father. Kate was so splendid

a figure at the time that Mrs. Villard thought she had never seen anyone like her. She was at once struck by the fact that no one ever referred to her as Mrs. Sprague, only as Kate Chase. She also observed
the number of cavaliers who paid court to her. And she had never forgotten the sight of her at a ball in a sensational crinoline gown, leading
the clumsy General Grant through the lancers, while dozens of young
officers stood at a respectful distance awaiting their turns.

Mrs. Villard felt sympathy rather than admiration for Kate when she
arrived at Dobbs Ferry. Before long the Civil War belle, apparently
realizing that her appearance was startling to her hostess, took refuge in
the story that she had been at the seaside and the salt air had stung her
eyes. In her heyday Carl Schurz had said that Kate's eyes always had the
liquid look of one about to weep, but without the reddened effect.
Now the picture was complete, whether it came from the tears Kate
had shed, the salt air or the illness that was soon to destroy her.

She visited Mrs. Villard again on December 1 and some weeks later
Fanny wrote to her brother Francis, summing up her impressions of
Kate:

Mrs. Kate Chase looks like a wreck of her former self. False blonde
hair, powder and paint and weary, half-closed eyes make a sad impression
on one. She has not yet got the money with which she is to keep her
daughters and herself from the pangs of starvation and she has few friends.
Harry has got the property she owns, saved to her by dint of hard work,
Seth Low helping at the last minute when the mortgage had to be paid
off. What she will do I don't know. When I first saw her, she was Queen
of Washington society.

By this time Villard had succeeded in swinging the deal for Kate,
raising $48,000 on Edgewood from his own pocket, with the assistance
of Low, Morton, Huntington, J. Pierpont Morgan and one or two
others. This covered the $40,000 mortgage. Kate was allowed $3,000 a
year from the balance for living expenses until the property could be
sold. When that time came—and she was still convinced it would
bring $100,000—the surplus would go to her after deduction of the
mortgage and the money advanced to her in the interim.

The wolf was driven from the door but death was at hand. Actually
Edgewood was sold a few months before Kate's end. But she had three

years of peace from the strain of supporting herself and Kitty, with the constant fear of being turned out of her home.

Her months in New York had revived some of her drive and spirit. It had been good for Kate to talk to men of affairs again, to dine at sumptuous tables, to discuss Lord Salisbury's criticism of the Monroe Doctrine and John Morley's defense of it on the Venezuelan question. Kate observed that the great days of the past were quite outdone by the magnificence of the nineties. She had dined at several of the mansions that now lined upper Fifth Avenue. The fruits of the fortunes she had seen being amassed were in evidence in art collections, in lavish entertainment, in jewels and household possessions. She found that her father's memory still was green in banking circles. A bank now bore his name.

Although Kate had not lived in New York since her school days at Miss Haines's, she had been a constant visitor there, both with her father in the early days of the war and with Sprague in the 1870's. She had always been an honored guest at the Stock Exchange as the daughter of Chase, the friend of Jay Cooke, the wife of the Cotton King of New England. She had come regularly to shop, to attend the Sanitary fairs and Union balls, to be a guest at large private parties, to sail for Europe. She knew all the luxury spots and had sampled the best of them. She was a familiar figure at art shows, at the opera, at first nights in the theater. Wherever the pulse of smart life stirred, Kate Chase was likely to be present.

She now experienced to the full the bitterness of fair weather friends. She wandered about the streets, no longer able to afford carriages. She walked, still slowly and gracefully as if on parade, through the streets of downtown New York, observing the men of finance, whiskered, carefully tailored, with stiff high collars and four-in-hands. There was a great snowstorm in February but Kate now had to be careful of her health and she stayed indoors.

During the weeks she was in New York waiting uncertainly for the success of Villard's plan, she viewed the new hotels but dined herself in frugal style at little coffee pots, except for the few occasions on which she was invited out. She saw that Sarah Bernhardt was playing in Magda but she could not afford theater tickets. Ada Rehan was appearing in The Countess Gucki at Daly's and James Hackett was starring in The

Prisoner of Zenda. But the poultry and pigeon show at Madison Square Garden was of more immediate interest to Kate, whose very subsistence now depended on her hens.

However, she noted with interest that on February 2 Mrs. William Astor gave a reception at her new mansion at Fifth Avenue and Sixty-fifth Street, followed by supper and cotillion at Perry Belmont's two blocks up the street. Mrs. John Jacob Astor gave a dance that same week, with seventy small tables sporting the racing colors of the Belmont stables. The favors were white leghorn hats trimmed with flowers and ribbons, twisted in one of the figures of the cotillion and, for the men, silver match boxes engraved with the date.

It all had a familiar ring to Kate, although she was now on the outside looking in. That was the way she had done it, too. She noted that the styles were ornate, but much less flattering than the crinolines of the Civil War. The leg of mutton sleeves, the umbrella skirts, the tilted hats with birds' wings, did not seem to Kate to flatter their wearers. She did not feel at home among these wasp-waisted women with high coiffures who looked at her with an air of disapproval. Nor did she fail to detect the touch of pity in the eyes of their husbands, to whom she still was a legend. Proud Kate evoking pity! It was all rather tiring. Most evenings she returned to her hotel, after her weary trek downtown, to read a while, then go early to bed and sleep—Kate, who once entertained or went out every night of her life; who danced until three in the morning; whose days were filled with acclaim and excitement.

When the future of her home was assured, she was glad to get back to quiet Edgewood, to Kitty and to her father's library, to the wide veranda where she sat in the evening and watched night descend on the Capitol. She no longer worried about tomorrow's food or strove over the farm.

Kate did not go into town for the inauguration of McKinley in 1897. She had no part now in the presidential picture, even though she approved of the McKinleys. But she read that a motion picture camera had clicked a record of the spectacle. The telegraph, the telephone, the phonograph, the cinematograph—how life was changing! In McKinley's first year gold was discovered in Alaska and Kate gave thought to Seward's Folly. Her hates and loves still were strong and Seward was one of the men she remembered as an enemy of her father.

In the following year the United States was at war with Spain, an
her old friend John Hay pushed through the "open door" policy fo
China. He was now Secretary of State, a most suitable appointmen
Kate believed, remembering the skill with which he had handled He
Satanic Majesty and the intelligence he had shown in all public matter
except in giving her father his due. Observing the pointed beard, th
glasses, the dignified elder statesman look of John Hay in the 1890';
Kate remembered the blithe and sometimes inconsequent young ma
who had ruffled all their hearts when he appeared in Lincoln's retinu
He had always been charming to Kate and it was a shock to see what h
and Nicolay had written about her father. She had lived long enough t
garner some of the early books on the Civil War.

Few could have told more than Kate herself. There was talk for
time that she was writing her memoirs. But there is no evidence tha
she seriously considered anything of the sort. Actually Kate was deepl
reserved, kept her secrets intact and left few records behind her, excep
some stilted letters and her newspaper defense of herself when she fe
overwhelmed by scandal. This was out of character, for Kate was s
reticent about her own affairs that only desperation could have drive
her to flaunting her domestic woes in the press. Usually when in troub
she relied on her inner strength to sustain her. Nor are there any recorde
instances of her revealing a political confidence, although the statesme
of the day trusted her with many secrets. She had been well traine
in the legal principles that were a matter of course with her father.

The habit of a lifetime prevailed and she kept her own counsel i
her declining years. Only toward the end did she break down in a wav
of reminiscence to a distant cousin from Ohio who visited her whi
passing through Washington. On this occasion Kate discussed matte
she had never dwelled on before. Not even to her father had she bee
able to bare her inmost thoughts or discuss her deepest sorrows. He ha
learned more by deduction and observation than he had from Ka
herself.

She was truly bereft of friends in the closing years of her life. No
that men no longer sought her out, she must have felt the need
feminine support. In spite of all the interesting women who had circle
around her in the days of her success, Kate had few close friends of h
own sex. She was essentially a man's woman and was used to toug

political thinking from the age·of sixteen. Such women as Mrs. Douglas understood her and could meet her on her own ground. She got on well with the very simple or the ultraworldly, but was at sea with a woman of earnest intention like Lucy Hayes.

Yet Kate had tact to an uncommon degree and could hold her own on any social level and interest all kinds of men and women. She was not scornful of her sex, even of those who succumbed to the vapors at the mere thought of an obstacle. Yet the average woman stood a little in awe of her and was not altogether at ease in her company. Kate lived with dash in the Victorian frame. She belonged essentially to the eighteenth century genre of realistic sirens with intellect dominating heart.

Her Civil War contemporaries commented first on her brains, second on her manners, third on her looks and clothes. All were memorable. She was dazzling to the young girls and officers' brides of the war days. Kate diffused her charm quite widely and gave the impression of having an angelic disposition. Her father, her husband and any who crossed her, knew better.

Her deference to older women of distinction gave her sound backing in the Washington scene. Flatterers surrounded her, as they did her father, until her wings were clipped by ruin and disgrace. She had been the most sought after guest in Washington and her own invitations the most prized, until the Conkling episode drew her into the headlines. From that time on, Kate found herself stranded on the shoals of social ruin. Her old friends were passing, one by one, or had moved away from the capital. Those who remained were deeply critical. She had lost touch with the school friends she used to visit in New York. Not one woman friend in Washington stood by Kate through these difficult years, although a few men championed her cause.

Her Ohio friends and relatives, particularly the McLeans, kept a thread of contact alive, both from a sense of loyalty and from deep admiration for Kate. All her life she had drawn her closest friends from her native state and in a number of instances had showered them with bounty. Knowing Kate's history from infancy, they had some understanding of her deep-rooted ambition and drive for power. These qualities had been evident quite early in her life and were taken to be a direct inheritance from her father and his family. Chase had grown up with the fixed idea that in all things he must be first. He was nationally known as a man of great ambition. His forebears had shown strength and drive in their chosen fields.

The circumstances of Kate's childhood had tended to foster these inherited qualities. As a motherless girl she was singled out for attention and flattery. Her father saw that she did not lack for intellectual stimulus and he drove her hard, continually demanding excellence in her studies. He talked to her about his own work and ambitions as if she were an adult. At the same time he showered affection on Kate and Nettie. His letters to his daughters and three wives all reveal a man of deep family tenderness and sympathy, even though the public viewed him as cold, aloof and self righteous.

Kate's already well developed ego received further stimulus when she became her father's hostess in Columbus at the early age of sixteen. She immediately became part of the political scene. His friends made much of her. She was an oracle in her own right and loved it. Again in Washington, at the age of twenty-one, she was swept along on a tide of excitement, with the Civil War beginning two months after her arrival, and the official set, from the President down, listening attentively to what she had to say. Altogether, Kate had more than her share of adulation, so that by the time of her marriage her ruthless will and her drive for power were already highly developed. Her inherited tendencies had had ample opportunity to thrive in this rich soil and to make her the unusual woman she was. Her Ohio friends accepted the fact that she was the natural inheritor of a proud man's ambition.

She had risen high. Now she had fallen low. But at the end Kate was without reproach for those who had deserted her, without rancor for the terrible snubs she had suffered. Tragedy had softened rather than embittered her proud nature. She welcomed friendly human contacts far different from any she had known in her more affluent days. To the tradesmen and small farmers who lived around Edgewood, she was an unfortunate and aging woman, penniless, with a sick child and utterly without friends. Seeing her need, they came to her door with small offerings. None of them knew the irony of the situation as Kate, within sight of the Capitol dome, accepted a sack of coal or a pound of tea with a warm glow of gratitude. But the old Negro retainers who made trips out to Edgewood to see her were well aware of it. Her servants had always adored her. Long after official Washington had forgotten her existence, they visited her. It was natural enough that they should also serve as pallbearers for the daughter of Salmon Portland Chase.

Another of her visitors toward the end was Gaius Smith, the baggage-master from Narragansett who had helped Kate to escape from Canonchet. As she slowly opened the door at Edgewood and peered around it, he was shocked to see what had happened to the glorious Mrs. Sprague. He had been offered large sums of money by newspapers and magazines to tell what he knew of the Conkling-Sprague fracas, but had always refused, out of respect for Kate.

She never mentioned the Governor in her last years. She had heard that his fortunes were rising again through Avice, but since his treatment of Willie she had blacked him out of her life with all the determination of which she was capable. Portia now was friendly with her father. Ethel had married Dr. Frank Donaldson, a surgeon with Theodore Roosevelt's Rough Riders. Their small boy, Chase, visited Kate at Edgewood during the last year of her life and brought her much joy. She led him around the farm, gathering eggs, showing him the hens and dogs. She told him of the chickens and kittens she had had as a child at Clifton Farm. Kate took special pains to impress on the small boy that he had had a noble grandfather, although he was much too young to understand.

Ethel's fortunes were to fluctuate, too. After her husband's death she joined the staff of a San Francisco newspaper. Her lodgings were wiped out in the great fire and earthquake. Kate's papers and souvenirs were lost, since they were in Ethel's possession after her mother's death. During the First World War she held a government post as a translator, using the languages which Kate had thought so all-important in her education.

For the last two years of her life, Kate was a martyr to pain. The liver and kidney complications which were to cause her death were gaining ground. She said nothing about it to anyone as her days drifted by in isolation and her agony grew worse. She did not get medical help until the end. Kate died at three in the morning on the last day of July, 1899, a few days before her fifty-ninth birthday.

Ethel saw to it that her mother lay in state in her grandfather's library, with its windows overlooking the garden where gay fetes had been held and historic figures had gathered around Kate. Her white hair was draped with rare old lace. The long lashes lay on the cheeks that had always looked like alabaster. Kitty wept inconsolably. The dogs barked and were removed from the house, but found their way back to Edgewood next day.

There were no famous names at Kate's funeral and few mourners. The Rev. Ernest Paddock, of St. John's Church, conducted services at Edgewood. Negro servants of Kate's in her more affluent days were the pallbearers. But President McKinley saw to it that a special car was assigned to take her body to Cincinnati for burial beside her father. Kate had often told Ethel that this was what she wished. No doubt she had told McKinley, too. Or John Hay knew. On her last visit to Ohio, she had gone to Spring Grove to lay flowers on her father's grave.

Now Ethel, Portia and Kitty stood beside hers, on the hot August day on which Kate was committed to the earth. They knew little of Cincinnati, but they saw the two-storied limestone house on Broadway, with a fanlight over the front door, where their mother was born. The farm at Clifton had been sold years earlier. Afterward, the three daughters headed sorrowfully back to Washington. Portia took charge of Kitty, then twenty-six and the image of her mother. She kept her until her death several years later. Ethel had her own small son and an ailing husband to cherish.

As Kate's body was borne away from the capital, the Marine Band was giving its usual weekly concert at the White House, playing the overture to *Poet and Peasant*, Sousa's marches and Negro melodies. Percival Spencer had crossed the English Channel in a balloon and President McKinley was planning a reception for Admiral Dewey. The races had begun at Saratoga. Newport was having a brilliant season, with yachting, polo, golf and tennis. *The Shamrock* was on its way from Britain to compete for the cup.

It was all part of the world to which Kate had belonged and which she had graced for many decades. The notice of her death in the middle of the summer season evoked editorial comment in many of the newspapers. Old clippings revived some of her glory. The violins played for Kate again. All conceded her grace and influence. Her romance with Roscoe Conkling figured in many of the notices. The Springfield *Daily Republican* bluntly observed: "Mr. Conkling was such a man as she should have mated with but there was no element of disgrace in his relations with her." The Philadelphia *Times* made the point that all that Kate had sought, all that she accepted, all that she gained, had turned to ashes on her lips—"the fate of Queen Guinevere was not more bitter because there is reason to believe that Roscoe Conkling was her Sir Launcelot." The Washington *Evening Star* commented: "The most brilliant woman of her day. None outshone her."

And the New York *Tribune*, owned by her old friend, Whitelaw Reid, carried a Washington dispatch on August 1, 1899, which summed up Kate's place in the sun:

No name could possibly be spoken in this city among the older residents that would evoke the reminiscences always started by the mention of Kate Chase. No woman so young ever held here the prominent and controlling position as leader that came to her as mistress of her father's household, nor has the most critical observer failed in according to her an exceptional personal brilliance.

The greatest trust and confidence existed between her father and herself, and the charm and grace of her manner were of inestimable advantage to him both socially and politically. When thus brought so prominently before the world Miss Chase was only sixteen years of age, and but a few years older when her father, taking the Treasury portfolio under President Lincoln, again needed her help as mistress of his Washington home. At this time began the social career with which her name was associated for so long. Her father occupied the house still standing at Sixth and E Streets, notable in these days for its spaciousness and the elegance of its furnishings, and where so many of the events which helped to make history of that period took place. Here Miss Chase held a court of her own and her reputation spread far and wide as the most brilliant woman of her day. The popular verdict declared her to be at the same time one of the most beautiful.

She had rare personal magnetism, a faculty of drawing out the best traits in others, and while shining herself pre-eminently, she was able to keep about her the most prominent leaders in politics, in society and in fashionable life. She had great success in arranging entertainments and while the hospitality of her day was on a much more simple scale than that which obtains now, hers was marked by an originality which gave it piquancy and flavor. Flattered by everyone and loved by many, Miss Chase's drawing room reflected in many varying moods the excitement then stirring hundreds of households in the early days of the war.

No one ever questioned Kate's influence, but it was subtly applied. While Susan Anthony and Victoria Woodhull were pounding hard for the vote; while Elizabeth Blackwell was determinedly pushing her way into the medical field; while Lucy Stone was openly campaigning for women's rights, and other feminists were beating the drums for one cause or another, Kate, beautifully gowned and lovely to look at, was influencing men for her own vain ends.

Her aims were personal, not humanitarian. They were direct and simple—top place for her father, but above all, for herself. As time went on, she grew to love politics for the game itself. But here, too, the personal equation prevailed. Kate the sibyl. The adviser of men. The prescient female. The fountainhead of wisdom. The molder of destiny.

Kate was without peer among American women in the boldness with which she played the political game for her father and worked to undermine his enemies. Her force was spent on men of intellect. She lived in a stirring era, held court, consorted with the leading statesmen of her day, got the best of their wit and knowledge—if not always their affection—and basked ever in the approval of her father. Kate knew great men in moments of crisis. She moved more political pawns than the public would ever know or than she would ever tell.

She had a strong and imperious nature, but she drove too hard and thus perhaps encompassed her own defeat. Her father mellowed as Chief Justice. His ambition declined with his health, but Kate would not give up. Her inheritance was irresistible. Her overmastering quality was pride. She was obsessed with one idea. It burned her up and made victims of those around her.

Time and the ruin of her life chastened Kate, but did not change her. The financiers who saw her in her last years caught the old spark of pride and determination. Scandal, failure, heartbreak, lost hopes, her son's suicide, bitter poverty and neglect, had not wholly broken her spirit. At least her father had not lived to see the ruin. Life was grim for Kate at the end, but it had held glorious hours for forty years. She had lived to the hilt and impressed herself on as many men of stature as perhaps any belle in American history.

Bibliography

AMES, MARY CLEMMER, *Ten Years in Washington*. Hartford, Conn.: A. D. Worthington and Company, 1873.

ANDERSON, MARY ELIZA VIALL, *The Merchant's Wife*. Providence: privately printed, 1876.

AUCHAMPAUGH, PHILIP GERALD, *James Buchanan's Administration and His Cabinet on the Eve of Secession*. Lancaster, Pa.: privately printed, 1926.

BANCROFT, GEORGE, *Oliver Hazard Perry and the Battle of Lake Erie*. Newport, R. I.: The Mercury Publishing Company, 1912.

BAYLES, RICHARD M., ed., *History of Newport County*. New York: L. E. Preston and Company, 1888.

BAYNE, JULIA TAFT, *Tad Lincoln's Father*. Boston: Little, Brown and Company, 1931.

BLAINE, JAMES G., *Twenty Years of Congress: from Lincoln to Garfield*. Norwich, Conn.: H. Bill Publishing Company, 1884-86.

BOWERS, CLAUDE G., *The Tragic Era*. Boston: Houghton Mifflin Company, 1929.

BOYD, BELLE, *Belle Boyd in Camp and Prison*. New York: Blelock and Company, 1866.

BRIGGS, MRS. EMILY EDSON (OLIVIA), *The Olivia Letters*. Washington: The Neale Publishing Company, 1906.

BROOKS, NOAH, *Statesmen*. New York: Charles Scribner's Sons, 1893.

CHASE, SALMON PORTLAND, *An Argument in the Case of Wharton Jones vs. John Vanzandt*. Cincinnati: R. P. Donogh and Company, 1847.

———, *Sketch of the History of Ohio*. Cincinnati: F. S. Benton, 1833.

CHESNUT, MARY BOYKIN, edited by Ben Ames Williams. *A Diary from Dixie*. Boston: Houghton Mifflin Company, 1949.

CHIDSEY, DONALD BARR, *The Gentleman from New York: a Life of Roscoe Conkling*. New Haven: Yale University Press, 1935.

COLVER, ANNE, *Mr. Lincoln's Wife*. New York: Farrar and Rinehart, Inc., 1943.

COMMAGER, HENRY STEELE, *The Blue and the Gray*. Indianapolis: The Bobbs-Merrill Company, 1950.

CONKLING, ALFRED R., *The Life and Letters of Roscoe Conkling*. New York: Charles L. Webster and Company, 1889.

DANA, CHARLES A., *Recollections of the Civil War*. New York: D. Appleton and Company, 1899.

DE CHAMBRUN, CLARA LONGWORTH, *The Making of Nicholas Longworth*. New York: Ray Long and Richard R. Smith, 1933.

DE LEON, THOMAS C., *Belles, Beaux and Brains of the Sixties*. New York: G. W. Dillingham Company, 1909.

EVANS, WILLIAM A., *Mrs. Abraham Lincoln*. New York: Alfred A. Knopf, 1932.

FORAKER, JOSEPH BENSON, *Notes of a Busy Life*. Cincinnati: Stewart and Kidd Company, 1916.

FORAKER, JULIA B., *I Would Live It Again*. New York: Harper & Brothers, 1932.

FRÉMONT, JESSIE BENTON, *Souvenirs of My Times*. Boston: D. Lothrop and Company, 1887.

FURMAN, BESS, *White House Profile*. Indianapolis: Bobbs-Merrill Company, 1951.

GOSS, REV. CHARLES FREDERIC, *Cincinnati, the Queen City*. Vol. I. Cincinnati: S. J. Clarke Publishing Company, 1912.

GREENBIE, MARJORIE BARSTOW, *My Dear Lady*. New York: Whittlesey House, 1940.

GREVE, CHARLES THEODORE, *Centennial History of Cincinnati and Representative Citizens*. Vol. I. Chicago: Biographical Publishing Company, 1904.

HAMLIN, CHARLES E., *The Life and Times of Hannibal Hamlin*. Cambridge: Riverside Press, 1899.

HARPIN, MATHIAS P., *Patterns on the River*. West Warwick, R. I.: Pilot Publishing Company, 1946.

HART, ALBERT BUSHNELL, *Salmon Portland Chase*. Boston: Houghton Mifflin Company, 1899.

HELM, KATHERINE, *The True Story of Mary, Wife of Lincoln*. New York: Harper & Brothers, 1928.

HENDRICK, BURTON J., *Lincoln's War Cabinet*. Boston: Little, Brown and Company, 1946.

IVES, A. A., *William Sprague Scrapbook of Rhode Island*. Providence: 1869.

JOSEPHSON, MATTHEW, *The Robber Barons*. New York: Harcourt, Brace and Company, 1934.

KECKLEY, ELIZABETH H., *Behind the Scenes*. New York: G. W. Carleton and Company, 1868.

KEMBLE, FRANCES ANNE (FANNY), *Journal of a Residence in America*. Philadelphia: Carey, Lea and Blanchard, 1835.

KINNAIRD, VIRGINIA, *Mrs. Lincoln as a White House Hostess*. Springfield: Illinois State Historical Society, 1939.

KNIGHT, BENJAMIN, SR., *History of the Sprague Families of Rhode Island, Cotton Manufacturers and Calico Printers*. Santa Cruz: H. Coffin, 1881.

LEECH, MARGARET, *Reveille in Washington*. New York. Harper & Brothers, 1941.

LEONARD, J. W., *The Centennial Review of Cincinnati*. Cincinnati: J. M. Elstner and Company, 1888.

LOCKWOOD, MARY S., *Historic Homes in Washington*. New York: Belford Company, 1889.

———, *Yesterdays in Washington; its noted men and women*. New York: Belford Company, 1889.

LUTHIN, REINHARD H., *Salmon Portland Chase's Political Career Before the Civil War*. Mississippi Valley Historical Review, June, 1942; March, 1943.

McCLURE, ALEXANDER K., *Our Presidents and How We Make Them*. New York: Harper & Brothers, 1902.

NEVINS, ALLAN, *The Emergence of Lincoln*. New York: Charles Scribner's Sons, 1950.

NEWBERRY, JULIA, *Julia Newberry's Diary*. New York: W. W. Norton and Co. Inc., 1933.

NICOLAY, JOHN G. AND JOHN HAY, *Abraham Lincoln, A History*. New York: The Century Company, 1890.

———, ed., *Complete Works of Abraham Lincoln*. New York: The Lamb Publishing Company, 1905.

PEACOCK, VIRGINIA TATNALL, *Famous American Belles of the Nineteenth Century*. Philadelphia: J. B. Lippincott Company, 1901.

PEARSON, F. B. AND J. D. HARLOR, *Ohio History Sketches*. Columbus: F. J. Heer Printing Company, 1903.

PECK, DR. GEORGE B., *The Life and Character of William Sprague*. Rhode Island Historical Society, January 30, 1919.

PHELPS, MARY MERVIN, *Kate Chase, Dominant Daughter*. New York: Thomas Y. Crowell Company, 1935.

PIERCE, EDWARD L., *Memoir and Letters of Charles Sumner*. Boston: Robert Bros., 1877-93.

POORE, BEN. PERLEY (AND REV. O. H. TIFFANY), *Life of U. S. Grant.* Cincinnati: Edgewood Publishing Company, 1885.

———, *Perley's Reminiscences of Sixty Years in the National Metropolis.* Philadelphia: Hubbard Bros., 1886.

PRYOR, MRS. ROGER A., *Reminiscences of Peace and War.* New York: The Macmillan Company, 1905.

REID, WHITELAW, *After the War: A Southern Tour.* New York: Cincinnati: Moore, Wilstach and Baldwin, 1866.

———, *Horace Greeley.* New York: Charles Scribner's Sons, 1879.

ROSEBOOM, EUGENE H., *The Civil War Era,* Vol. IV. Columbus: Ohio State Archaeological and Historical Society, 1944.

ROTHSCHILD, ALONZO, *Lincoln, Master of Men.* Boston: Houghton Mifflin Company, 1906.

SANDBURG, CARL, *Abraham Lincoln, The War Years.* New York: Harcourt, Brace and Company, 1939.

———, *Mary Lincoln, Wife and Widow.* Letters, Documents and Appendix by Paul M. Angle. New York: Harcourt, Brace and Company, 1932.

SCHLESINGER, ARTHUR MEIER, *Salmon Portland Chase, Undergraduate and Pedagogue.* Columbus: F. J. Heer Printing Company, 1919.

SCHUCKERS, J. W., *The Life and Public Services of Salmon Portland Chase.* New York: D. Appleton and Company, 1874.

SCHURZ, CARL, *The Reminiscences of Carl Schurz.* New York: Doubleday, Page and Company, 1909.

SEWARD, FREDERICK W., *Reminiscences of a War-Time Statesman and Diplomat.* New York: G. P. Putnam's Sons, 1916.

SHOEMAKER, HENRY W., *The Last of the War Governors.* Altoona, Pa.: Altoona Tribune Publishing Company, 1916.

SMITH, T. C., *Life and Letters of James Abram Garfield.* New Haven: Yale University Press, 1925.

SOULE, RICHARD, JR., *Memorial of the Sprague Family,* Boston: James Munroe and Company, 1874.

STARR, JOHN WILLIAM, JR., *Lincoln's Last Day.* New York: Frederick A. Stokes Company, 1922.

STERLING, ADA., ed., *A Belle of the Fifties, Memoirs of Mrs. Clay of Alabama.* New York: Doubleday, Page and Company, 1904.

STERN, PHILIP VAN DOREN, *The Life and Writings of Abraham Lincoln.* New York: Random House, 1940.

STODDARD, WILLIAM O., *Inside the White House in War Times.* New York: C. L. Webster and Company, 1890.

STOWE, HARRIET BEECHER, *Men of Our Times.* Hartford, Conn.: Hartford Publishing Company, 1868.

STRYKER, LLOYD PAUL, *Andrew Johnson; A Study in Courage*. New York: The Macmillan Company, 1936.

SWISSHELM, JANE GREY, *Half a Century*. Chicago: J. G. Swisshelm, 1880.

TAFT, CHARLES SABIN, *Abraham Lincoln's Last Hours*. Privately printed, 1934.

TILDEN, SAMUEL J., *The Writings and Speeches of Samuel J. Tilden*, edited by John Bigelow. New York: Harper & Brothers, 1886.

VILLARD, HENRY, *Lincoln on the Eve of '61*, edited by Harold G. and Oswald Garrison Villard. New York: Alfred A. Knopf, 1941.

———, *Memoirs of Henry Villard*. Boston: Houghton Mifflin Company, 1904.

WARDEN, ROBERT BRUCE, *An Account of the Private and Public Services of Salmon Portland Chase*. Cincinnati: Wilstach, Baldwin and Company, 1874.

WELLES, GIDEON, *Diary of Gideon Welles*. Boston: Houghton Mifflin Company, 1911.

WILLIAMS, T. HARRY, *Lincoln and His Generals*. New York: Alfred A. Knopf, 1951.

WINDLE, MARY JANE, *Life in Washington, and Life Here and There*. Philadelphia: J. B. Lippincott and Company, 1859.

WITTENMYER, MRS. ANNIE, *Under the Guns*. Boston: E. B. Stillings and Company, 1895.

Magazines

Atlantic Monthly
Harper's Weekly
Harper's Magazine
Ladies' Home Journal

Leslie's Weekly
New England Magazine
Pathfinder

Newspapers

Cincinnati *Commercial*
Cincinnati *Daily Chronicle*
Cincinnati *Gazette*

New York Times
New York *Tribune*
New York *World*

New York:

New York *Evening Post*
New York *Herald*
New York *Independent*
New York *Sun*

Washington:

Washington *Daily Chronicle*
Washington *Evening Star*
National Republican
Daily National Intelligencer

Index

297

Set in Linotype Electra
Format by Katharine Sitterly
Manufactured by The Haddon Craftsmen, Inc.
Published by HARPER & BROTHERS, New York